EMMA CURTIS HOPKINS

New Religious Movements
J. Gordon Melton, *Series Editor*

Emma Curtis Hopkins
From *High Mysticism*

EMMA

FORGOTTEN FOUNDER

CURTIS

OF NEW THOUGHT

HOPKINS

Gail M. Harley

WITH A FOREWORD BY
Danny L. Jorgensen

Syracuse University Press

The paper used in this publication meets the minimum requirements of American National
Standard for Information Sciences—Permanence of Paper for Printed Library Materials, ANSI
Z39.48–1984.∞™

Library of Congress Cataloging-in-Publication data for this book is available upon request
from the publisher.

ISBN 0-8156-2933-8

Manufactured in the United States of America

In memory of

Beatrice Wolfe Harley,

Sarah Harley Lybrand,

Sally Rice Dawson,

Lottie Drone,

and

Jean Harley Miller

Gail M. Harley is a teacher-scholar at the University of South Florida. She studies religions of synthesis and minority movements in the Middle East. She has written extensively on facets of U.S. religious history and authored "New Thought and the Harmonial Family," in *America's Alternative Religions* (SUNY Press, 1995). She has written entries for *The Encyclopedia of World Religions, Encyclopedia of Prayer* (forthcoming from ABC-CLIO Press), and *Women Building Chicago, 1770–1990: A Biographical Dictionary* (Indiana University Press, 2000). She serves on the editorial board of the *Journal of the Society for the Study of Metaphysical Religion* and is also a member of the American Academy of Religion.

CONTENTS

FOREWORD

Danny L. Jorgensen

$\mathcal{G}$ ail M. Harley's biography of Emma Curtis Hopkins is the first in-depth, scholarly inquiry into the life of a little-known but genuinely remarkable turn-of-the-century American woman. In several notable respects, Emma Hopkins is similar to three much more familiar women: Ann Lee of the Shakers, Helena Petrovna Blavatsky of Theosophy, and Mary Baker Eddy of Christian Science. Hopkins, like all of them, was a renowned teacher who attracted dedicated students. She was instrumental in developing and establishing a new religion in the United States. Hopkins facilitated the formal organization of "New Thought." New Thought, not unlike Theosophy, Christian Science, and perhaps even the Shakers, has demonstrated a certain organization, stability, and durability. Hopkins, much like Ann Lee and Mary Baker Eddy, envisioned a feminine aspect of the divine (this issue probably is irrelevant to Blavatsky, but she certainly was a feminist in her own way). Hopkins, like Blavatsky and Eddy, was a prolific writer whose published works remain influential. Yet, unlike Lee, Blavatsky, and Eddy, Hopkins largely is unknown, even to ardent students of U.S. religion.

So what? you may be wondering. The world is full of interesting women and peculiar, alternative religions. Who cares? Why should this matter to anyone except perhaps to Hopkins's New Thought followers? Why, other than some frivolous curiosity about unusual people and strange religions, does Emma Hopkins's life make any difference at all? What is New Thought anyway? Why and how is it consequential? What, if anything, is to be learned from the study of minor, socially marginal religious experiments in the United States?

It may be useful to reflect, at least briefly, on the questions and issues. My purpose is to call to your attention an intellectual context and certain grounds for understanding this biography of Hopkins, as well as its significance for the study of religion, new religions, and indigenous U.S. religious innovations.

New religions in the United States are monumentally important for religious studies as well as related disciplines and fields of inquiry for a variety of sound theoretical reasons. In talking about "new religions" in the United States, I am referring to those religions that are uniquely innovative and substantially different from the country's most essential religious traditions: Protestantism, Catholicism, and Judaism. Fresh, innovative religions are collective, humanly meaningful responses to conventional, socially established, and legitimated images of what people hold to be "real"; what people think, feel, and do, based on existing cultural designs; and how these matters are structured and organized socially. New alternative religions, like all religions, advance and defend culturally meaningful and socially organized ways of thinking, feeling, and doing as matters that somehow are sacred, divinely sanctioned, supernaturally legitimate, and of ultimate, cosmic significance. Essentially, religious innovations are a critical response to traditional religion, culture, and society. New religions, to a greater or lesser extent, usually are protests against established, traditional religions and the social order advanced and supported by them.

New religions are exceptionally potent because they constitute a tremendously powerful means of *resisting* or *promoting* (or both) fundamental changes in human institutions. Religious innovations challenge conventional images of reality as well as the basic structure and organization of the established society by promoting fresh, creative, and sometimes extremely radical, reactionary, and revolutionary choices and options. New religions, for example, often advance novel alternatives to the customary ways in which gender, marriage, family, child rearing, education, economics, ethnicity, politics, health and healing, and many other aspects of human existence are envisioned and enacted by people in a particular culture and society.

New religions are an especially interesting feature of contemporary, modern societies, such as the United States. The world has been increasingly disenchanted and secularized as a consequence of modernity. With the rationalization, industrialization, urbanization, and individualization of human existence over the past several hundred years, the location and role of religion in modern cultures have changed dramatically. Religion in most of the Western world today is less central, influential, and determinative of the basic social fabric and its arrangement.

Religion, however, has not disappeared from Western societies or the U.S. scene. Religious belief and practice may be more private and individualized than in the past, but by the relevant indications, more Americans today truly are religious than in any previous period of the country's history. We are among the most religious people on this planet, and religion continues to exert weighty influence in matters of the utmost importance to public life and the social order. New religions, in particular, have proliferated and flourished in the United States. They, along with the persistent meaningfulness of traditional religions to Americans and their way of life, confirm that religion is highly resilient. Religion, in the United States and elsewhere, exhibits an enormous propensity for adapting to particular sociocultural circumstances and, thereby, changing—reforming, transforming, and revolutionizing—itself.

Studying new religions also promises to enhance our understanding of old religions. All of the old, traditional religions obviously were at some time new religions. In most cases, however, their precise origins, early formulation (or formulations), establishment, institutionalization, and other subsequent developments are at least partly obscure and sometimes exceptionally difficult to reconstruct from today's vantage point. Consequently, researching new religions provides scholars with outstanding opportunities to examine concrete, readily observable instances of the emergence and development of religion. New religions that are or are not successful are *experiments,* the study of which promises to yield exciting scholarly data about the dynamics of religion in general.

Almost from the beginning, the United States has produced several different kinds of new religions. There are many reasons, primarily the American commitment to religious freedom as well as the diversity and pluralism of religion in the United States. Most of the first European colonists had religious motives for coming to the Americas. Many of them were in search of a new land where their belief in and practice of minority religions—ones that conflicted with the socially dominant, established religions of particular European countries—could be done freely. The ideal of religious freedom attracted subsequent immigrants and their religions, eventually resulting in greater and greater religious pluralism. The constitutional prohibition against governmental establishment of or support for any particular religion fostered and secured the country's religious diversity and pluralism. In the United States today, all of the world's major religions are represented to some extent, and a bewildering array of other religions finds ample expression.

Hundreds, perhaps even thousands, of would-be new religions appear every decade or so in the United States. Most of them, however, fail to survive more than ten years. Few new religions attract sizable followings, and only a scattering of them outlive their founders. Religious innovations that deviate too radically from the conventional culture, on the one hand, thereby limit their appeal; new religions that are not perceived as a genuine alternative to existing religions, on the other hand, are unlikely to attract much public interest. Furthermore, if a new religion is to be successful, it must somehow acquire and mobilize sufficient human and material resources, and create a viable, enduring social-organization form.

When new religions are successful, they are almost always perceived as a threat to traditional religions and to the larger culture and society that the established religions commonly support and legitimate. Even in the United States, notwithstanding the constitutionally mandated freedom to subscribe to any religion or none at all, novel religions frequently provoke criticism, hostility, conflict, and sometimes even violence. Only under the most exceptional circumstances does a new religion overcome the obstacles it inevitably faces, gain public recognition, and survive for more than a hundred years.

There are at least three basic varieties or ideal typical forms of new religion in the United States. Each of these different types is interesting and informative in its own way. One type is defined by instances in which a traditional or socially established religion, such as Hinduism, Buddhism, or Islam, is transplanted and adapted to U.S. culture. Although these imported religions may be old within their home cultures, they differ substantially from the traditional religions of the United States, and they are commonly adjusted and expressed distinctively as U.S. religions.

Another form of new religion derives from socially marginal, underground, or deviant cultural traditions, as in the cases of Western magic, esotericism, occultism, and assorted paganisms. Although these beliefs and practices may be old and even derived from what at one time were socially dominant traditions, they commonly appear to be new and novel when they are revived by contemporary religionists.

The third most unusual and strongest form of new religions is made up of the ones, such as Mormonism, Seventh-day Adventism, Jehovah's Witnesses, Christian Science, New Thought, and Scientology, that uniquely are products of U.S. culture and society. They, consequently, promise to supply enticing insights into both religion in the United States and the sociocultural environments that produce them.

New religions in the United States have attracted considerable scholarly attention, although there remains a strong tendency among students of traditional religions to dismiss new religions as minor curiosities. Study of most, if not all, of the principal instances of new religions imported from other cultures, especially the East, has resulted in numerous major works. Esoteric traditions—particularly the periodic revival of assorted Western occultisms and the recent emergence of a substantial neopagan and Wiccan (or witchcraft) movement—have consistently fascinated academics in various disciplines. There is a sizable body of valuable literature on this type of new religion. Mormonism—the largest, most successful, and fastest-growing new religion born in America—has been studied thoroughly. The scholarly literature on Mormonism clearly demonstrates that there are monumentally important lessons to be learned—about religion in general and U.S. religion in particular—from an earnest examination of new religions, especially the ones born here.

None of the other new religions created in the United States has been researched as thoroughly as Mormonism. Conversely, none of the other major new religions born in the United States is as neglected as New Thought. There probably are reasons for this situation: its teachings and practices have not been perceived as especially offensive to traditional religions or the larger society; it has not generated much public protest or opposition; it is commonly viewed as part of a larger, highly complex, and diffuse metaphysical movement, perhaps being merely a derivative of Christian Science; and, therefore, it does not seem to be particularly distinctive or important in its own right, among other possibilities. Whatever the reasons for this scholarly neglect, it is unjustified. New Thought is one of the more successful and significant new religions produced in the United States. What it has to tell us about U.S. religion, culture, and society will remain unknown until New Thought has been described, analyzed, and interpreted by serious, concerted scholarship.

Here, then, is an intellectual context, and some of the more conspicuous theoretical grounds, for reading and understanding Gail M. Harley's biography of Emma Curtis Hopkins. It is more than simply a biography of an interesting but neglected American woman. Harley's interpretation of Hopkins's life contributes to a more comprehensive understanding of New Thought and its relationship with a much larger religious movement; it enables us to grasp the organizational dynamics of New Thought more completely; and it teaches us important lessons about the role of women in new religions, the establishment and development of new religions produced in the United States, as well as our culture, society, and religion in general.

In presenting Hopkins and making her more readily available for scholarly consideration, Harley boldly advances and more than adequately defends the thesis that Hopkins was the founder of the organized New Thought movement. This heretofore obscure and neglected founder of one of the more substantial new religions born in the United States now may be located alongside a few other principal architects of U.S. religious innovation, especially women such as Ann Lee, Helena Blavatsky, and Mary Baker Eddy. Harley supplies a solid basis for thinking more about why and how women have been especially prominent in new religious movements.

Harley sketches Hopkins's life story selectively, concentrating on those aspects that are most pertinent to New Thought. She develops, in detail, Hopkins's relationship with key persons and events. By doing so, she reveals the social history of a diffuse religious movement, characterized by an innovative emphasis on metaphysical healing, which eventuated in Christian Science and, subsequently, New Thought. She clarifies these relationships, and helps untangle some of the complexities of metaphysical religion in the United States, particularly as it relates to New Thought. Her account of the relationship between Hopkins and Eddy is original and invaluable, and it documents Hopkins's role in both of these new religions. Harley presents Hopkins as a feminist theologian, and links her image of a feminine principle of the divine with the ideas of Ann Lee and Mary Baker Eddy. Scholars of religion will find Harley's treatment of Hopkins's life and teachings particularly useful for examining issues of profound concern to women and feminism.

In reconstructing Hopkins's biography, Harley has thoroughly examined the primary sources of New Thought, including new and obscure materials by and directly related to Hopkins. Excellent summaries of the relevant secondary literature are used appropriately to critically analyze and interpret the primary data. Harley also supplies an interesting account of people who knew Hopkins or who had special knowledge of the unusual woman. Harley's brief, almost ethnographic account of this data collection further illustrates the meticulous character of her investigation. One of the greatest strengths of this book is Harley's skillful collection and scholarly presentation of primary-source materials. Her research is a solid foundation for building what, it is hoped, will become a much larger body of knowledge about the founder of New Thought, and the new religion organizationally established by Hopkins. This book again, in turn, promises to teach us more about new religions born in the United States, the culture and society that produce them, as well as religion in general.

PREFACE

*Y*ears ago, I came across a book that had a picture of an elegant Victorian lady on the back cover. My curiosity was aroused, and I tried to learn more about who this mysterious lady was and about her achievements and accomplishments.

Little was known about her either in New Thought circles or in the academic arena encompassing U.S. religion. Information about her seemed reverent and intriguing. So began my research. The odyssey to recover Emma Curtis Hopkins began, and subsequently I was able to reclaim her for a significant place in U.S. religious history. I traveled across the United States and abroad to England. Other groups and people came to my assistance and researched where I could not travel.

J. Gordon Melton, director of the Institute for the Study of American Religion, had been intrigued by Hopkins and had done extensive research and recovery of material for the nine years that Hopkins had lived in Chicago. I traveled to the institute in Santa Barbara and worked in the archives for several days as we collaborated. He generously shared his findings with me, pleased that I had come along to research her earlier and later years and to write the book about her.

I planned to write about Hopkins for my Ph.D. dissertation at Florida State University, with Leo Sandon, chair of the Department of Religion and director of American studies, who was directing my committee. It was he who suggested I contact Melton. He had also invited Robert Ellwood of the University of Southern California for a guest conference, and Ellwood supported my research project with scholarly enthusiasm, saying so little had been done in New Thought and it was certainly time. I was fortunate to have these eminent scholars as an academic support system.

The New Thought movement has been an understudied phenomenon in the United States, considered by many a marginal religion not worthy of serious scholarship and a major investment of research time. I am grateful to be a trailblazer in the original scholarship of new religious movements and the first person to work with some of the primary-text materials that illuminate the life and work of Hopkins. Despite the long odyssey and the many years of research, there are still nearly twenty years of Hopkins's life of which I know little. My hope is that those people who have information or documentation may someday share that material with scholars of U.S. religion.

The enigmatic quality about the pursuit of original research is that you never know what you may uncover, as was the case with Hopkins and New Thought. Hopkins was not in her own time recognized as the feminist founder of organized New Thought. She was considered the "teacher of teachers," a prolific metaphysical and mystical writer, and somewhat of a sainted figure in New Thought circles. In U.S. history, her own accomplishments and achievements were eclipsed for several reasons. First, she founded a religious movement that was considered by mainline groups as less than legitimate. Second, the intense polemics that surrounded Mary Baker Eddy and what the press termed the "Boston Craze" shrouded New Thought and its developments, especially in the Midwest, because the New England press focused on Eddy in Boston.

Today, Hopkins's influential work casts its ambiance into mainstream religions synthesized by sacred and secular groups that have no idea where their principles, precepts, or concepts originated, appropriating the ideas from the wide pluralistic milieu of contemporary culture.

My work has been made easier by the support of those embracers of New Thought who have also developed a critical consciousness about their movement and promote scholarship in that area. It is my hope that New Thought and the metaphysical movement will encourage serious scholarship among its members and prompt them to examine their origins. Preliminary research indicated that this lesser-known movement has had more impact on the broad cultural milieu of the United States than was previously suspected.

It is important to recover and claim those people who have earned a rightful place in history. Their legacies live on through the lives of people who have been touched or shaped by their principles. Our society has been enriched by the mystical and metaphysical tributaries created by those theological mavericks, their sterling ideals igniting an imminent quest for the infinite here amid rapid technological achievements. For women's history, it is important to recognize and reclaim women who were powerful people in their own rights as pathfinders who became watersheds for advancements in human consciousness. For universal history, noteworthy people who answered a transcendent call and sacrificed their personal lives for the good of humanity need to be recovered as part of the heroic history of the human race. Hopkins, as biblical exegete and pioneer of her religious movement, revivified for many the healing aspects of the Christian faith. Hopkins, as a mystic, is reported to have captivated the hearts and minds of her students, galvanizing them with her spirited presence and leaving them with a body of writings on her version of New Thought that is still being printed and sold to a younger generation of searchers and seekers.

I hope this book will fill some of the gaps about the life of the enigmatic Hopkins and her pivotal contributions to U.S. religious history. I anticipate that this basic addition to contemporary scholarship will be fleshed out to the fullest by scholars who are yet to come.

ACKNOWLEDGMENTS

*M*y friends, family, and colleagues supported me in various ways during the research and writing of this book. Much scholarship is done alone, and I am thankful for those people who assisted while knowing so little about what I was doing.

I am grateful to the late Mary and Aaron Geiser, Chris Geiser, Nancy Hollis, Kathy Kelly, and Zane O'Keefe in California for the many kindnesses through the years.

My friends Linda Bennett-Elder, Loretta Armer, Dennis Tishken, Sue Austin, the late Jean Bermingham, and Sandi Landis were helpful through the Tallahassee stage of work.

Four generations of the extended Harley family in South Carolina have, over a lifetime, been a source of spiritual renewal. My late grandfather Jamie R. Harley of Beaufort, South Carolina, generously subsidized portions of my graduate education and research costs, which my budget would not cover. From him, I learned the love of books and the value of the written word, the dignity of all peoples, and reverence for the holy. My children, Jamie and Cary Sprague, offered praise and kind words when needed. Maxine Dunnett was steadfast and more than supportive during my journeys to my home state for brief periods of respite.

I wish to thank specifically the Reverend William L. Lamb of Tampa, Florida, for his invaluable assistance in locating and contacting people who were working with Hopkins's material and his continued support of New Thought scholarship.

Chris McCown, Ethel Ross, Patricia Sanna-Jody, Margaret Holland, Susan Boriello, Barbara Kazanis, Jan Davis, Virgie De Salvo, Ruth Wheelock, and Haywood Thomas were particularly helpful in the Tampa Bay area.

Alan Schwartz, Robert Glazer, and Carl Fierstein were supportive through various stages of research and writing as the years progressed and the book took final form.

The Reverend Marge Flotron was helpful and hospitable in the Chicago area while sharing the history of her ministry with me.

Margaret Weaver, town historian of Killingly, Connecticut, did a marvelous job of locating information on Hopkins's early life and photographing the family grave site until I could get there myself. Hannah Ward and Jennifer Wilde were more than accommodating while I was engaged in research in England, as was the staff at Holy Trinity House.

So many people at Florida State University (FSU) extended themselves. Barbara Reis was extremely helpful during the dissertation process.

My dissertation committee—Leo Sandon, Ruth Katz, Jean Bryant, and Ardis Nelson—all made concrete suggestions to enhance the project. Maureen Tilley gave me pointers that facilitated the research as well.

Bruce Bickley and Walter Moore were instrumental in keeping me teaching so I could support myself, the research, and the writing of the dissertation.

The members of the interlibrary-loan staff at Strozier Library of FSU gave me the greatest service in locating old manuscripts and books.

I remember with special appreciation the interview granted me by the late centenarian Louise P. Ramey of Tampa and her insights of New Thought in the 1920s and 1930s. I especially thank her grandson, Stephen Ramey, for his kind donation of many precious old books from his grandmother's estate to the library at Unity Progressive Seminary, Clearwater, Florida; and the Institute for the Study of American Religion, Santa Barbara, so that scholars today and in the future have access to these documents.

Becky Ridge and the late Gary Nunn wished me well and cheered me on from their long distances away.

Some of my family and friends saw me partway through the long project. The late Corene Bunton provided encouragement through the early stages of planning. The late Lucille Foutz of the University of South

Florida (USF) was instrumental many years ago in directing me on an academic path. Robert Ellwood and J. Gordon Melton mentored me in areas too numerous to name with their knowledge of the New Thought arena as an integral component of U.S. history. Timothy Miller and Catherine Wessinger of the New Religious Movements Group of the American Academy of Religion provided a forum to introduce Hopkins's achievements and accomplishments in order to correct existing inaccuracies and stimulate additional research in the area.

Thomas Johnsen and Herbert Dresser of the First Church of Christ, Scientist, in Boston, were more than helpful in providing information on Hopkins and her association with that group.

Patricia Delks, Lynn Anderson, and Betty Jean House of the International New Thought Alliance sent material. House gave me material from her own personal collection, and Ferne Anderson released material not included in her master's thesis on Hopkins.

Patricia Willis was helpful with the Luhan material housed at the Beinecke Rare Book and Manuscript Library at Yale University.

Sharon Patterson, librarian at the Unity School of Christianity, shared any material she thought would enrich the project.

My latest indebtedness goes to those people who supported the detailed publication process as the dissertation evolved into a book. Special thanks to Amanda Porterfield, Mary Farrell Bednarowski, and, again, Catherine Wessinger who read the revised manuscript and made creative suggestions that enhanced the book.

At the University of South Florida, Dell deChant was a prime motivator to get the book out. The Reverend Leddy Hammock of the Unity Church of Clearwater has always supported scholarship in the New Thought arena and generously supported mine. Beverly Coe offered suggestions and unfailing loyalty to the work on Hopkins. Wanda Kirby, Louise Boehme, Laura Wever, Carol Rockwell, Helen Hause, Arline Erdrich, Jana Lindner, and Buzz Coe remained positive throughout the project. Carl Lincoln and Maureen McDevitt generously offered the veranda at Otter's Restaurant in Weeki Wachee, Florida, for rest and relaxation, allowing me time to socialize with wonderful friends and return to the work refreshed.

The faculty of the Religious Studies Department at the University of South Florida was instrumental throughout the long years in supporting my academic career. I particularly thank William C. Tremmell, James F. Strange, Mozella Mitchell, and Darrell Fasching for their loyalty to me as a former student, and then acceptance of me as a returning colleague.

William Shea and Nathan Katz while on faculty at USF and Lawrence Cunningham while on faculty at FSU charged me to work as a scholar in the understudied area of U.S. religious history called New Thought.

James Rosenquist and Hamilton Stirling provided quiet, pristine rural locations to rewrite and polish the book. Chandra Manasingh helped with the last stage of research, as did Louise Boehme. Teresa Finley served many laborious hours as word processor, learning the academic formats. Max Griffin-Maya refined them and reformatted the text for the final submission to Syracuse University Press. He deserves more than simple words for his dedication to such a complex task. Margo Smith did the final edit before the book went to the publisher.

Robert Mandel and Mary Selden Evans at Syracuse University Press were valuable facilitators for the publication process.

My students through the years at both FSU and USF have continually challenged me and recharged my batteries. A healthy balance between teaching and research is sometimes difficult to maintain, and the students strengthened this flow between the two worlds. To them I am grateful.

There are people too numerous to name who expressed interest in the research and writing and wished me well along the way. To them, I give a hearty thank-you!

EMMA CURTIS HOPKINS

INTRODUCTION

Who Was Emma Curtis Hopkins?

*E*mma Curtis Hopkins (1849–1925) influenced the New Thought movement in various areas of its historical and religious development. For thirteen months during 1884 and 1885, she was assistant to the editor and then editor and again assistant editor of the *Christian Science Journal* under the direction of Mary Baker Eddy. In November 1885, Hopkins was suddenly discharged. To broaden her perspective and continue the commitment she had made to metaphysical healing, she relocated to Chicago, where she founded an independent Christian Science theological seminary. She taught that the third person of the Trinity was the Holy Mother or Comforter,[1] and actively assigned women a prominent place in her ministry as ordained pastors. As chief executive officer, she actively supported feminist organizations through her coast-to-coast network of healing groups. Although she founded no specific New Thought ministry, she taught and ordained others who did. Myrtle and Charles Fillmore, whom she ordained in 1891, established the Unity School of Christianity, perhaps the most visible and well-established New Thought group. Malinda Cramer and the Brooks sisters cofounded Divine Science after studying with her. In 1924, a young Ernest Holmes came to her for individual sessions. He later founded Religious Science.

Hopkins's teachings were widely disseminated, achieving primary importance in the arena of mental healing or the "mind-cure" movement, as William James, a psychologist turned philosopher at Harvard, called it in *The Varieties of Religious Experience.*[2]

After serving as creative catalyst and innovative consultant in developing New Thought, Hopkins moved to New York for the remainder of her life. From 1895 until her death in 1925, she maintained an extensive private practice in metaphysical healing. It was during this phase of her life that she became a trusted adviser and spiritual mentor to members of the artistic, dramatic, and literary intelligentsia of the United States.

Hopkins was educated in the public school system of New England,[3] and self-educated through classical literature in the world's great religious traditions. She was a prolific writer and exegete of biblical material. Her first book, originally published in pamphlet form, *Class Lessons, 1888,* launched her career. As the years progressed, her writing became more complex so that it is best to read her work in sequential fashion. Her magnum opus, *High Mysticism,* was completed in stages from 1908 through 1915. This work challenged her senior students and disciples to actively engage in the life, study, and interpretation of metaphysical and mystical experiences.

In the mid-1880s, Hopkins corresponded with Mary Baker Eddy. These letters are housed in the Church History Department of the First Church of Christ, Scientist, in Boston. They illuminate the primary reason Hopkins became interested in healing and religion. From 1917 until 1924, Hopkins carried on a correspondence with the socialite and author Mabel Dodge Luhan. Today, these letters, shared with me through the courtesy of the American Literature Collection at the Beinecke Rare Book and Manuscript Library at Yale University, are a rich source of personal insight into Hopkins's personal thoughts on astrology, the occult, male-female relationships, important persons, her mother, and other intriguing topics. Reclusive by nature and mystical by temperament, Hopkins withdrew from organizational power positions and administrative leadership as soon as she was satisfied that New Thought was successfully established in U.S. society and had become a uniquely packaged U.S. spiritual export to other countries. The multidimensional effects of Hopkins's influence in U.S. history have gone unrecognized because she shied away from self-promotion and the pursuit of celebrity status. She perceived her mission, as a dedicated servant for the Second Coming of Christ, to be of divine importance and lived her life from that perspective.

Elements of New Thought

William James, at the turn of the twentieth century, spoke of New Thought in his discussion of the religion of healthy-mindedness. He traced various philosophies and theologies that, through time, contributed to the principles of New Thought, namely, the New Testament gospels, the idealism of Berkeley, the theory of evolution, transcendentalism, Hinduism, and Spiritualism. The most significant feature of New Thought that James defined was the "intuitive belief" in "healthy-minded" attitudes. James, poised at the beginning of a new era committed to scientific and technological advances, had a unique position from which to observe the development of certain independent strains and mind-cure tenets. He discerned that mind cure rests on a pantheistic foundation. James posited that the result of this pantheistic infrastructure results in an absence of a doctrine of grace because "we are already one with the Divine." James said, "[W]e find [in it] . . . traces of Christian mysticism, of transcendental idealism, of vedantism, and of the modern psychology of the subliminal self."[4] Hopkins assimilated these strains and became a purveyor and practitioner of spiritual healings, positive attitudes for life, health, and prosperity, which she simplified and organized into lessons that any adult could master. *High Mysticism* became an illustrious volume brimming with her symbolic imagery as a spiritual pathway to the Divine.

Certain ideas of the transcendentalists influenced New Thought. As Catherine Albanese stated in *The Spirituality of the American Transcendentalists,* "Transcendentalists thought and wrote in distinctive ways, they revealed the extent of their commitment by *acting* distinctively." According to Albanese, this group "experimented" in different and new lifestyles and "devoted themselves to contemporary efforts for social reform." They also "desired to seek within themselves the divine fountain of life," thereby engaging in mystical experience. The worldview of the transcendentalists "was based . . . [on the] ancient idea of correspondence."[5]

In brief terms, correspondence presupposes that the microcosm is a reflection of the macrocosm, and therefore there is "no radical break between the sacred and the profane and . . . therefore all of human life [is] religious." This idea cemented the notion that "living in tune with the divinity within oneself . . . meant cultivating the ground for mysticism." Albanese further observes that it was these theories that "suggested the universal consciousness that has accompanied so much of mysticism." One implication of the law of correspondence was that "human beings were divine; and empowered by their divinity, they should live expansively, learning to control and order the world."[6] Hopkins believed that it was one's responsibility to live in touch with one's divine nature. By developing a ministry that focused on healing, Hopkins was able to empower others to "use their divinity" and to "control and order the world."

New Thought also builds on earlier forms of metaphysical idealism developed by Emanuel Swedenborg, Phineas Parkhurst Quimby, and particularly Mary Baker Eddy. However, New Thought, in its early years, assumed the shape of Hopkins's prophetic vision, inasmuch as there was no organizational structure until Hopkins actively assumed the role of innovative developer.

Evolution of Current Scholarship

The scholarly attention to Hopkins's life is fairly recent. Ferne Anderson wrote the first study of Hopkins's accomplishments in a master's thesis submitted to the University of Denver in 1981. Anderson's work, titled "Emma Curtis Hopkins: Springboard to New Thought," is the first academic treatment of Hopkins's person and work. Anderson is a practitioner of New Thought, and had first encountered the work of Hopkins in religious texts. So little was known about Hopkins's personal life that Anderson decided to gather together what she could to contribute to a better understanding of Hopkins and her role in the establishment of New Thought. She received a small travel grant from a women's group that allowed her to conduct some personal interviews and do archival research at the Unity School of Christianity near Kansas City, Missouri.

J. Gordon Melton of the Institute for the Study of American Religion in Santa Barbara, California, has researched a number of new religious movements in the United States and has compiled and written numerous reference works, such as biographical dictionaries, directories of U.S. religious bodies, and encyclopedias of religious groups and creeds. As a historian of religion, one of Melton's special interests is new religious movements that surfaced in U.S. society in the nineteenth and twentieth centuries. Through his research, he discovered that many contemporary groups had roots that extended back to Hopkins's teachings. Subsequently, he presented a paper, "New Thought's Hidden History: Emma Curtis Hopkins, Forgotten Founder," at the American Academy of Religion's annual meeting in Boston in 1987.

I based this biography on critical library research, personal and telephone interviews with New Thought practitioners, and several research trips to Killingly, Connecticut (the natal home of Emma Curtis); Boston (the first site of her professional affiliations); Chicago (where she established the Christian Science Theological Seminary); and other relevant geographic areas. My research has not identified anyone who knew Hopkins. There is, however, a nebulous body of knowledge circulating in New Thought circles labeled the "oral tradition," which attempts to flesh out those aspects of Hopkins's life that are not factually established. Some of these reports seem plausible; others are clearly erroneous. There is less written about Hopkins than about more visible members of the metaphysical family who were active in her time. Few libraries contain her books and articles in their collections.[7] Her works—if marketed at all—are generally found in New Thought bookstores and can be special-ordered through several commercial chains.

Historian Gerda Lerner, who is concerned with the development of a universal history that is free of patriarchal bias, argues that there is an urgent need to study how women shaped historical events through the creation of local and national organizations.[8] Men and women both made unique contributions to the evolutionary development of humanity. The historical documentation of men's achievements has long been a primary focus in patriarchal culture. If women are judged by patriarchal standards, they do not, predictably, compare favorably with men. This study measures Hopkins's influence without gender bias.

Lerner describes "the true history of women [as] . . . their ongoing functioning in that male-defined world on their own terms."[9] This definition serves as an analytical tool in the reconstruction of Hopkins's achievements. Documents delineating her specific contributions reveal Hopkins as a woman who adroitly maneuvered herself and her organizations through a patriarchal culture on her own terms. Furthermore, once she established New Thought, she lived in mystical retreat on her own terms. She served as a role model and pathfinder for women to move from the home environment and share their skills and talents with female-oriented movements before moving onward to serve or lead patriarchal institutions.

Hopkins was an ardent feminist who believed in the goodness and innate spirituality of women. Assuming the function of a bishop, Hopkins ordained 111 and possibly even more of her advanced graduates (both male and female) in the independent New Thought (Christian Science) ministry. She sent these ministers into the religious milieu of the United States and other countries as evangelists, pastors, and missionaries. She graduated another 350 or more persons in the basic course and sent them forth as healing practitioners of the ministry of Christ. Hopkins created the first national network of New Thought organizations while establishing the first seminary to ordain women in large numbers.[10] Her support of feminist values in religion during the turbulent era of nineteenth-century social-justice causes was clearly countercultural to mainstream religious thought and practice. Hopkins's life and work illustrate a monumental paradigm shift for her and her followers as she challenged the dominant patriarchal mores of the time.

This analytical and critical biography places Hopkins in a conceptual framework that permits her to make history as a writer, editor, healing practitioner, feminist, missionary, mystic, mentor, adviser, biblical exegete, and prophet who stridently ushered in a novel religious movement heralding the Second Coming of Christ for an urban technological world.

1

THE NEW ENGLAND YEARS

Hopkins's Early Life

*E*mma Curtis Hopkins was born Josephine Emma Curtis in Killingly, Connecticut, to Rufus Curtis and Lydia Phillips Curtis.[1] Here, for the sake of clarity, she will be called Emma until after marriage and her professional association with Christian Science. Then, I will call her Hopkins for the remainder of the text.

There has been confusion about Emma's correct birth date. Many existing sources are erroneous. According to both the *1850 United States Census Bureau Report* and the *Commemorative Biographical Record,* Emma was born September 2, 1849. Charles S. Braden, in *Notable American Women,* reports her birth as September 2, 1853. Rosemary Ruether, in *Women and Religion in America,* reports 1853 as the birth date, as does Kali Herman in *Women in Particular.* An article in the *New Thought Bulletin* by Margaret Cushing states this date of birth also. A tribute to Emma Curtis Hopkins, written by an unnamed source and placed after the foreword in her *Class Lessons, 1888,* gives this erroneous birth date also. The inaccurate dates of birth given for her would change her place in the family constellation from first born to third child. The changed birth date confuses Emma's birth with that of a younger sister, Janette Phillips, born August 12, 1853. Emma was the oldest of nine children and enjoyed a special relationship with Estelle, who was the fifth child, born eight years after her.[2]

The attempt to portray Emma as younger than she was might have gone undiscovered except for the *1850 United States Census Bureau Re-*

port and the *Biographical Record* for prominent citizens of her home county.[3] In another apparent conspiracy to hide Emma's true age, her date of birth was deliberately omitted from the stone marker at the Dayville Cemetery, and only the date of her death was given. The family monument records the dates of birth and death, or their ages when they died, for every other family member.

Rufus Curtis was a farmer and part-time realtor who had seen service in the Civil War as a soldier of Company K of the Eighteenth Connecticut Regiment. In the Battle of Piedmont he was wounded in the leg and taken prisoner. His leg was amputated. After his release from active duty, he returned home to run a successful dairy farm for thirty-five years. "His record as a brave and efficient soldier reflects honor upon him and he is one of the most respected citizens of the community."[4]

Rufus's mother, Margaret Greenman Curtis, was from "an old family of prominence in Rhode Island." Her father, John, had seen service in the Revolutionary War. Her mother, Annie, lived to be more than one hundred years old. Rufus's father, Norman, was born in New York, but came to Connecticut as a young man and bought a farm. "He possessed the respect and confidence of his friends and was an honest and useful citizen."[5] Rufus married Lydia Ann Phillips. She was born in Providence, Rhode Island, on January 29, 1828. From 1860 until 1870, death claimed three children of the Curtis family: James D., age four months, died on July 24, 1860; Anna R., age thirteen years, died on October 1, 1864; and Frederick W., age two years, died September 2, 1870. Emma's birthday was September 2. The day her younger brother died, Emma turned twenty-one years old. Anna R., the sister closest to her in age, died when Emma was fifteen and she thirteen. The tragic deaths of her siblings and the amputation of her father's left leg created an indelible imprint on the young Emma. These rueful events would shape her life, spark her ideals, and prime her career.

Lydia Curtis, Emma's mother, was well respected in the community. It is perhaps a testimony of her strength to note that during the Civil War, with her husband away, she "faithfully nurtured and reared her children and in their hearts has a place most dear to them."[6] Emma was twelve and the oldest child at the onset of the Civil War. No doubt she was actively involved in the running of the farm and the raising of the younger children. Despite the hardships of the times, Lydia Curtis lived to be ninety-two years old.

The *Biographical Record* indicates that education was valued by the Curtis family and that Rufus gave his children "every educational opportunity." According to the *Biographical Record,* Emma and all but two of her sisters who survived to adulthood were teachers. Lewis Lincoln Grant (the youngest child and only son to reach adulthood) was conceived and born after Rufus returned from the Civil War. He graduated from Phillips-Exeter Academy in New Hampshire.[7]

The *Biographical Record* states that "Emma taught for some time at Woodstock Academy" in Connecticut. Margaret Cushing's spring 1945 article in the *New Thought Bulletin* indicates that young Emma attended Woodstock Academy and was so accomplished that she was retained as a teacher. Records of the institution that were checked at the time of Ferne Anderson's master's thesis on Hopkins do not support this statement. I spoke with Robert Smith of the Woodstock Academy on two separate occasions. He researched catalogs, recital lists, and registration forms, finding no mention of any person named Curtis for the time period Emma might have been there. The school was closed during the Civil War. Afterward, enrollment peaked when the school reopened. Again, Emma was listed neither as having matriculated nor as having been employed there. Had she been so employed, it would have been as an assistant to the teacher.[8]

It is certainly in keeping with the profile and values of the Curtis family to suggest Emma's presence at a local educational facility, if not at that specific school. In fact, Killingly had an academy that is now defunct, and the *Biographical Record* states that Emma was educated at the Killingly High School. Smith said most young people of that time attended school near their homes. For Emma to commute to Woodstock for school or work would have required a daily six-hour round-trip horseback ride.

Emma married George Irving Hopkins on July 19, 1874. They had a son named John Carver, who was born June 8, 1875, and died in 1905, probably in an influenza epidemic. Census records indicate that George Hopkins was a high school English teacher. Reports circulated through oral tradition to Ferne Anderson that he taught as a professor at Andover College could not be confirmed.[9]

The 1880 Census reports Emma; her husband, George; her son, John; and her younger sister Estelle living in Nantucket, Massachusetts. Emma was identified as a housewife. George Hopkins's occupation was listed as high school teacher. The *Census Report* does not tell why her younger sister Estelle was residing with them. However, in later years, it was Estelle who brought Emma home to die and who continued her work after her death. Closeness between the sisters was a lifelong pattern. Emma and her husband, George, did not reside together permanently after the mid-1880s. Braden states they were divorced, and Emma's death certificate agrees. The newspaper death notice for her mentions no divorce, but portrays Emma as the widow of a professor. Emma and George lived separately to pursue individual career goals that placed them in different locations. George initially accompanied her to Chicago, attended several meetings of the Hopkins Association in Chicago in the late 1880s, and is not mentioned again in New Thought literature.

The *Census Report of 1900* records Emma as residing in Manhattan, stating that she had been married for twenty-six years, though was not living with her husband. She reported her true age. She is listed as a lodger in the home of a married couple. Later that year, in mid-November 1900, George sought a divorce from Emma. He was residing in Manchester, New Hampshire. He petitioned for a divorce, charging "abandonment." At that time, he and Emma had not lived together in nearly fifteen years.

It would be five more years before Emma's son died as a young adult. When not residing with his mother, he can be presumed to be living independently or perhaps with Emma's mother or sisters. The Curtis family was close, and the extended family network was a source of family stability. In fact, Emma's mother preceded her in death by only five years. Much of what has been discovered about Emma's personal feelings regarding her family comes from recently recovered letters she wrote to Mary Baker Eddy, Myrtle Fillmore, and Mabel Dodge Luhan. The letters reveal that Emma was a dutiful daughter who shared close bonds with her mother throughout her life. In her late sixties, Emma stated in her letters to Luhan that she journeyed to the family farm in Connecticut to see her mother despite her own failing health.

Meeting with Mary Baker Eddy

Between 1881 and 1883, Emma Hopkins and George Hopkins moved from Nantucket, Massachusetts, to Manchester, New Hampshire. Little is known about Emma and her lifestyle prior to 1883. Oral tradition reports that Emma had a health problem related to breathing and was healed by a Christian Science practitioner in 1881. Although this report contains some truth, it is not entirely accurate. In October 1883, Emma was a guest in the home of Mary F. Berry in Manchester, New Hampshire. Mary Baker Eddy was also a guest there and gave an "impromptu talk" on Christian Science healing.[10] At that time, Christian Science was a new religious movement created by middle-aged Eddy in response to a spontaneous healing she reported after a severe fall on ice in 1866. Eddy was reading a biblical passage when the healing occurred and subsequently founded a church that embraced physical healing with its religious tenets. She had been exposed to and was healed earlier by Phineas Parkhurst Quimby, a pioneer mental healer in the New England area. When Emma met Eddy, there was great controversy over what the press called the "Boston Craze," or Eddy's version of divine healing.[11]

In a letter to Eddy dated December 12, 1883, Emma wrote, "I want to tell you that the beautiful theory you advanced has taken . . . so firm a hold on my heart that in a late serious illness I had no other medical advisor but your friend Mrs. Berry. . . . I am now anxious to learn more of the science . . . directly from your own lips."[12] According to other statements Emma wrote, she was a skeptic at first, and then after being healed (sometime between October 23 and December 12, 1883) was motivated to contact Eddy for more information on her specific modality for Christian healing.

It was in this letter to Eddy that Emma shared her aspirations, dreams, and "the hope of my life." Near the farm in Killingly, Connecticut, where she grew up, there was, Emma said, "a spot of land . . . selected by me when a mere child as the site for a hospital for sick, destitute children." Emma carefully described her plans for the ideal establishment for the care of ailing children, and then she wrote, "What if my dream shall come to pass and the little ones . . . shall be restored by the healing thoughts of your God endued disciples!" Obviously, she hoped this vision of a hospital would become a reality. The enthusiasm for divine healing and building a hospital for ailing children was no doubt sparked in part by the deaths of her young siblings. Wistfully, she added, "But see how far off from such an undertaking my circumstances and prospects seem!" She took Eddy into her confidence and shared with her the reason her hopes and dreams were "far off." Emma stated, "I am happily married to a young man . . . and have one sweet little son. . . . [M]y husband is heavily in debt first for his college education and then an obligation to pay a heavy note which he endorsed for a near relation." She says that because of these financial commitments, she could not "command a single dollar."

Not wanting to add to her husband's already monumental indebtedness, she discussed with Eddy an agreement whereby she could pursue the curriculum at the Massachusetts Metaphysical College and pay Eddy for the course work. After she was graduated and working as a practitioner, she suggested that Eddy "take all my first fees for . . . payment." After paying off her indebtedness to Eddy, she could then work "toward the hospital I wish to found." She signed her letter "Mrs. Emma J. Hopkins, Manchester, N.H., December 12, 1883." She had switched her first and second names and was not yet using her maiden name as a middle name as she would in later writing.

This letter began an ongoing correspondence with Eddy. Unfortunately, only one side of the correspondence is represented. Less than one week later, on December 17, 1883, Emma again wrote to Eddy. From the contents of the letter, one can infer that Eddy must have written a reply to Emma's letter of December 12, and charitably offered that she could study at her college, "paying as it seemeth one's duty under the circumstances." It is at this time that Emma responded to an apparent statement by Eddy in her letter. She said, "You say you are alone in this work—do you suppose I could learn to assist you?" Emma said she could "catch ideas fairly well . . . having been a teacher." Then in a statement both reverent to Eddy but naïve in reality, she wrote: "I would charge nothing but would feel it my privilege" to serve as an assistant. In this letter, one gets a rare glimpse of the Victorian gentleman her husband must have been when she says to Eddy that "he is discreet, reserved, silent" about the business arrangements and personal commitments of others.

Ten days after writing this letter, Emma journeyed to Boston and took the primary course in Christian Science healing under Eddy. According to Bates and Dittemore, there were four women (including Hopkins) and four men in the December 27, 1883, class.[13] This class marks the official beginning of Emma's association with Mary Baker Eddy and Christian Science.

Several months later, Emma contributed to the February 2, 1884, issue of the *Christian Science Journal,* or the *Journal of Christian Science,* as it was called originally. She advertised her business card as a practitioner of Christian Science healing in this and the next two issues. She apparently traveled back and forth from Manchester to Boston. The address on the card is not Christian Science headquarters, and it can be presumed that Emma was financially supported in Boston by her husband's earnings while he was still living in Manchester.

Several weeks prior, Emma had a positive experience that validated for her that she was on the right track in pursuing the cause of spiritual healing. In a January 1884 letter to Eddy, Emma said George had become extremely ill with "a raging fever, great head ache and sore throat—a man who is never ill." She continued, "I soothed the fever in a few minutes, [and] completely annihilated the head ache." She drove the pain to one side of the throat, and the swelling nearly choked him. Still, she permitted no one in his room and refused to call a physician. She and Mary F. Berry, who was more experienced, treated him. During the acute phase of his illness, Emma must have gotten a letter from Eddy requesting she come to Boston. She answered and questioned Eddy, "Shall I stay to conquer or come to you at once? . . . [I]f it is work on the journal you want, I can write right here in my husband's room." To delimit her literary ability, she stated, "I never write poetry, though." Toward the end of the letter, she vowed, "I give myself and all my time to the Master's work wherever it lies, here, there, or yonder." Although she was committed to the work of spiritual healing, there was a personal desire to stay near her husband during his illness. George's recovery from what might have been a quinsy sore throat was an event that helped convince her that this type of healing was a blessing from God.[14]

By April 18, 1884, Emma attempted to have her church membership transferred by letter from the Congregational Church of Killingly to Eddy's First Church of Christ, Scientist, in Boston. The minister must have been reluctant, for she said he asked her if she still insisted. "I assured him solemnly I did," she told Eddy.

Hopkins Becomes Editor of the Christian Science Journal

On April 5, 1884, Hopkins contributed an article to the *Journal of Christian Science* titled "God's Omnipresence." She demonstrated an eclectic proclivity, viewing both Eastern and Western religious traditions as providing a viable theoretical framework for her own point of view. At Eddy's behest, Hopkins assumed full editorship of the fledgling journal three issues later, on September 6, 1884. The journal became a monthly publication. Seven months later, in April 1885, the name was changed to the *Christian Science Journal.*

In a letter to Eddy dated August 16, 1884, Hopkins shared her fear that "I must go to Boston without letting anybody (my relatives, I mean) know that I go as editor of a paper without salary." Knowing that her husband, George, was struggling financially to support them might have made her relatives question her willingness to work without pay. Probably, in the infancy of her career in Christian Science, she was reluctant to discuss any of the details of her affiliation with family members.

Sarah Crosse, who assisted Eddy with the rental of rooms at the Massachusetts Metaphysical College, sent a letter to Hopkins offering her a room at the college for six dollars per week for the times of the month that she needed to be there. She also offered to refer new patients to her. Hopkins, hoping for a way to afford the rent, realistically expressed her fears, "If I find I cannot earn my way, I shall have to go home, of course." It seems that Eddy suggested that the students at the college provide Hopkins with the necessary financial support to remain in Boston. Hopkins wrote, "Mrs. Crosse has loaned me the first week's expenses. . . . I am to pay when I earn more by healing." Hopkins ended the letter by saying that after she found somewhere to place her son in her absence, she could start out for Boston and the training period that would lead to her formal assignment as editor of the journal.

Hopkins was the first person besides Eddy to hold the rank of editor of the *Christian Science Journal*. Her predecessor, Arthur Buswell, was acting or assistant editor to Eddy. Hopkins moved to the college for part of the month and had both a room and an office on the premises. She last advertised her card as a practitioner in the June 7, 1884, issue. Her administrative and literary duties as editor assumed first priority, as she commuted to Boston to ready the journal for publication. This editorship was a portent that writing would be one of the two main expressions of her lifework. In *Mary Baker Eddy*, Bates and Dittemore credit Hopkins with being a "much more efficient and capable journalist [than Buswell or Eddy]. Under Mrs. Hopkins [the journal] was enlarged and issued as a monthly. Its experimental days were over." [15]

In the 1880s, Christian Science was a new religious movement with a focus on spiritual healing. Eddy was having difficulty retaining control of persons who had studied with her or other Christian Science teachers. Robert Peel, a biographer of Eddy, says factionalism was rampant in the mind-cure subculture; it was the pettiness or "drag of the small-minded rivalries that would have kept Christian Science a quarrelsome sect." [16] In an effort to ensure adherence to her doctrines among recalcitrant disciples, Eddy personally confronted those people in residence who violated her standards. For persons beyond her immediate reach, the power of the written word was brought to bear. The *Christian Science Journal* was designed to offer inspirational and instructional articles. It also operated as a literary forum to publicly address rivals in the arena of metaphysical healing and those individuals or groups whose precepts were viewed as deviations from orthodox Christian Science.

Under Hopkins's novice editorship of the *Christian Science Journal*, people who violated or appropriated the teachings of Eddy were frequently taken to task. She was staunch in her support of Eddy and loyal to the movement Eddy had created. Referring to Eddy's text, Hopkins stated that there were many students who could "give the letter of the law, as written in the book *Science and Health*," but were not able from the standpoint of their own spiritual development "to venture a single statement or explanation" of how this healing worked. She argued that these students were not "qualified to teach Christian Science, except rudimentarily." [17] In the July 1885 issue, Hopkins took to task the Reverend A. J. Swarts of Chicago. Swarts, a former Methodist minister, had attended some of Eddy's lectures in Chicago. He was charged by Eddy with blatantly synthesizing techniques from her teaching with spiritualism and other healing modalities. Hopkins clarified for journal readers that Swarts's avowed association with Christian Science was minimal and that he had not completed a formal course of study with Eddy, but had attended only several of a series of lectures. Bates and Dittemore list him and his wife as having attended five lectures. [18]

Hopkins Is Discharged by Eddy

Hopkins later had cause to regret the strength of her support of Eddy, when she was suddenly discharged from her post at the *Christian Science Journal* and became the object of Eddy's anger. In an undated letter to Eddy, Hopkins said, "I received a peremptory message from Dr. Frye [Eddy's secretary] to vacate my room at the college, accompanied by a notification from Mrs. Crosse that my services were no longer necessary on the *Journal* in view of the lack of funds." Apparently, this reason was given to Hopkins for her abrupt discharge, but it was not the real reason. Braden says, "Just what happened is not altogether clear, but she was dismissed as editor in October of 1885 and succeeded by Mrs. Crosse. Why?" The only answer he gives to this question is the one supplied by Bates and Dittemore: "She began to read other metaphysical books besides Mrs. Eddy's writing." [19] This particular theory sounds plausible. That Eddy would take umbrage after thirteen months is not entirely logical, however. In "God's Omnipresence," Hopkins had mentioned by name almost every major religious tradition and its sacred literature. Surely, her eclectic taste could have been no surprise to Eddy.

In her undated first letter to Eddy after the abrupt discharge, she seemed to accept the reason for the firing as financial. "I was with my mother in the country and hastened quite a little journey to comply with Dr. Frye's request. . . . I wanted to take leave of you. . . . I had feared to take leave of you formally." She left clear directions regarding works she had in progress for the next edition of the journal. She offered to help Eddy in her endeavors "not for the science (though I am one with its precepts) but for yourself." Speaking of her dedication and commitment, Hopkins said, "I gave you more than all the friends or relations I ever had . . . received." Hopkins signed it, "Lovingly Your disciple."

Apparently, on that inauspicious day, Hopkins went along with the reality of events as they seemed to be. In contrast, Braden offers the hypothesis that her "independence and her indisposition to bend to the will of her superior probably lay at the bottom of [her discharge], though I have seen nothing from Mrs. Hopkins herself to reply to Mrs. Eddy's attack upon her. . . . She could not accept the role assigned to her . . . [and] became an independent teacher."[20] Braden is postulating what to him seemed a likely probability. Hopkins's letters reveal that it did not happen exactly this way. Hopkins did not wish to leave Christian Science; she revered Eddy and had been neophyte enough not to see the employment crisis for what it was.

Stephen Gottschalk, a Christian Scientist and scholar, writing independently of church sanction, stated that Hopkins, after being fired by Eddy, launched out on her own because of her "tendency toward spiritual freewheeling."[21] If by "spiritual freewheeling" he means that she had the worldview of the eclectic teacher who saw Truth in all religions, then he might be accurate. This description appears, however, to be only part of the issue. Upon meeting Eddy, Hopkins was a ready disciple. Nearly one year after they met, in her November 4, 1884, letter to Eddy, she says, "I am at your service." She signs it, "Lovingly, your disciple."

Peel says that Hopkins was a "young woman of . . . brilliant potentialities." Both Peel and Gottschalk minimize Hopkins's loyalty to and feelings for Eddy, yet Peel records portions of a letter that Hopkins wrote to Eddy that demonstrated she had maternal feelings for her teacher: "You seem so often like a tired sobbing body . . . and no mood moves me to other than a sheltering tenderness for one whose life has been so stormy."[22]

Hopkins was eclectic, Eddy more focused, in her theological approach. In reading the first issues of the *Journal of Christian Science* under Eddy's editorship, however, one is impressed with the variety of religious and philosophical articles. When Hopkins became associated with Eddy, she wrote to her on January 14, 1884, that "I lay my whole life and all my talents, little or great, to this work." After assuming the editorship of the journal, she saluted Eddy in one of her first editorials as one who pioneered "upon Puritan, conservative soil."[23] Gottschalk believes Hopkins's theological orientation encouraged her to embrace universal values in her literary and religious thought. Examination of the *Christian Science Journal* before and after Hopkins's editorship demonstrates that the inclusion of a variety of articles was standard operating procedure under both Hopkins and Eddy. Particular issues published under Hopkins's editorship appear to be no more varied in topics than the ones preceding or subsequent to her tenure.

Hopkins's Departure from the Journal Fueled by Plunkett's Presence

Peel says that toward the end of the women's relationship, Eddy could see that Hopkins was being wooed away from her by the enterprising Mary Plunkett. Eddy had enrolled Plunkett in her basic class of September 14, 1885, without realizing that she was a possible rival and potential source of trouble because of her entrepreneurial nature.[24] Peel's theory is that when Eddy realized that a friendship existed between these two unlikely souls, she discharged Hopkins from her position as editor of the *Christian Science Journal,* replaced her with Sarah Crosse, and had Calvin Frye, her male secretary, evict Hopkins from her residence on college property. On November 4, 1885 (after her discharge), Hopkins described to former colleague Julia Bartlett how her various experiences in Christian Science had been instructional: "I shall never serve a cause or a person without sharp business arrangements again, and shall hold strong guard over personal reverence and worshipful feeling at every point." Hopkins was hurt because her mentor had banished and abandoned her. That she felt unsupported by the others is evident. In the same letter, she said, "I do not think I had a single enemy among the scientists." Time would demonstrate that she did.[25]

On November 4, 1885, Hopkins formally resigned from the Christian Science Association. Ironically, another of the reasons Hopkins was fired seems to have been an article she had written in support of Eddy, called "Teachers of Metaphysics." Eddy thought her particular doctrine was not sufficiently supported. In the November 4 letter to Julia Bartlett, Hopkins acknowledged that she was being watched. "I really was under heavy fire mentally." She perceived herself as being on a fact-finding mission: "I was digging for facts. . . . I was always ferreting out . . . with my critical, cynical gaze." Hopkins's letter does not mention Mary Plunkett. Yet, Peel believes that it was the close alliance with Plunkett that caused Eddy to discharge Hopkins.[26] It is impossible to prove whether this assumption is correct, because Peel does not document the sources he used to arrive at the conclusion that Eddy was jealous and suspicious of the relationship between Hopkins and Plunkett.

If Peel is correct, factors centering around Plunkett may have served to fuel the discharge of Hopkins. Plunkett had an energetic, entrepreneurial spirit when she came to study and take classes with Eddy in September 1885. According to Peel, Eddy did not realize that Plunkett's husband was not the father of her two children, an assumption that Peel does not document. The enthusiastic Plunkett proved ambitious and hard for Eddy to control. One can suppose that Eddy and Plunkett would not see eye-to-eye. Peel says that Plunkett closely allied herself with Hopkins. There is, however, nothing in Hopkins's letters to indicate this affiliation.[27] Eddy perceived an alliance between the flamboyant Plunkett and the charismatic Hopkins and believed it bode no good for her.

That Eddy was eminently sensitive to what she perceived as renegade Christian Scientists teaching her revelations is evident in a response she wrote for the "Questions and Answers" section of the *Christian Science Journal*. The month before she discharged Hopkins, she said, "There never was a science as abused as Christian Science..,.[O]wing to false teaching . . . the student who understands it best is . . . least likely to pour into the community his primary sense of it." With this qualifying statement, she set the stage in the readers' minds for suspicion of people who openly taught their own variations of Christian Science and paved the way for discrediting other defectors. The most vocal may not be the most effective as teachers. Eddy may have had premonitions that Hopkins's spiritual, mystical, and oratorical talents would propel her into the limelight, and she was trying to preserve the purity and sanctity of her system of Christian Science from philosophical and territorial encroachment by Hopkins and other excommunicants. A Hopkins-and-Plunkett team less than exclusively committed to Eddy's teaching was threatening to her authority. In anticipation of a possible defection, she promoted herself and her text *Science and Health* "as far more advantageous . . . than the spurious teachings."[28]

In later months and years, Eddy did not speak well of Hopkins. She said she was one of the "unprincipled claimants" who took her thoughts and said that "dishonesty—yes, fraud—is conspicuous" in her teachings.[29]

The Arens and Quimby Controversy

In the decade before she and Hopkins became associated, Eddy had already lost several of her significant students and had initiated court action against some of them for using her work. The lawsuits against Edward J. Arens, a former student of Asa Gilbert Eddy, the husband of Mary Baker Eddy, served to increase Eddy's sensitivity to what she thought might be plots of malicious magnetism against her. Eddy had a belief that thinking evil thoughts against someone could harm them. She termed it *malicious magnetism*. Julius Dresser charged, in the *Boston Post* of February 1883, that Eddy had pirated the work of Phineas Parkhurst Quimby and used it to create Christian Science. Quimby was a pioneer mesmerist and healer in Maine who experimented with various methods to heal without medications. Eddy's reply in the *Post* followed, and for several years great controversy raged between the opposing factions. The same argument was revived by the son of Julius many years later, when Horatio Dresser wrote and published *A History of the New Thought Movement* in 1919.[30] The polemics of the Quimby-Eddy controversy was a major factor that eclipsed the contributions of Hopkins to the spiritual-healing movements. Another factor was Hopkins's commitment to her mission that did not include an egoistic need for self-aggrandizement.

Part of Hopkins's self-appointed fact-finding mission while acting as editor of the *Christian Science Journal* was to investigate for herself whether the charges by the Dressers or others against Eddy were tenable. After close association through months of residential and educational contact, Hopkins wrote, "I found [Eddy] free to her own original . . . inspiration. I saw all the letters said to be written to Dresser and Quimby and not one of them could be held as argument against her supreme originality."[31] The material she was privy to via her short sojourn with Christian Science must have satisfied her that Quimby and Eddy had not utilized identical principles in healing and that Eddy had not deliberately appropriated Quimby's work and labeled it her own.

Assuming that Eddy had become aware that Hopkins was "digging for facts" to satisfy her "critical, cynical gaze," she may have fired her for being curious enough to investigate the charges. Eddy's belief in malicious magnetism would have led her to jump to the conclusion that Hopkins would turn on her and use inside information to support the Dressers' claim that she had copied the healing practices of Quimby. Eddy does not seem to have been a particularly patient person who would have waited for Hopkins to complete her "house" investigation on the assumption that Hopkins would be able to help vindicate her or come into the controversy as a strong ally. Probably, if Hopkins had made public her findings that she found Eddy "true to her original . . . inspiration," the Dressers would have discredited her as a close associate who was an Eddy employee and had a reason to be supportive. They might even have seen her as a serious contender to replace Eddy on her retirement as the head of the Christian Science organization and would have attacked her as having a vested interest in strengthening Eddy's position. This statement supporting Eddy's position was made by Hopkins in late 1885 after nearly two years of editorship of the journal. It was also made after she was abruptly fired by Frye on Eddy's orders. She had no reason to protect Eddy or whitewash any issue pertaining to the Quimby controversy.

Today, after the passing of more than one hundred years and the deaths of all who had major interests on either side of the quarrel, the issue over the Quimby controversy can be examined more objectively. For instance, after evaluating the disputed material, Melton says in the *Encyclopedia of American Religions:* "An examination of Eddy's writings and the publications of the Church of Christ, Scientist, reveals an essential difference between Eddy's teachings on healing and those of Quimby and finds the major similarity to be in the area of terminology, and the attempt to struggle with some of the same questions of religion and health." [32]

Based on this assessment, it looks as if there may have been a similarity of terms that clouded the picture at the time, confusing the issues and veiling Hopkins as an emerging leader in the establishment of what would become the New Thought movement.

Aftermath of the Discharge

It is evident that the discharge of Hopkins by Eddy was a complex event, fraught with issues and innuendoes not easily deciphered by Hopkins then, and certainly not now on the basis of the available evidence. However, it seems the major factor in her discharge was her association with Plunkett.

As Hopkins evolved, grew, and expanded the parameters of her developing system, a separation from Eddy had to occur in order to preserve the integrity central to them both. Eddy chose to hasten the inevitable break with Hopkins out of her own sense of insecurity. Ann Braude, in "The Perils of Passivity: Women's Leadership in Spiritualism and Christian Science," notes that "Eddy censured any who emulated her by aspiring to religious authority." Gail Thain Parker, who has explored literary avenues of New Thought, says in *Mind Cure in New England,* "The number of prominent early Scientists who either split with Mrs. Eddy or were excommunicated reflects . . . [a] come-outer spirit operating within an authoritarian framework." She lists Emma Curtis Hopkins and Ursula Gestefeld as prominent excommunicants who became leaders in New Thought. As Braude states, "Christian Science did produce a number of powerful female leaders" who would carve a niche in nineteenth-century religious thought.[33] Their rejection by Eddy or refusal to comply with her authoritarian regulations served to pave the way for them to become more innovative with their theology. In Hopkins's case, the term *excommunicant* is much more appropriate than *defector* or *apostate,* because she was fired from her position by Eddy's lieutenants on her orders.

Fourteen months after being fired by Eddy, Hopkins, in a conciliatory effort, wrote to Eddy of her successes in Chicago.[34] She assured her former teacher that she spoke highly of her and promoted her text *Science and Health.* Hopkins, smarting from Eddy's earlier rejection, was attempting to mend torn fences. Holding up her overwhelming acceptance in Chicago as a trophy for Truth, she said to Eddy, "Oh, if you could only have been mental enough to see what I might be or do and given me time to work past and out of the era through which I was passing." Hopkins missed Eddy as a mentor, teacher, and leader. There was nostalgia in her letter, as Hopkins tried to salvage remnants of their previous relationship: "You were very wise to write me what you had heard . . . thus giving me the opportunity of flatly denying the charge of speaking ill of you." [35]

Ferne Anderson states, "By 1887 Hopkins was constantly . . . attacked by Eddy" and refused to rebut the attacks. In fact, in the April 1887 issue of the *Christian Science Journal,* Eddy said Hopkins was "deluding the minds she claims to instruct." Hopkins's refusal to rebut would certainly be in keeping with the New Thought tenet of not wanting to give energy to negative behavior. With a wise silence, Hopkins did not create more conflict. The passage of time and the relocation from Boston to Chicago healed Hopkins from the trauma of the abrupt discharge. As a process of renewed vision, she later "saw Eddy as just another version of age-old truths." [36] The perennial philosopher could emerge full-blown in Hopkins. Released from stultifying loyalties, she was free to expand horizons, explore multidimensional spirituality, and focus her own prophetic vision on Truth.

Hopkins Accused of Piracy

Because of internal dissension and what she perceived as defections, Eddy attempted to institute administrative and educational objectives that would selectively make it harder to learn her methods. She developed plans to protect the copying of her work by dividing her program. To ensure the exactitude of her detailed curriculum and thwart the efforts of "every cheerful rascal" who wished to use her ideas, Eddy began the normal class at the college in August 1884. There were ten students enrolled. In February 1885, a group of people traveled from Chicago to Boston to participate as students.[37] Several of this group had come east in February 1884 for the primary course. They, along with some others, had taken Christian Science ideas back to Chicago. The introduction of metaphysical healing proved a great boon for Hopkins when, a year later, she took up residence in Chicago.

Peel believes that Eddy intended for these students who commuted to Boston to return to their home bases upon graduation and found "institutes" to teach students locally. The main office of "Authentic Christian Science" was Eddy's Massachusetts Metaphysical College. The tuition for the preliminary class for practitioners was one hundred dollars. The stated fee for the normal or advanced course for teachers was three hundred dollars. Members of the clergy were charged no tuition, as Eddy wanted to make converts of mainstream ministers. Husband-and-wife teams were admitted two-for-one. She charitably waived payments from people, such as Hopkins, whom she deemed in need of financial assistance.[38]

Gottschalk writes that Hopkins and Plunkett pirated a portion of a "system of metaphysical instruction" from Eddy. He cites no references for this accusation, but it is reminiscent of the Dressers' allegations that Eddy pirated her system of healing from Quimby. Although that particular issue is not to be debated here, it may help to state briefly that Braden reports that critics claim the term *Christian Science* was alleged to have been one of Quimby's that Eddy copied. Stillson Judah, an early historian of New Thought whose scholarly contributions are foundational in the understanding of the metaphysical movements, said that this claim "cannot be supported on the basis of present manuscripts."[39] Because Quimby's coining of the term cannot be proved through the literature, Judah observes that it does not "preclude the possibility that Quimby used the term [verbally]."

The following observation by Judah is well put and helpful in dealing with accusations of piracy from one party to another. Judah reiterates that in examining "the inspired sayings or revelations of all great historical religions, [one] will have distinctive features . . . built upon the religio-cultural blocks of the past." He also makes a useful statement that helps define the relationships between Quimby and Eddy, and Eddy and Hopkins. Allegations of one person having dependence upon another "need not discredit [another's] revelation."[40] The religio-cultural ethos of the 1880s was fertile territory for the "divine missions" of the mind-cure prophets, none of whom had captured the exclusive corner on Truth.

One wonders how carefully guarded any method of instruction can possibly be that is openly practiced and discussed. These allegations of piracy from one party to another lead one to believe that there is a perceived monopoly on Truth and healing. Judah uses this example of the Quimby controversy: Eddy tried to denounce her association with Quimby, recant her eulogy of him, and thereby minimize any influence he had upon her, wishing to be perceived as the sole beneficiary of revelatory knowledge and sole discoverer of Christian Science. Judah says, "It is unfortunate that Christian Science has made such an issue concerning the uniqueness of Mrs. Eddy's revelation."[41] Using Judah's insight and applying it to Hopkins's situation allows each new proponent a religio-cultural block from the past as a foundation for further innovation. Admitting to a shared history does not diminish the originality of a newer revelation; in fact, it is the natural and perhaps the most objective way to understand the evolution of metaphysical healing in U.S. religion and culture. That there are connecting links between proponents is undeniable. Quimby was experimenting with metaphysical healing in the 1850s and 1860s. Eddy further developed the process by adding other dimensions in the 1870s, and Hopkins taught metaphysical principles coast to coast in the 1880s. Metaphysical healing itself is a paradigm shift from the allopathic school of medicine that presupposed a germ theory for sickness. This shift brought the locus of control back to individuals who could "doctor" themselves through right thinking about health. The mind-cure prophets, by removing the power of established medical practitioners to treat disease, were blazing a new trail through the healing arts late in the nineteenth-century United States, and creating an innovative avenue for women to legitimately participate as healing practitioners in a normative culture hostile to women in the medical profession.

In her short tenure as editor of the *Christian Science Journal,* Hopkins had sufficient time to assimilate portions of Eddy's teachings into her own expansive worldview. Hopkins remained reverent toward her teacher. She also became aware, as her own metaphysical sophistication increased, that Eddy could not be the only "[t]eacher sent from God."[42] To be a clone of Eddy would deprive Hopkins and others who would come after her of their own creativity and sense of divine mission.

Hopkins would leave Eddy's organization believing that the process of spiritual transformation coupled with the healing tradition should be taught as an independent or generic Christian Science and that no one individual should lay claim to a monopoly on divine healing.

Eddy's Personality

Gottschalk, in defense of Eddy's militant stance about her particular revelation, says she had "a central dynamic that must be grasped," describing her as "a woman of religious vision" who believed "that she had discovered basic religious truth and had a divinely appointed mission to expound it."[43] Eddy believed that she alone had been chosen by God for a divine mission. In contrast, Hopkins believed she too was fulfilling a transcendent call from a power greater than herself and that there were others with equally divine purposes on earth. It is interesting to note that disciples of Eddy rescue her from charges of appropriating techniques from Quimby, then use the same charges to vindictively accuse Hopkins. Christian Science writers, such as Peel and Gottschalk, draw no parallels and apparently see no pattern in the accusations.

In defense of Eddy, Gottschalk states that few people in the Christian Science movement itself understood Eddy. "[H]er brand of humor . . . tended toward irony and . . . sarcasm. . . . [S]he . . . was in her later years . . . a lonely woman." Eddy lived at a high "level of spiritual intensity." His defense of Eddy attempts to present her in the best light. Unwittingly, he also provides the reasons so many of the bright and promising students left or were forced to leave Christian Science (Hopkins being no exception).

In the final analysis, Eddy thought she had such a monopoly on Truth "that when my students become blinded to me as the one through whom Truth has come to this age, they miss the path."[44]

Eddy's predilection for paranoid thinking takes the forefront in her feelings for Hopkins. Dissension and defection were common denominators among her students. As previously stated, the Christian Science movement was rent with rebellions. In 1888, two years after Eddy fired Hopkins, there was a handful of people in Boston who owed allegiance to Eddy's movement.[45] The mind-cure movement fueled by the independent attitudes of its adherents had vociferously expanded into Christian Science territory and caused mass defections.

In my opinion, it would have been naïve of Eddy to expect that Hopkins would sink into "historical oblivion" and disappear from the religious scene because she fired her. Eddy believed there was a deliberate move among the "mind quacks" to create turmoil in the Christian Science movement so they could draw away the Christian Science students, and thereby swell the ranks of the mind-cure movements. She believed her best and most promising students had been so mentally abducted. Eddy concluded that Hopkins had been kidnapped in this way. She thought the person responsible for this feat of mental ability, whom she believed to be A. J. Swarts, had bragged that it had "taken him six months to bend [Hopkins] to his purpose." It has been reported that Eddy told Hopkins, "You are so full of mesmerism that your eyes stick out like boiled codfish."[46] Apparently, Eddy had no compassion for those students like Hopkins whom she believed had been duped this way. Therapeutic intervention and crisis management were not part of Eddy's treatment plan for these "mentally abducted" victims.

For Eddy, "mind cure" meant a belief that the Divine Mind, God, could cure. Healing occurred as divine power and not as the action of one mind or another. The mind curer healed through "human mind power," a form of malicious magnetism. In its severest form, Eddy called it "malicious animal magnetism." Insightfully, Catherine Wessinger suggests that perhaps this idea postulated by Eddy was a precursor of the brainwashing theory as a method of procuring converts for various religious movements. Christian Science, Eddy argued, was faith healing. She said that other methods of healing were not divine, but were one person's belief displacing another's. She thought Christian Science was based on the concept of Divine Mind, not a human mind.

Use of the Term Christian Science

Hopkins, the excommunicant, went the way of many of the apostates of Christian Science. Believing there was no corner on Truth, Hopkins and others of that time continued to use the generic title of *Christian Science*. This usage has served to confuse those people, including scholars, who have tried to delineate organizational boundaries among contending factions. There were many magazines, newspapers, and journals using *Christian Science* as part of their titles in the 1880s. Most had no formal affiliation with the Christian Science of Eddy. An example of how this use might have confused both the scholars and the laity is seen in Braden's book *Christian Science Today*. Charles Fillmore's use of the title *Christian Science Thought* for his periodical in 1890 might have caused Braden and others to associate the Fillmores with the Christian Science of Eddy. Braden makes the statement that Emma Curtis Hopkins and Charles Fillmore of Unity both came out of Christian Science. In fact, only Hopkins was associated with Eddy. Fillmore studied with several metaphysical healers and was ordained by Hopkins in 1891 in Chicago. Neither Myrtle Fillmore nor Charles Fillmore can be found on the class rolls of Eddy's Massachusetts Metaphysical College. In *The Household of Faith,* James D. Freeman, a Unity writer, states clearly that the Fillmores were never students of Mary Baker Eddy.[47]

The following evaluation of the pioneers of New Thought helps clarify the issue of terminology. Melton describes how the generic use of the term *Christian Science* came about. He argues that in the 1880s, the students were doing two things: They were acknowledging that some of their teaching had derived from Eddy. (In a sense, then, Eddy's former students were acknowledging similarities in thought with her. Eddy, of course, had long since disowned the apostates and considered "their use of the term illegitimate.")[48] They were also attempting to remain separate from competing religious systems, such as Spiritualism and Theosophy.

By using the term *Christian,* early members were acknowledging their Christian heritage while attempting to bring New Thought forward and couple it with scientific advances in human thought.

Hopkins's Affinity with Eddy and Margaret Fuller

The issue of eclecticism was not the sole or perhaps even the primary reason for what could have been an undercurrent of tension between Hopkins and the group surrounding Eddy and Eddy herself. Hopkins knew from the beginning how different their worldviews were: she associated Eddy with "Puritan, conservative soil" in her first editorial. Hopkins had ascertained that Eddy was at heart a Puritan. Peel says this statement by Hopkins indicates that she possessed an "unconscious hankering for lusher intellectual fields and more modish company." [49] Peel's insinuation that Hopkins craved the trendy and fashionable and was feeling intellectually undernourished seems inaccurate. Hopkins used the term *Puritan* descriptively, not as a pejorative assessment of Eddy and the particular mind-set that nurtured her theological development.

Hopkins was a generation younger than Eddy and influenced by the transcendentalist thinking that permeated the cultural milieu of her youth. According to the letters that Hopkins wrote to Mabel Dodge Luhan, her lifelong role model was the transcendentalist freethinker Margaret Fuller. [50] It was to Fuller's transcendentalist spirit that Hopkins resonated. Her earliest book, *Class Lessons, 1888,* and previously mentioned letters to Luhan reveal how much she admired Fuller. Among other achievements, Fuller was the first female war correspondent and writer for a major newspaper. She was an avowed feminist who ardently lived her principles. The prevailing nineteenth-century Victorian ethic promoted the piety and submissiveness of women and lauded their purity. That ethic, to say the least, was repressive and aimed to keep women from challenging the norms of patriarchal culture.

There are parallels in the lives of Hopkins and Fuller. Fuller served as editor of the *Dial* (the publishing organ of the transcendentalists) without pay. Hopkins served as editor of the *Christian Science Journal* without pay. They were both renowned for their speaking abilities. Fuller made history by hostessing her Saturday-morning "Conversations" for women. She wished to alter women's images of themselves. Hopkins was in demand as a speaker and teacher from her late thirties until her death. All that exists today are their written works, which are purported to portray only a fraction of their natural talents. Both supported revolutionary movements: Fuller took part in the Italian revolution, and Hopkins promoted religious and spiritual revolution through her ministry. Fuller had at least one mystical experience that paralleled the type Hopkins had had. Both were catalysts for social justice in their respective generations. Fuller encouraged women to define and pursue goals and to control their own destinies. According to social historian Barbara Welter, when Fuller preached that women were divine and could manage their lives, this idea of "women before God and man was sound Transcendentalist doctrine."[51] Fuller was a philosophical idealist who lived and died in the generation before Hopkins.

Eddy, however, reared in a more puritanical mode by a father who had Calvinistic leanings, was a live, flesh-and-blood reality, a prototypical example of heterodox religious thinking. Eddy was conservative in her personal life, yet founding a contemporary religious movement provided a working paradigm that proved effective for Hopkins to emulate. In *Sex and Power*, contemporary historian and writer Donald Meyer says Eddy "did not do what revivalists did, go out on the highway and preach the Gospel. She wrote a new gospel." Her tenacity and perseverance in the face of hardship eventually earned for her "the longest entry in the entire three volume dictionary of *Notable American Women*."[52] It was this ability to function decisively that charged Hopkins to action.

Both Hopkins and Eddy were raised Congregationalist in New England, but here the similarity ends. In a telephone interview on March 8, 1990, Thomas Johnsen of the Christian Science Committee on Publications in Boston stated that his doctoral study, "Christian Science and the Puritan Tradition," emphasizes the Puritan ethic embraced by Eddy. A common thread through all of her writings is selected aspects of a Puritan tradition that provided a narrower framework than Hopkins's own views. Albanese supported this idea when she said that Eddy was "more loyally Calvinist" than other thinkers of her time.[53]

Hopkins and Eddy were philosophically destined at some point to have disparate theological positions. Eddy, the senior in the relationship by some years, was clearly the authority figure. Hopkins respected this determined, dedicated woman who had persistently persevered in the face of all hardship to share and to teach her religious point of view. At one intersection, for nearly two years, the paths of Hopkins and Eddy converged. Each would ultimately struggle to provide a stable infrastructure for separate arteries of what was then known as the mind-cure movement. According to Johnsen, from Eddy's perspective, the gnosticized New Thought teaching bespoke a radically different sensibility, one cut off from the heart and depths of Christianity. It was this sensibility that Eddy fought to preserve.

To honor her mentor was in keeping with Hopkins's own positive view of Eddy's role as a divine prophet who would reveal spiritual truths for dissemination by the current generation. Many students complete an educational process in which they acquire new skills and knowledge, and then advance to self-directed innovative development.

In an unpublished Ph.D. dissertation, Penny Hansen comments that Eddy, as part of a developmental process of her growth, grew beyond her dependence on men and refocused that dependence on God. It was "the loving God of her mother" that she came to depend on.[54] This statement is the key to understanding the spiritual affinity and connection between Eddy and Hopkins: they both saw God as a triune deity incorporating the feminine energy principle. Their deity was not the traditional male trinitarian deity of mainline Christianity. This specific doctrine provided the model that motivated Hopkins to explore creative avenues in radical thinking.

Eddy was a Victorian female in a patriarchal culture. Because of her persistence, the union of religion with a healing movement allowed women to take health into their own hands, rise above dependence on the male-dominated medical establishment, and surmount an orthodox religious system. Hopkins had met the model-mentor she needed to inspire her to new heights of accomplishment. She could combine spiritual and pragmatic development in the pursuit of social reform through religion. The thirteen months of Hopkins's professional association with Eddy on the *Christian Science Journal* proved pivotal for Hopkins's career. It does not detract from Eddy's unique contributions to U.S. religion to say that both women would make history on their own terms, Eddy in Christian Science and Hopkins in New Thought.

Hopkins's Differences with Eddy

Each woman had a significantly different feminist agenda. For instance, Eddy gave support to some women's issues, but never overtly joined forces with the suffragists or feminists. She surrounded herself with male subordinates. According to R. L. Numbers and R. B. Schoepflin in "Ministries of Healing," the power positions in Christian Science were male dominated. Eddy never adopted a daughter, only a son. Bright and ambitious women had difficulty staying in her movement, and her most "celebrated apostates" were women. Her theological stance concerning the feminine aspects of deity contradicts the practical application of her beliefs that supported the patriarchal structure. Today, her inability to allow women political and administrative power might be termed the *queen-bee syndrome*. Yet, according to Hansen, in Eddy's eyes, "Women had the right to worship, to act benevolently, to work, and to pray." Eddy had an ideal of women that permeated her religious thinking. Not only were women "innately equal," but they were also more "spiritual." Eddy's ideal, according to Hansen, was "not feminism," though there was a devout "sense of feminine worthiness imbedded in the heart of the doctrine."[55] It was this "sense of feminine worthiness" that provided the impetus to catapult the celebrated apostates into realms of power and prestige in pulpits previously occupied by men. Hopkins was no exception.

Eddy clearly considered herself a revelatory prophet on a divine mission, functioning on a path parallel to the prevailing patriarchal religious system. Eddy sought legitimacy, for she wanted mainline acknowledgment of her perceived discovery of the Science of Christ. The theological and philosophical differences between Eddy and Hopkins were due not just to Hopkins's "freewheeling" eclecticism in spiritual affairs, but also to basic differences in worldviews. Although the issues between them vary because of age differences and different experiences, there is a primary problem that is more pronounced than others, namely, Eddy was not a feminist—and Hopkins was.

Eddy had struggled amid religious ridicule and social ostracism. Her allusions to "malicious animal magnetism" suggest a paranoid temperament that carefully guarded what she perceived as her divine revelation of Christian Science. Nonetheless, Eddy's accomplishments are not meant to be minimized here. Attacks on Eddy that used character assassination as a tool for psychological warfare perhaps were initiated by men who felt personally and culturally violated because Eddy "was a woman out of her place" in the nineteenth and early twentieth centuries.[56] Having shaped her perspective through suffering and struggling, Eddy was not going to allow Christian Science to develop haphazardly. Her desire for autocratic control of her emerging institution required vigilance in her choice of students, officers, employees, and supporting personnel.

Hopkins's skill in analysis and critical reconstruction is apparent. One sentence of the November 4, 1885, letter to Julia Bartlett reveals her disposition: "But they could not understand my complex way of explaining myself, nor know that I was digging for facts."[57] Here, in one phrase, is the fundamental difference between Hopkins and the typical disciple: her "complex way." Her own operational guidelines are the ones of a well-versed teacher, accustomed to comparative thinking. It would not have been appropriate for her to accept any new faith on face value. Her letters indicate her initial skepticism but openness to explore this new healing modality.

Peel notes, "Significantly, Mrs. Eddy never made [Hopkins] a teacher." Peel means that it was a sound value judgment on Eddy's part not to entrust Hopkins with a class. It is ironic in light of Peel's evaluation that Hopkins's stellar teaching qualities allowed her to shine brightly as a "[t]eacher's teacher." It is certainly not her lack of talent in teaching that Peel seems to be pointing to. In a backhanded compliment, he recognized her "good service as an editor" of the *Christian Science Journal*. Charles Fillmore, a student of Hopkins and cofounder of the Unity School of Christianity, supported this statement of Hopkins's teaching ability: "She is undoubtedly the most successful teacher in the world." One of her listeners reported to Fillmore that he had heard many of the nineteenth century's great contemporary orators and said Hopkins "had surpassed them all . . . with never a criticism of any sect or school." [58]

Conclusions

Hopkins saw the truths of Christian Science in all the great traditions of the world. The feminist eclecticism that placed her at odds with Eddy also led her to believe that Eddy "did not discover Christian Science, she merely presented it anew." [59] With an energetic, spiritual purpose, Hopkins moved her base of operations to Chicago for what would be the most dynamic years of growth in her career. There her innovative policies fortified the foundation and provided the organizational structure of the New Thought movement in the United States. Hopkins's feminist value system would influence important national events and support the emergence of a consciousness that accelerated the emancipation of women.

2

THE CHICAGO YEARS

The Transition Period

*A*fter her separation from Eddy, Emma Curtis Hopkins looked to the expanded frontiers of the Midwest as fertile territory for the free expression of metaphysical healing, which she continued to call Christian Science. The choice of Chicago proved fortuitous for Hopkins. Administrative management was not of special interest to Hopkins, and she formed an alliance with Mary Plunkett. Plunkett assumed the role of promoter and organizer, and Hopkins was probably glad to have the forthright Plunkett manage the nuts and bolts of their operation. After several months in Chicago, Hopkins would focus on teaching, which was her forte. Gottschalk stated that Plunkett and Hopkins founded the International Christian Science Association in 1886, implying they set this group up to rival Eddy. This assertion is not true. The International Christian Science Association was formed by Plunkett alone in New York in the spring of 1888 as a rival enterprise to the national network of Hopkins Associations.[1]

As mentioned in chapter 1, Christian Science had already been introduced into the Midwest. In fact, Christian Science had spread from Boston westward to San Francisco. People who became independent of Eddy's group wanted to keep a healing emphasis within the parameters of religion, but did not want to retain her ideas of the perceived dangers of mortal mind or her beliefs in malicious animal magnetism. Many of the freelance independents rejected an autocratic centralized structure such as the one found in Eddy's Church of Christ, Scientist. In a nutshell, Eddy's teaching became subject to syncretism.

Hopkins Edits Mind-Cure Journal

When Hopkins and Plunkett looked west, Edward J. Arens and others had already laid the foundations of metaphysical healing. Arens had taught George B. Charles who in turn taught Bradford Sherman. The Shermans (a husband-wife-and-son team) then journeyed to Boston to study directly with Eddy in the class of February 25, 1884.[2] As a result of their affiliation with her, they returned to Chicago and were founders of the First Church of Christ, Scientist. They were appreciative enough of Eddy and her teaching to send her a handsome Christmas present. The Shermans remained personally and professionally loyal to Eddy, even as their work, along with Arens's and some others', acquainted Chicago with metaphysical healing prior to the arrival of Hopkins. One can see a convoluted example of the splintered lineage here: Arens, a student of Eddy's husband, and Charles, whom he taught, became independents, neither of whom was taught by Eddy herself; yet, Charles's students, the Shermans, traveled to Boston and became members of Eddy's orthodoxy.

When Eddy made her pioneering journey to teach a class in Chicago in May 1884, Hopkins remained in the East to edit the *Christian Science Journal*. During this visit, Eddy encountered Swarts. He founded the rival Illinois Christian Science College. He also founded the first literary publication to challenge the *Christian Science Journal*, the *Mind Cure Journal* (later *Mental Science Magazine*).

As mentioned previously, Hopkins, as editor of the *Christian Science Journal*, devoted several pages of journal space to a castigation of Swarts. In an article titled "What Is Plagiarism?" she said Swarts was "the editor of an obscure little publication in Chicago" who was using Eddy's work "without crediting the same." She further stated that she had been the editor of the journal from September 1884 to April 1885 and that she, not Eddy, was responsible for the statement in the February 1885 issue in which she called Swarts's journal a "pretentious little publication" and reminded him of the Arens plagiarism case in Boston. Hopkins, to demonstrate what she meant by plagiarism, then lifted passages from his periodical that sounded similar to passages from Eddy's *Science and Health*. She warned him that the fact that "quotations are not verbatim doesn't signify" they are not pulled from older original work. In the final paragraph of the article, Hopkins militantly challenged Swarts to honor "Ingersoll's Strategic Command: Put up, or shut up." She stated that she had "obeyed the first half of his oracle's injunction" by demonstrating how he had borrowed Eddy's work. It was up to Swarts to "show his wisdom by following the second" injunction, which was to "shut up." [3]

When Hopkins relocated to Chicago, she did not, upon arrival, establish an independent center of Christian Science healing.[4] According to Melton, she worked temporarily as a practitioner, and for at least five months in 1886 she edited the same *Mind Cure Journal* she had so roundly denounced a few months before. In a letter dated December 25, 1886 (fourteen months after her October 1885 discharge), to Eddy, Hopkins said that a letter she had received from Julia Bartlett on November 4, 1885, at the time of the discharge was "absolutely malicious." This letter is the clue to why Hopkins edited the *Mind Cure Journal*. Because of the vituperative nature of the letter, Hopkins decided "to take up . . . the offer of editing the *Mental Science Magazine* while its editor [Swarts] was in Kansas." In the same letter, she told Eddy, "I was not well used by the management of affairs in Boston. . . . The charge against me of mesmerism is puerile and ridiculous. Your students make themselves simple by such attempts to damage me." [5]

The editorial position that Hopkins assumed after leaving Eddy seems to have been engineered by Plunkett. Swarts was Plunkett's friend. There are no records available of the conversation between Hopkins and Swarts as they negotiated her editorial position on his magazine, so one assumes that Plunkett, with her persuasive techniques, was able to mend the breach between them. Apparently, Swarts was magnanimous in his forgiveness of Hopkins for attacking him and calling his articles in the *Mind Cure Journal* "plagiarisms." It is most likely that Hopkins's protective ardor toward Eddy cooled when she left the editorship of Eddy's *Christian Science Journal*. She no longer felt the need to vindicate Eddy when she herself felt victimized and "not well used by the management of affairs in Boston." However, she never spoke ill of Eddy in any of her writings. In fact, when she referred to "my teacher," it was with respect.

Hopkins Founds College of Christian Science

Hopkins had been in Chicago several months when she decided to branch out. In the spring of 1886, she founded the Emma Curtis Hopkins College of Christian Science in central Chicago.[6] Plunkett was the administrative president and Hopkins the teacher. Class work totaled twelve lessons for the month. Hopkins delivered a sermon at the Ethical Culture Society Hall each Sunday. After the graduation of the first class from the Emma Curtis Hopkins College of Christian Science in 1886, a student association was organized called the Hopkins Metaphysical Association. The energetic Plunkett became the first president.

This association, though it was started by Hopkins's students, was an open forum for people interested in metaphysical healing. Melton says "metaphysicians, including spiritualists and theosophists," were permitted membership.[7] The organization was loose, but despite the casual ambiance of the association, it became a model for metaphysical schools and branch associations. Plunkett resigned as president of the association in 1887, and Ephraim T. Castle, one of the few prominent males in the group at this time, became the second president.

The Emma Curtis Hopkins College of Christian Science graduated its first class in June 1886. Melton states in his paper that no records remain for the original class, but he has reconstructed a list of the thirty-seven participants from a synthesis of other sources. Among them were Helen Wilmans and Ida Nichols, who later founded and edited *Christian Science,* the literary vehicle for Hopkins's student association; Mabel McCoy, who introduced Fannie James to Christian Science; and Kate (Mrs. Frank) Bingham, who introduced metaphysical healing to Nona Brooks. McCoy, James, Bingham, and Brooks were instrumental in founding Divine Science.[8] Each of these students became a teacher of extraordinary influence in New Thought. This premier class of students became key figures who founded organized groups to develop and institutionalize the healing ministry. Each person Melton mentions became a recognized teacher or editor who influenced the healing movement in its early development and facilitated the rapid growth of the establishment of New Thought centers or churches. The first class of 1886 cemented Hopkins's reputation as a teacher of teachers, and she built the primary New Thought network that established her nationwide ministry on this early foundation.

Hopkins's influence had transnational importance due to the pioneering zeal exhibited by her students as evangelists. As a result, Hopkins was a threat to Eddy's version of Christian Science and to the supremacy of Eddy. A little more than a year after her relocation to Chicago, Hopkins was attacked by Sarah Crosse, who had assumed the editorship of the *Christian Science Journal* when Hopkins was discharged. Crosse wrote an article titled "Beware of False Teachers." She said, "Mrs. Plunkett and Mrs. Hopkins are traveling over the land, professedly teaching Christian Science, and deluding their victims. . . . [B]e it said that their journeying is done for the ducats, and not the interest of the Cause." Another charge that Crosse brought to bear against them was that "they both belong to a theosophical society. Theosophy is only another name for Animal Magnetism." Fear of Hopkins as a potential rival in the Christian Science arena was the motivating factor behind the attacks. The accusation that Hopkins and Plunkett were Theosophists was probably provoked by the inclusive nature of the Hopkins Metaphysical Association. The vitriolic attacks were attempts to stem what Eddy perceived as a furious tide of defectors. According to Bates and Dittemore, Eddy "coined the phrase 'Mind Quack' to describe Julius Dresser, A. J. Swarts, Mrs. Hopkins, and another recent renegade, Mrs. Mary Plunkett." [9]

In a section of the *Christian Science Journal* called "Questions Answered by Mary Baker Eddy," there is an obviously planted question: "Emma Hopkins tells her students that Mrs. Eddy teaches mesmerism. Is that true?" Eddy's roundabout answer was: "She took a Primary Course at my College, but was not permitted to go farther. . . . [She] is not qualified to teach Christian Science, and is incapable of teaching it." There is an admonition for students to check credentials "because of unqualified teachers." [10] In Eddy's view, a qualified teacher taught her version of Christian Science and acknowledged her as the sole discoverer and founder. The developing mind-cure movement gathered momentum. Despite Eddy's frequent attacks, it was beyond her control to manipulate. Once Hopkins was at the helm, New Thought lost its loose configuration and began to develop organizational structure under her direction. What had been independent metaphysical thought began to show the influence and direction of Hopkins's distinct feminist theology.

Despite Eddy's assault on her teaching credentials, Hopkins earned the label "Teacher of Teachers" of the New Thought movement because of the prominence of those people whom she taught. This title is found in both New Thought periodicals reverent to her and in critical scholarly works by Braden and Judah. Hopkins's success with that first Chicago class left an indelible imprint on the religious history of the late-nineteenth-century United States. That this imprint carried over into the twentieth century is not surprising. Catherine Wessinger, in the introduction to *Women's Leadership in Marginal Religions: Explorations Outside the Mainstream,* states, "Contemporary feminist spirituality and theology have strong roots in the metaphysical movements." Mary Farrell Bednarowski, in "Widening the Banks of the Mainstream: Women Constructing Theologies," denotes that these women, who were in some cases theological mavericks, applied their creativity "as artists whose medium is the theology of their own particular tradition." [11]

The Rapid Development of Hopkins's Career

Eddy "closed her metaphysical college and surrendered the charter" just as Hopkins was achieving her greatest success as a teacher. According to a short news brief contained in the second 1889 issue of *Modern Thought,* a journal edited by Charles Fillmore, Eddy closed the doors of her metaphysical college on October 29, 1889. The reason she gave for the closing was that Christ's teaching does not support material methods of learning but should be "of a spiritual foundation." (I think she means by "material methods" a classroom situation where students are charged tuition for the course work.) Eddy provided her own explanation of why the college closed in the November 1889 journal: "The First and only College of Christian Science Mind-healing, after accomplishing the greatest work of the ages and at the pinnacle of prosperity is closed. Let Scientists who have grown to self-sacrifice do their present work awaiting with staff in God's commands." By closing the doors of her college, she removed herself from any direct competition with Hopkins.

In the same issue of *Modern Thought,* there are several references to Hopkins, including her six treatments for every day of the week (but Sunday), which seem to be her own development in metaphysical healing. There is an announcement that "the eminent Christian Science teacher . . . will open her class January 6 [1890]" in Kansas City. A Dr. Thacher indicates, "A larger room will have to be secured in order to accommodate the many" wanting to attend the lectures. The author of the article (probably Charles Fillmore) closes it as follows: "This is good news and we hope to see a grand metaphysical rally such an [*sic*] has never been seen in this part of the country." The next news brief indicates that during the last half of December, meetings would be held in Kansas City, "preceding the advent of Mrs. Hopkins."[12]

Several scholars working today acknowledge Hopkins's importance in the last century. In an unpublished Ph.D. dissertation titled "Horatio Dresser and the Philosophy of New Thought," Alan Anderson said, "In the so-called metaphysical movement's development one of the most important figures was Emma Curtis Hopkins." He perceived her "as a link between Christian Science and New Thought and as a teacher in her own right." Hopkins's "meteoric career" began in 1884, according to Peel, who said she was "a young woman of . . . brilliant potentialities."[13] In the ensuing years, scholarly work built on these and other ideas about Hopkins's influential role has served as inspiration for the recovery of the material that documents her contributions.

As Hopkins moved out of orthodox Christian Science, she continued to develop the eclectic ideas she had expressed in one of her first articles, "God's Omnipresence." Her own theory was that Christian Science was another manifestation of "Life, Truth, Holiness-Health" and that there was "Truth in every religious system of the world, else it would find no followers."[14]

Hopkins emerged as a theological force to contend with in Chicago. While recovering from her abrupt discharge in Boston, she had the presence of mind to assess her own peculiar strengths and weaknesses and formulate a working plan for the dissemination of Christian Science Truth as she perceived it and had dedicated her life to it. Hopkins, even though a product of nineteenth-century Victorian culture, answered a transcendent call and took on the role of radical feminist. Accompanied by her husband and son, she left for an unfamiliar destination in the Midwest. This decision to relocate and establish a feminist ministry had to be based on a spiritual cause. Her final decision to make a monumental move may have been predicated on the reawakened vision from her childhood to found a hospital for "sick, destitute children." As Dell deChant states, the development of a "religious technology" by the metaphysical family of religions was in part a response to modernize religion through what were perceived as scientific methodologies.[15] Hopkins heard the transcendent call and became a pivotal figure in the structuring of this "religious technology," centralizing the spiritual-healing precepts tantamount to her specific vision.

Periods of Success and Trial

The first full year after Hopkins relocated to Chicago was 1887, and it proved foundational for her and for New Thought; in fact, it was critical for her ministry. In October 1887, Hopkins attended a two-day meeting in Boston of the various eclectic factions of the mind-cure movement. Peel reports that at this meeting, "No one agreed with anyone else, but everyone got a hearing." (If his assessment is correct, the group was democratic in process. He does not specify his reasons for this conclusion.) At this meeting of the independent healers not affiliated with Eddy, Hopkins was introduced by physician Luther Marston as the "star that rose in the East and has spread its glory throughout the West." Melton says this prominent introduction by Marston, who was a leading independent in the Boston area, proved Hopkins's "emerging role as the dominant voice among the independents."[16]

Several factors led to Hopkins's dominance. There was a growing population of students who were finding their way to Chicago for the monthly classes sponsored by Hopkins College. New branch affiliates of Hopkins Associations were springing up each month in various parts of the country. Also, during 1887, Hopkins made three major teaching trips. In April, she journeyed to San Francisco to teach 250 students. This class held the record for the largest of any Christian Science (or New Thought) teacher for many years. In October, Hopkins traveled to Milwaukee to teach, and in November she taught another large class at New York's Murray Hill Hotel. Her most notable student in this class was Harriet Emilie Cady, the homeopathic physician who would later author *Lessons in Truth*, a classic text for the Unity School of Christianity that is still in use today. At the end of 1887, there were seventeen branches of the Hopkins Metaphysical Association from Maine to California.

Hopkins's skill in teaching and public speaking allowed her to rise above the many independent practitioners who had left Eddy's Church of Christ, Scientist. Most independent teachers who established schools were limited to a small practice in their specific location. Due to student demand, Hopkins College was able to schedule regular monthly classes at the Chicago headquarters and send teachers on missionary assignments to other U.S. cities. It is for these reasons that Hopkins emerged as the most dynamic figure in the new movement. Having the only organized coast-to-coast ministry secured for her the pacesetter position. To complicate matters, Plunkett, for reasons unknown, decided to promote both Eddy and Hopkins at the 1887 meeting. She told the assembly, "People have tried to get truth in various ways, but the world never knew how to get it until it came through *Science and Health*." [17] During the same conference she also praised her partner, Hopkins. This confusing move by Plunkett was not understood by either party because many of the attendees were apostates of Eddy's movement or ones who had disagreed strongly with her. It seemed out of place for Plunkett to praise someone who had excommunicated her and called her a "Mind Quack." In November 1887, one month after the Boston meeting, Plunkett founded a publishing company and monthly journal called *Truth, a Magazine of Christian Science*. This magazine would serve both the school founded by Hopkins and Plunkett and the student association.

When Hopkins returned to Chicago from Boston, she instituted changes in living space. The house on Michigan Avenue that had served initially as headquarters had been rented. Moving rapidly, Hopkins purchased a large home as the permanent facility for the college. The new building was dedicated on December 1, 1887. Making the commitment to purchase housing was a sign of triumph from Hopkins. In 1883, as a novice under Eddy's tutelage, she could not have "commanded a single dollar." The year 1887 had been good for the growth of New Thought and the emergence of Hopkins as a foundational figure in the movement. It was on the strength of this success that Hopkins took the economic risk of expanding her growing ministry to include a sizable facility as a home base.

There was a downside after the initial success of 1887. The Hopkins-Plunkett liaison dissolved early in 1888, when Plunkett relocated to New York. Her fame in the metaphysical healing community there prior to her association with Hopkins had earned her the title of "High Priestess," as she flamboyantly taught her own brand of Christian Science healing.[18] Plunkett seemed to have innate tendencies that gave her talent as a promoter. After moving to New York, she continued for a short while to return to Chicago for student meetings, but soon stopped. She withdrew support from Hopkins's college, taking the magazine named *Truth* and, with it, the subscription list. Melton states that "by the summer of 1888, Plunkett formed a rival 'International Christian Science Association' and renamed *Truth* the *International Magazine for Christian Science,* [an] organ for Plunkett's new work."[19] The defection of Plunkett from Hopkins's forces meant that the journal designed to transmit messages between Chicago and Hopkins's outreach satellites in various states was no longer operative. A result of this loss of communication seems to have been that many outreach locations became independent or aligned with Plunkett's New York association.

In 1888, additional problems manifested through the Hopkins organizations, as personal and internal dissension whittled away the student population. Hopkins did not like administrative management and had allowed laissez-faire ideas to develop. This experiment in freethinking seems to have fragmented the loyalty of the students and promoted sibling rivalry. Helen Wilmans, a noted suffragist and one of Hopkins's followers, said the discord was responsible for her selling her magazine and relocating to Georgia. Hopkins, regretting the lack of structure, used this critical time to reorganize and redesign her ministry.

By 1889, Plunkett in New York was far removed from Hopkins in the Midwest. Plunkett's problems, however, were just beginning. Though still married, she involved herself with A. Bently Worthington, professing that a "spiritual-marriage" existed between them. Concomitantly, she attempted to identify herself as a student of Eddy, as if doing so would insulate and protect her from public opinion. Desperately seeking legitimacy for her strange affair, she tried to use passages from Eddy's *Science and Health* to promote the clandestine arrangement of a "spiritual" husband. (Eddy had at one time explained her marriage to A. G. Eddy as a "spiritual marriage" on behalf of the cause. However, she would never have recommended eschewing legalities.) Peel does not give sources for the following information, but he says that Worthington was "exposed as an embezzler wanted on an old charge and a bigamist with a child and several wives in other states. Quickly he melted away."[20] Consequently, Plunkett's career ended in shambles, and her publication folded.

Peel reports that it was at this time, in 1889, after the "spiritual marriage," that "Hopkins dropped [Plunkett] like an asp discovered in her breakfast cereal." He does not seem to grasp that as early as mid-1888, Plunkett and Hopkins had formally separated. Hopkins had for a year or more been disassociated from Plunkett when Plunkett committed the "monumental indiscretion that assured her downfall." Gottschalk does not check the time frame either, stating that "at the beginning of the affair, Mrs. Hopkins . . . bowed out." There was no "bowing out" for Hopkins to do: Hopkins and Plunkett had already parted company.[21] Plunkett had set herself up as a competitor in metaphysical healing when she absconded with the subscription list to *Truth*. In fact, the convention in Boston in late 1887 where Plunkett praised both Hopkins and Eddy may have been the harbinger of Plunkett's defection. This time-frame oversight by both writers seems to be an indirect way of attempting to associate Hopkins with the alleged sexual excesses and unstable behavior of Plunkett.

The period of trial for Hopkins had a gloomy financial side. She had already taken substantial economic risk to purchase a large house. With the dissolution of her partnership with Plunkett she was left to manage the nuts and bolts of administration and teach. Ida Nichols described the situation: "Here was the position: A large, expensive house, necessity for expensive help, very few patients, no pupils to speak of, no friends, no one to help." People who had promised help for this venture fell by the wayside. The students who had not abandoned Hopkins questioned her about the situation. She advised them to use the energy of their anger constructively by focusing on healing those people in need of treatment. To stew about their situation was a waste of energy: "Take the anger that chokes you like a reed in the wind. In the heat of your anger, treat some sluggish paralytic."[22]

Several events occurred as a result of the short-lived professional relationship between Hopkins and Plunkett. After the split, Hopkins assumed the presidency of the college and association and gave it new direction. She reevaluated the task of integrating physical and mental healing with religion. Melton said, "She concluded that her work must stand out and become more than merely the training of alternative healing practitioners." He quoted her as saying, "Christian Science is not a business or a profession, it is a ministry." Because Hopkins viewed her mission as sacred, the advanced course would no longer be taught in a classroom setting, but conducted as a tailor-made curriculum in "Theology and Practical Ministry" on a one-on-one basis with the senior student. This decision to work individually was a portent of the type of teaching-healing to which Hopkins devoted the last twenty-five years of her life. As a response to her renewed dedication to healing and religious doctrine, Hopkins remodeled the school she had founded. She made the leap from a college to an ecclesiastically structured seminary. By the summer of 1888, the school under her direction had made the transition to "Theological Seminary for the Preparation of Students for the Christian Science Ministry."[23]

Hopkins's second pioneer project for 1888 was to institute weekly Bible lessons in *Christian Science,* beginning in October 1888 with a commentary on passages found in Josh. 3:5–17. This project followed quickly on the heels of the transition from college to seminary.[24]

The third project that commanded Hopkins's attention during 1888 was the replacement of the magazine *Truth,* which Plunkett had taken. This situation was resolved when Ida Nichols, a senior student of Hopkins, inherited some money. After a discussion with Hopkins, Nichols agreed to found and fund with her inheritance a magazine called *Christian Science.* According to Melton, "The premier issue of *Christian Science* appeared in September 1888 with an initial press run of ten thousand copies."[25] The magazine's appearance marked the end of a time of trial. The days and months of hardship were passing. With equanimity at the September meeting of the association, Hopkins thanked the people who helped in her organization's plight and the ones who did not. The loyal members of the association who pulled together had found strength in their ability to handle adversity. The ones who had not helped had forced them to gather their own resources and re-create, solidifying the foundations of their New Thought ministry.[26] Hopkins, despite her dislike of administration, had become an able executive in "turn-around management."

By the fall of 1888, with the lean months of trial behind her, Hopkins optimistically said in *Christian Science* that "we ought to send missionaries out. . . . [O]ther cities need us." She was now a seasoned veteran, ready to supply national groups a working model for the establishment of new ministries. The year 1888 had been one of monumental change for Hopkins and her students. Acting zealously in the wake of her success, she dispatched her eager students as missionaries. Although some of the outreach components had aligned previously with Plunkett, various locations were responding to the missionary efforts of Hopkins. New people became interested in the Hopkins Association and traveled to Chicago to study at the seminary. By the time the seminary was in operation for a year, the missionary focus was stable and well organized. In *Sex and Power*, Meyer says, "Old churches opened few doors to women, the new ones many."[27] Hopkins, with others of her time, had created a viable avenue for American women who wished to be not only an integral part of a religion, but also the controlling forces within it.

Helen (Nellie) Van Anderson and Jane Yarnall took the lead in missionary activity. Van Anderson would later found the first stable New Thought Center in Boston. Yarnall reorganized the branch in St. Louis. Classes at the seminary were scheduled to allow the faculty to move around the country teaching classes in outreach areas. Melton said that by the time the first class graduated from the seminary, the work "again assumed national proportions." For instance, activity was reported in Dayton, Ohio, led by Nina V. Hughes; Louisville, Kentucky, led by Angela Crippen-Davis; and in Denver, Colorado, led by Mary J. Butler. John S.

Thacher headed the College of Christian Science in Kansas City in March 1887. Kate Bingham taught in Pueblo, Colorado. There were associations in Sedalia, Missouri; Madison, Wisconsin; and Olney, Illinois. There were people in the first graduating class from St. Paul, Minnesota; Janesville, Wisconsin; Philadelphia, Pennsylvania; Peoria, Illinois; and Cedar Rapids, Iowa. The times of struggle for Hopkins had paid off. The establishment of specific academic goals to emphasize the sacredness of her mission had succeeded.

The Evolution of New Thought

The development of the New Thought movement was a gradual evolution from several sources. As mentioned earlier, Phineas Parkhurst Quimby (who died in 1866 and had treated Eddy) is sometimes mentioned as the founder of New Thought. For instance, Braden, who was writing in the early sixties, credited him with founding "New Thought and the Metaphysical Movements in America." Albanese states in recent work, "Quimby was surely the harbinger of a new age." She finds that his creative mind "hammered out a confused—but still commanding theology of healing, for a character document for American metaphysical religion." Judah, who wrote several years after Braden, says Quimby was the "forefather of the mental science healing groups." His influence is undisputed. No one questions the authenticity of his contributions to the New Thought movement. Nonetheless, recent scholarship encourages a careful reevaluation of Braden's position. Melton, who has done critical assessments based on primary-text materials not available to Braden, illustrated Quimby's exact role within metaphysical healing. He states, "New Thought historians frequently overlook the point that until the 1880s, no movement existed. Quimby gathered only a few pupils, taught informally and never published his material."[28] The work of Phineas Parkhurst Quimby, though vital, was clearly limited in scope. There was a twenty-year period between Quimby's death and the development of organizational New Thought. In light of current research, it seems more apropos to say that Quimby was the father of New Thought ideas or the "forefather" of New Thought.

In his discussions of the various tributaries responsible for the development of New Thought, Melton says, "Often overlooked is the role of Emma Curtis Hopkins. She remained closer to Eddy in her teaching than Quimby and helped make New Thought the uneasy synthesis of Eddy and Quimby, which it is today." Hopkins is cited in Melton's work as "the teacher of the great New Thought leaders, from Ernest Holmes to Charles and Myrtle Fillmore." Although no one disputes the position of Hopkins as teacher of teachers, Christian Science does not like to admit there is a linkage between New Thought and Christian Science. Nevertheless, "the two movements are historically related," according to Melton. "New Thought was . . . built upon the work of Eddy's early students, particularly Emma Curtis Hopkins." In fact, Melton asserts, Hopkins came into the movement in December 1883, when Eddy's group was splintering.[29]

Alan Anderson raises another question in "Contrasting Strains of Metaphysical Idealism Contributing to New Thought," a paper presented at the American Academy of Religion meeting in Boston in 1987. He notes that Hopkins's "references to science do not seem to follow the usages of Quimby and Eddy."[30] It looks as though in Hopkins's particular case, there was an independent development of the idea of "science." Anderson's assessment of the various strains inherent in New Thought and Hopkins's originality seems to support the idea that Hopkins was an innovator whose ideas were not cloned from either Quimby or Eddy. Certainly, the radical feminist points of view that she quickly implemented in her network of ministries bear little or no resemblance to these forebears. Quimby was preoccupied with the healing of individuals. Eddy was preoccupied with creating institutional Christian Science and refining her major work, *Science and Health*. Hopkins's focus was the dissemination of Christian Science Truth as a catalyst for spiritual, social, and economic change.

Hopkins nurtured New Thought from its embryonic inception to the successful implantation of metaphysical healing concepts (which she called Christian Science) into coast-to-coast affiliated networks. She decreed the movement fulfilled the prophecy of the Second Coming of Christ into the contemporary world. She threw her ministry into social activism because she believed the mission marked a paradigm shift that supported radical change and improvement for the status of women in the religious arena and society at large. Rosemary Radford Ruether and Rosemary S. Keller observe that after the Civil War, there was "the beginning of a massive effort to win rights for women in politics, in the legal system, in church hierarchies, and in professional employment." Hopkins, through her New Thought ministry, vigorously supported these efforts. Women at that time were attempting to achieve parity in the mainstream denominations. Some of the first women who were successful in seeking ordination did so in the period after the Civil War. Anna Howard Shaw was the first woman ordained to the ministry in the Methodist Protestant Church in 1880, but few others followed in her footsteps. Hopkins supported the ordination of women not as tokens of parity, but as models of female empowerment that were ordained by God. Her commitment to the Second Coming of Christ catapulted her movement to the forefront of social-justice activity. In this respect, Hopkins served as a cultural and religious catalyst. She, her ministry, and the movement that can be traced directly to her classes—first at the college, then at the seminary—were foundational supports for many "women at the close of the nineteenth century [who] felt a keen sense of their own power within a large world." [31]

Hopkins and New Thought

In the period of the 1890s, the term *New Thought* became prominent for groups not associated with Eddy's Christian Science. Today, the Christian Science movement is emphatic about the separation between Eddy's Christian Science and New Thought groups developed elsewhere. The twentieth century saw the arteries diverge even more, as these two components of the mental-healing movement segregated for all time. During the early twentieth century, men assumed roles as editors, teachers, publishers, writers, and historians in New Thought. Because of the decentralization, the feminist impulse was diluted and Hopkins's role obscured. [32]

There were many diverse groups and noteworthy people who made pertinent contributions in the pioneer days of the mind-cure movement in the nineteenth century. Yet, Gary Ward suggests that Hopkins was the primary founder of New Thought, noting that the Hopkins Metaphysical Association had twenty-one branches coast to coast by the latter part of

1887. He credits Hopkins as the person who "establishe[d] the first national New Thought network."[33]

As previously noted, Hopkins was not the only teacher of New Thought. There were many practitioners who were working, writing, lecturing, and training others. What distinguished Hopkins was the people who attended her classes as pupils. Ward says, "[E]ither [Hopkins] or her pupils taught the founders of virtually every major surviving New Thought group today—Unity School of Christianity, Homes of Truth, the Divine Science Church, and the Church of Religious Science."[34]

As discussed earlier, the annual meeting of independent practitioners in mental healing was held in Boston in the latter part of 1887. An example of Hopkins's oratorical power is supplied by Melton who quotes a witness to her speech: "Other speakers may give the impression that Science is a good thing. She gives the impression that it is a true thing."[35]

On December 17, 1883, Hopkins, in her second letter to Eddy, defined her skills and talents and asked Eddy if she might become her assistant. She said, "I do not speak extemporaneously (I never tried)." In a period of four years, she would polish speaking in public and private to a fine art. She said to Eddy in the same letter, "If the science is really really true I am in love with it and will do you no discredit in the future." Her own conviction as to the verity of mental healing satisfied her and hence others in later years. The numbers of new members (some traveling great distances) to join her classes indicate that Hopkins's reputation quickly became foundational in New Thought circles. Her first three letters to Eddy in 1883 and 1884 prove that she became dedicated to the new healing process after her first skeptical encounter at Eddy's lecture in New Hampshire. Ultimately, Hopkins lived her entire life "in love with" healing and teaching. In Hopkins's third letter to Eddy, dated January 14, 1884, she says, "I am abundantly qualified with courage. . . . I lay my whole life and all my talents . . . to this work." It was this single-minded sincerity of purpose that fueled Hopkins's success as a Truth teacher.

Hopkins's eclectic background as a well-educated, well-read teacher (for that time period) provided her intellectual framework. It was this all-encompassing eclecticism that made her attractive to others also. In her letter of December 25, 1886 (fourteen months after her abrupt discharge), Hopkins explained to Eddy, "My knowledge of the older philosophies as corroborative evidence to this has drawn around me literary people." In fact, this statement is a key to understanding the influence Hopkins had not only on the religious aspects of New Thought, but also on the secular aspects of the movement. Most of the "literary people" Hopkins spoke of were the "movers and shakers" of the late 1880s and '90s.

Hopkins possessed a decidedly feminist consciousness, and as a result of her pivotal position in New Thought, she gave early New Thought a self-conscious feminist foundation. The "literary people" who were drawn to her were also feminists and representatives of the women's movement. They were probably interested in Hopkins's monistic philosophy that transcended denominational lines. Because of the eclectic focus of her ministry, it had a strong propensity to be generalized into a secular format, which could be a diffuse catalyst for social justice. For instance, Hopkins did not approve of alcohol consumption, so her teachings fit into the temperance movement. However, she saw alcoholism not as a moral problem or physical disease, but as a spiritual hunger for Truth.

Ruether and Keller conclude that Christian Scientists (in the New Thought movement) shared some "millenarian or spiritualist perspective with utopians." They assert that these people believed they were "an avant-garde of a new redeemed age of humanity, anticipating and leading the transformation of the world toward a new level of spiritual perfection." [36] That these ideas dovetail into social reform is no accident.

Many of the people who surrounded Hopkins in these years were already influential in suffrage circles. They included, for instance, women "who were already making a contribution to the secular phase of the women's movement, such as physician Alice Stockham, editors Helen Wilmans and Elizabeth Boynton Harbert, poet Ella Wheeler Wilcox, and author educator Abby Morton Diaz." [37] There is a difference between what Hopkins was doing and the typical social club of the day. Hopkins deliberately directed New Thought to the forefront of feminist activism. As Hopkins revealed in the essay "Ministry of the Holy Mother" and her other early work written at this time, she and her companions asserted their feminist principles, lived by them, and organized their world around them. As will be seen later, Hopkins clearly assumed roles and duties normally ascribed to males alone, particularly the power to ordain clergy.

Hopkins's broad educational background adds credibility to the role of wise adviser. At the time she wrote the December 25, 1886, letter to Eddy, Hopkins, no longer a novice, was thirty-seven years old and had just entered her prime as a major proponent of New Thought. Her experiences in Christian Science for the thirteen months of her professional affiliation and nearly two-year association with Eddy strengthened her formal skills as an editor, teacher, and writer for the years of challenge, trial, and triumph ahead.

Hopkins's Role Obscured in the Development of New Thought

According to Melton, the development of independent or generic Christian Science can be traced to the October 1881 "resignation of eight of Eddy's students." Miranda Rice, one of the eight who resigned, relocated to San Francisco the next year and became the first healing practitioner on the Pacific Coast. She was a seasoned veteran who had initially studied in Eddy's class of 1872. After eleven loyal years, she withdrew membership from both the Church of Christ, Scientist, and the Christian Science Association, claiming, along with the seven others, that she could no longer submit to the "frequent ebullitions of temper, love of money, and the appearance of hypocrisy." [38]

Several of Eddy's more ambitious students, such as Edward J. Arens of Chicago, formed healing practices and schools based on the model of Eddy's Massachusetts Metaphysical College. Arens persevered in establishing the University of Spiritual Science in order to teach his synthesized healing modality, called "Old Theology." By 1883, generic or independent Christian Science had crossed the country.

Actually, Eddy's fight with Arens, claiming he had plagiarized important metaphysical material from Eddy's husband and murdered him through malicious animal magnetism, raged through the newspapers. This argument had monumental import in the history of the metaphysical movement because it served to obscure Hopkins's contributions to New

Thought for nearly a century. In fact, several important events that happened at about this time led Melton to conclude that "New Thought was born in the midst of an intense polemic."[39] The history of the times was troubled in terms of stability of existing groups. As mentioned previously, Eddy's organization suffered severe splintering during the 1880s. Many of her brightest and best students took their talents elsewhere. It was at this time that Julius Dresser moved to Boston. Dresser and Eddy had met in the 1860s because they had both known Phineas Parkhurst Quimby and were interested in his healing methods. It was at the time Eddy's movement was splintering that Dresser attacked Eddy for being a plagiarist who had taken the thought of Quimby and thereby created Christian Science. Arens, quick to see an ally, promptly aligned himself with Dresser. He claimed that because Eddy had copied Quimby, she had no right to the material. Arens lost the plagiarism case in the Boston courts.

Although this factor was significant in the overlooking of Hopkins's role in New Thought, other equally important points deserve mention. Namely, the Quimby-Eddy controversy was strengthened by the ahistorical nature of the movement itself. People were preoccupied elsewhere with other principles and did not pursue the truth of the matter. There was little time for self-reflection within the movement because New Thought centers its metaphysical foundation upon "the present realization of an eternal changeless truth." The practical applications of that "Truth" are to life situations that exist here and now, such as day-to-day poverty, sickness, and sorrow. Therefore, self-reflection on its past has not been a significant feature of New Thought development. Keeping track of events, situations, and people has not been a historical focal point in New Thought.

Another factor in the lack of systematic coverage of the history of New Thought has been its neglect by the mainstream of the U.S. religious community. Moreover, as Melton recognized, the alternative religious traditions in the United States have generally been understudied. Because New Thought was treated as a "cult" and "less than legitimate religious movement," it has remained relatively obscure as an integral facet of U.S. history. Alternative movements receive little academic attention. Usually, the mainstream refutes their legitimacy because it is believed unlikely that they

could make any significant contribution to religious thought. Consequently, New Thought's tenets have not been studied, its journals and
publications have been ignored, and libraries and historical societies have
refused to acquire New Thought literature to place on their shelves for
public use.

Due to this lack of historical documentation, Melton believes that Horatio Dresser, Julius Dresser's son and "an otherwise competent philosopher," had to do the historical work that a professional using the
methodology of a historian should have done. Dresser, in an attempt to
make up for the historical void in New Thought, "performed as an ama-
teur and in an amateurish manner." In a critical assessment of Dresser's
1919 book, *A History of the New Thought Movement,* Melton pinpoints
the inherent weakness that looms large to a historian. Specifically, Dresser
recorded groups that were familiar to him and his family in the East, and
neglected "the more significant aspects of New Thought" that had developed in the West and Midwest.[40] In other words, Dresser's research was
limited; thus, not only was his presentation of the salient features of New
Thought limited, but so was the validity of his conclusions. He did not realize that Hopkins's ministry from 1887 to 1894 was an epicenter of organized New Thought. Because Dresser wrote the first and only history of
New Thought, for more than forty years the position he assumed from his
father, Julius—that Quimby actually founded New Thought—became
standardized.

One can see from the sequence of events concerning the splintering of
Eddy's group, the Quimby and Arens controversy, and lack of a documented history of New Thought that it was easy for Hopkins's contributions to get lost amid the intensity of various polemics. The more
sensational situations always get the press and serve to focus public opinion on those specific issues. For instance, the allegations that Eddy borrowed heavily from Quimby became a focal point for the press and for
Dresser. Thus arose the idea that Quimby was the founder of New
Thought—because Julius Dresser pushed the idea in an attempt to discredit Eddy. Hopkins never joined the fray. Believing her mission sacred,
she taught and healed while others fought.

Hopkins's Healing Concepts

Hopkins's primary assumption was a belief in the oneness of all things. *Class Lessons, 1888* demonstrated how she saw the religious truths of "the East and the West": "They make the world round . . . of one blood all the nations. . . . Let us marry the still East to the forward moving West . . . for the sons and daughters of God." [41]

Hopkins had an idea similar to the collective unconscious of Carl Jung, for she mentions race law in *Class Lessons, 1888*. Early in her healing career, while still associated with Eddy, she was called to treat a young girl who had severe rheumatism and was sick. She reports in the lesson that her patient's forefathers had had the same physical problem. Apparently, Hopkins believed that "inherited traits" are brought on by "ugly tenacity." She doubted her ability to heal and said, "How could my feeble word meet the race-law? Suddenly, the memory of my teacher's [Eddy's] words concerning denial, recalled to me my judgment. No! I said in the silence . . . at every statement [the patient] made." Hopkins believed there were five problems inherent in the patient's present condition: "1) heredity, 2) race laws, 3) direct influence, 4) cause and effect laws, and 5) direct contact or communication with others." She also believed that communication existed through the process of "thought transference, whereby the mind received thought impressions, as the tympanum receives sound impressions." First, in order to treat, Hopkins denied the rheumatism, then mentally assured her patient she was well. "Because God is your health, you cannot be threatened with diseases." [42]

Hopkins mentioned Eddy's book, *Science and Health,* and said it helped her think about "the making manifest of Mind or Spirit, with all its powers." Then she said, "what error common to the race mind is the regular second error of mortality?" She told the rheumatic girl, "You are free from race deception. . . . You are perfectly well. You are free. You are spirit. You trust God." Hopkins reported that the young woman was able after several treatments to change her countenance and tell her she "felt like a new creature." Later that evening, after being busy in her private practice, Hopkins mentally treated the young woman again, using the same process of denial and affirmation. (This style is called absent treatment, when the patient is not in the presence of the practitioner.) Hopkins concluded the lesson by saying her success in what she believed to be an obstinate case led her teacher to request she write an article "for the little Christian Science Journal [*sic*]." [43]

In the next chapter of *Class Lessons, 1888,* Hopkins again picked up the story of the girl with rheumatism. The family history indicated that "the father and grandfather had been violent and cruel tempered men." She said, "It is a good sign for a patient to trust you with his secrets. The spirit is motherly and forgiving, and draws the broken heart to lean upon it for comfort, if it shines through you." In discussing the case with the girl, Hopkins told her how Christian Science treats such errors. Calling her in the silence, Hopkins told her, "You are not suffering . . . as the result of your parents' sinfulness or your own sinfulness. . . . Neither can the whole race mind of error be reflected upon you; the selfishness of the race mind cannot make you selfish." [44]

In the following chapter, Hopkins spoke again of the divine as female when she said, "We are an infant on the bosom of the Infinite Mother God." In order to heal children who are sick, she advised the use of this prayer: "Wilt thou, blessed Mother, present this little one now before us all perfectly sound and well? I Thank Thee that Thou didst make her perfect from the beginning, that she is perfect now, and evermore shall show forth as Thou madest her. . . . I leave her with Thee in perfect trust that Thou hast heard my prayer and hast served her to perfect health in our sight. Amen." [45]

Hopkins spoke of involving other practitioners to pray for difficult cases "if there is a lurking desire to have the credit of healing the patient yourself. Pride is a bad ingredient of the mind in the healing practice." Further on in the chapter, she said, "Christian Science . . . accomplishes a three-fold cure . . . bodily health, moral reformation, quickened intelligence." [46]

Hopkins's mystical inclinations show clearly in this case. She concluded that the rheumatic girl was cured because "I have struck the key note to her spiritual nature and physical body, or mortal mind, by the same word. A body resounds when its key note is struck." She says sound that is steadily paced and continuously delivered can cause a body to lose its cohesiveness and "go to pieces." As an example of how potent sound is, she stated, "Joshua struck the key note of the walls of Jericho with seven rams' horns blown by seven priests for seven days . . . so we cause [the] mind to vibrate when we strike its peculiar error by a word of truth."[47]

Hopkins claimed that the process of silent communication to the sick or afflicted is based on an old idea practiced in the East. Hopkins related that silent communication "is an introduction into Western practice of an ancient Eastern system of instruction. The guru or teacher of the Orient, sits silently in the presence of the chela or student, and informs him by un-voiced speech."[48] Because Hopkins was not writing or teaching for an academic audience, she did not use footnotes to document her statements; hence, it is impossible to trace some of her eclectic ideas to the original sources.

This early text, the most seminal of this period, written three years after she left Eddy, clarified Hopkins's position regarding the relevancy of Christian Science in the world:

> Every statement made by the Christian Scientists is an almost verbatim quotation from some ancient thinker. I do not believe the Christian Scientists live any more truly by these teachings than did those who formerly proclaimed them. And as for healing the sick, theirs are far below the works accomplished by former healers by formulas. The only credit the Christian Scientists can take . . . is that they have boldly determined to compel the world to listen . . . and see how . . . they coincide with the teachings of the Bible writers and Jesus of Nazareth.[49]

I think it is important to emphasize that Hopkins took Christian Science back to ancient times. Although she was aware of the Arens controversy that raged around her during the Boston years, she did not support the idea that Eddy had pirated the ideas from Quimby. Her ventures into the older philosophies of the Hermetic tradition convinced her that Christian Science (or New Thought) was a restatement of age-old truths.

Although Hopkins denied the unique role of Eddy as sole divine purveyor of revelation, she never lost her respect for Eddy as a teacher of Truth. Melton seems to think that Hopkins lost faith in what Eddy perceived as her divine mission because Eddy placed emphasis on "mortal mind, the illusory world of error where according to Eddy, evil has its origin."[50] This arena is where "animal magnetism" and "malicious animal magnetism" are said by Eddy to originate. Hopkins never spoke of these two concepts in any of her later writing or teaching and certainly never supported them in her theological system. In *Class Lessons, 1888,* Hopkins mentioned Berkeley, Fichte, Plotinus, the Zohar, and Plato, who spoke about Ideas being the only real things and said that God was the ruling Principle. There was no room here for belief in the mortal mind that Eddy saw as evil.

Hopkins originally delivered her class lessons in a series of twelve sequential lectures that she had printed in pamphlet form. One of the first students to write about them was Frances Lord. In her book *Christian Science Healing,* published in 1888, she stated that Hopkins had given her permission to quote extensively from her teaching. Lord, a native of Great Britain, wasted no time in publishing her version of this healing method. She also took the book to England for dissemination there, which seems to be the earliest documentation of international missionary activity by Hopkins's inner circle of students. As it happened, however, Lord's work mainly served to prepare England for the advent of orthodox Christian Science. She taught classes there from October 1887 until July 1888, based on Hopkins's model. Her work helped fertilize the area and introduce the topic of metaphysical healing. Eddy's students arrived and began classes in November and December 1888.[51]

Hopkins's lessons were collected and published later in book form as *Class Lessons, 1888.*[52] Hopkins, in her missionary zeal, wanted to cross the ocean with her teaching as forthrightly as she had spanned the continent. Her students stumped the United States unceasingly. To promote taking the message overseas, she permitted Lord to be creative in the way she presented the material.

Hopkins, like Eddy, did not believe in matter as reality. The only true reality was God, and everything perceived as matter was illusion. God did not create the world and stop. Creation was an ongoing process. Evil cannot exist because it opposes the power of God. Hopkins called the lessons of science "twelve baskets full of eternal food—the bread and meat of life." She ended the last session with the statements: "All is one. There is only one. We are one." She believed that Truth could be found in any variation of human religious expression, oral or written. This universality separated her from Eddy.[53] Hopkins believed that more than one person could be chosen to implement various stages heralding the Second Coming of Christ.

The actual healing techniques that Eddy used, such as the affirmation of truth and denial of error, were used by Hopkins, as well as the twelve lessons. These processes later came under some revision as various students changed some of them and substituted others.[54]

Hopkins paid particular attention to her choice of examples to demonstrate Truth. Her eclectic method may be best described in the words of Arthur Christy, who conducted a special study on Emerson, Thoreau, and Alcott while teaching at Columbia: "It might even be said that eclecticism is the method of cosmopolitanism. It is naturally best suited to men [or women] who wish to range the whole gamut and history of human thought, accepting the congenial and rejecting that unsuited to their needs." Hopkins, for example, liked to roam the literary collections of the world's religions, picking and choosing from philosophies that supported her position. Alan Anderson says in his paper "Contrasting Strains" that Hopkins was well read for her time, although he did not know "how well she understood" the philosophical points of view of some of the writers.[55]

Hopkins was not an academician writing or teaching in a style designed for scholarly argument. What was more important to her mission was that she could take various ideas she found relevant and simplify them so that the ordinary person could grasp the meaning and make practical use of the principles. Hence, her eclecticism, ranging "the whole gamut . . . of human thought," was in service to what she perceived to be the Truth; she believed she had a mission of universal importance to share with the world. The divine mission was to herald and complement the Second Coming of Christ to a suffering world.

Hopkins as Seen Through the Eyes of Van Anderson

Helen (Nellie) Van Anderson, a student of Hopkins, organized the first New Thought group in Boston with full-time ongoing leadership in 1894. This "Church of the Higher Life" grew by leaps and bounds. The group provided a multitude of services. Braden said it supplied pen pals, a "Young Peoples Club, an Emerson Study Club, mothers meetings, spiritual training classes, and healing services each Sunday." Van Anderson also wrote a book titled *The Right Knock,* about which she said, "It is a book of facts, not fiction, although wearing the dress of fiction." Van Anderson quoted Carlyle: "'If a book come from the heart, it will contrive to reach other hearts.'" Her book was presented as having "come from the heart." [56] It is from *The Right Knock* that one gets a glimpse of Hopkins as she was seen by her early students.

Chapter 12 is titled "Mrs. Pearl's Lecture"; this thinly disguised story is about one of Hopkins's lectures. Mrs. Pearl addresses the issue of evangelical need based on "lifting the burdens of sickness, sorrow and sin." She praises the efforts of Christian Scientists (or New Thoughters) for their "marvelous or speedy results." In a later paragraph, she says it is "a better method of dealing with intemperance than any other class of reformers . . . because neither women nor men have learned the true principle of moral reform." Toward the last part of Mrs. Pearl's lecture, she states, "We now have thousands of Christian Scientists all over the country who are striving as never before to live a higher life, to work for humanity according to the Master's teaching. . . . Send your thoughts out to the grand reformers. . . . Sow the seed diligently."

This idea of working for humanity has some parallels and shares some concepts and similarities with the social-gospel movement that developed during the same period and came to its greatest influence in the first decade of the twentieth century. Both movements asserted that by following the social ethics and actions of Jesus' ministry to the poor and sick, human sorrow could be alleviated.

An interesting comment is found in the early part of the chapter. One of the characters says that the Christian Scientists have one noticeable characteristic: "bright, happy faces . . . full of repose and trustfulness." Mrs. Pearl has "this faculty of gathering and holding the thoughts of her audience and I could not help noting the calm and satisfied expression as they went out after the lecture." The character says that "there is a common chord of sympathy, which if rightly touched, will cause the many to think and feel as one, and herein lies the secret of a teacher's power." Hopkins's ability to create the Oneness and underscore the intimacy among her congregates was no doubt a linchpin of her oratorical success.

In a feminist statement on the nature of the divine, the same character states in a letter, "The nature of God embraces every good quality of masculine and feminine character, as also the impersonal life principle. It is . . . proper to use the masculine, feminine or neuter pronoun when referring to Deity." In chapter 15, Anderson notes, "When Mrs. Pearl came into the class room, all turned to look at her and every ear was ready to listen."

These early New Thought proponents were attempting through fact and fiction to do what is done in critical reconstructions of the Bible today: they were interpreting Scripture in an inclusive way that not only left room for the divinity of women, but also expounded upon it. The ideas of Hopkins's early group were not unlike the ones of contemporary feminists and egalitarians in their inclusion of the feminine as sacred. Although not scholars, they were using the tools available to them in an attempt to order their universe and convert the mainstream to their points of view.

The New Thought group acknowledged the power of the male to provide social and religious sanction. For example, in Hopkins's article on the Trinity, a male philosopher speaks in favor of the female.[57] In Van Anderson's book, a male gives spiritual meaning to the Lord's Prayer; he prays to the "all pervading Father-Mother Spirit." The fact that Hopkins and Van Anderson used the male voice indicates their willingness to adapt to the norm of the prevailing culture to convey their missionary message. Though definitely feminist in content, the male voice also represents a conciliatory effort to include men in the broader parameters of the organization. Clearly, neither of these pioneers had a negative agenda that excluded males from participating in the great venture that trumpeted the Second Coming of Christ.

Christian Science Theological Seminary

Hopkins established the Christian Science Theological Seminary because she believed in the importance of a structured scholastic environment established along ecclesiastical lines; students must have a place to gather and study as in seminaries of mainstream denominations. The formal establishment of these colleges and seminaries helped the graduates "obtain the sanction and seal of their companions in the faith." Hopkins created socially instituted norms in New Thought ministry by offering ritualized legitimization following the familiar patterns of mainline churches. For example, the healing course at the seminary and the advanced course for ministerial training each cost fifty dollars. (The advanced course fitted one "for teaching and platform speaking.")[58]

Hopkins was clear that in her theological seminary, she was launching a missionary movement of universal dimensions. She said, "The world is their church." In the interest of social justice, she said the missionaries were to address the needs of "people lying under the shadow of the mistaken needs of the past." Freedom from oppression and exploitation was the goal. Hopkins spoke of the "Father-Son-Mother Principle of the Godhead." Here she asserted the femaleness of God: "They know that the Mother God is the Holy Spirit of Scripture. They discern the signs of the times in the uprising of woman." She believed that the reign of this female principle, "the Holy Spirit, the Comforter promised to guide into all truth," was the beginning of new ideas about the presence of evil in the world. Hopkins stated that women should reject the notion "that evil is a necessity in God's kingdom." She perceived this rejection of the false belief in evil by woman as "the second-coming of the Christ." She demonstrated just how clearly she felt about the female principle and its significance when she called "woman's voice—the mother heart of the world [that] now proclaims the omnipresence, omnipotence and omniscience of the good, in whose universal presence is no evil." She concluded the ordination address by charging the graduates: "We send you forth to the world. . . . [Y]ou have been tried and not found wanting. . . . [Y]ou can heal . . . by . . . speaking. . . . You are the spring forth of that ministry prophesied by the sages of old."[59] The *Chicago Inter-Ocean* newspaper, dated May 30, 1889, ran a detailed story stating that "a large gathering of people witnessed the ordination of students at the Christian Science Theological Seminary." Hopkins, as a prophet, had proclaimed to this gathering the Second Coming of Christ and heralded the significance of women as trailblazers of the new spiritual order.

Melton says that in 1893, the only recovered catalog of the theological seminary indicated that 350 students had completed the basic course in healing, 111 of whom had taken the entire course and been ordained as ministers. How many more were graduated or ordained after that date is not known. After graduating, some of the brightest and most advanced students were offered positions on the faculty of the seminary.

These teachers generally taught the basic courses, such as biblical hermeneutics and math. According to Melton, the first person to come aboard was Annie E. Rix. She held the position of mathematics professor. Estelle Nichols, who like Rix was from San Francisco, was added next. Stanley Van Epes was added to teach hermeneutics. Other additions made to the faculty included Nellie Van Anderson, George Burnell, and Mary Lamereaux. The advanced course, which was taught by Hopkins one-on-one, as a tutorial, was a requirement for ordination. Melton makes the analogy in his paper when he says that Hopkins, much like John Wesley in the previous century, "assumed the role of a bishop and ordained her students to the Christian Science ministry."[60]

As the years passed, Hopkins's theological seminary was no longer the center of power. Decentralization had occurred with the establishment of missionary—and outreach-network branches. The seminary had formed a branch in New Orleans in the early 1890s. By the time Hopkins decided, in 1895, to close the doors of the seminary forever and relocate to New York, a new feminist religious movement of international importance had been created.

In the November 1888 issue of *Christian Science*, one can see Hopkins's radical thought evidently and succinctly. In a short synopsis of her philosophy, she states, "Now that we are wearying of . . . the pulpit's preaching, let us listen to the voice of the Comforter . . . the teachings of the true motherhood of this hour . . . the sacredness of marriage and the home-great symbol of Divine Trinity."[61]

Hopkins based her decidedly feminist content on Isa. 51.[62] Hopkins used the entire chapter and interpreted it to be a prophecy of the old fading away as the new came into being. Although she does not specify the exact passage that first inspired her, one may presume that it begins with verse 2, which states, "Look to Abraham . . . to Sarah who bore you; for when he was but one I called him and I blessed him and made him many." She asserts that "all the people of the world are looking for a great and mighty change," and "woman, the silent sufferer and meek yoke-bearer . . . is stepping . . . out of her old character" and "hurling herself against the age with such force . . . as to make even her friends stand aghast." One cannot help but wonder how autobiographical this statement was for Hopkins. She had stepped "out of her old character" by taking up the cause of Christian Science (or New Thought). She had left the home of her spouse to whom "she was very happily married," found surrogates who could care for her son in her absence, and negotiated a verbal contract with Eddy at *Christian Science,* which sparked her career in a controversial healing modality incorporated into a radical religious doctrine.[63]

Hopkins "hurled herself" out of her former lifestyle in the quest for religious Truth with such force as to "make even her friends stand aghast." It was atypical for a housewife of the 1880s to leave home to go even a short distance to school, let alone for a woman to lead her family to a distant city and set up a feminist religious movement that ran counter to the prevailing patriarchal norms. Emma Curtis Hopkins and George Hopkins may qualify as one of the first dual-career marriages. They may also have been casualties of that arrangement. George Hopkins, who eventually returned to Manchester, New Hampshire, to pursue his career as a teacher, is mentioned twice as a special guest of the Hopkins Association in Chicago;[64] he then quietly disappears until Hopkins mentions him in her letters as an elderly lady. By 1890, Hopkins used her maiden name, Curtis, as a middle name. In contrast, when she first wrote Eddy in 1883, she used the initial of her given name and signed the letter "Emma J. Hopkins."

In her letters to Eddy, Hopkins's references to her husband were always respectful. She spoke as a dutiful wife and mother: "Just now my husband is with me and I am devoting all my time to him." Yet, in the same letter, she discussed with Eddy the time frame whereby she could leave Manchester for Boston and work on the journal. Here is a portent of the absolute dedication and determination of Hopkins, which eventually fueled her strength to live separate from her husband. She said to Eddy, "I have not 'conferred' with [my husband] about the change: have simply told him my decision." [65] It was not common for a Victorian wife to not confer with her spouse about leaving home to begin a career; however, it is this same resolute willpower that permitted Hopkins to pursue the un-trodden path as a pioneer feminist in New Thought. How or why their marriage collapsed remains an enigma. Hopkins mentions in a letter later in her life that he used to go insane and strike her. Thus, whether career responsibilities or personal problems led to separation is unknown. However, this dogged willpower to follow her own decisions based on the vision from her childhood is the first indication that she is responding to a transcendent call that will have more power to influence her choice of lifestyles than any human being possibly could.

Documentation of Christian Science Theological Seminary in Chicago

In 1965, two diplomas of the Christian Science Theological Seminary were recovered. One was dated December 10, 1890, and signed by Emma Curtis Hopkins, Annie E. Rix, and F. S. Van Epes; it had been awarded to Mary Lamereaux. The other had gone to Charles Burnell (who later married Mary Lamereaux), and had been signed by Emma Curtis Hopkins, Annie E. Rix, Francis Perry, and Paul Militz. It was dated December 16, 1891. The left sides of these impressively designed diplomas bore the seal of the Christian Science Theological Seminary of Chicago. The diplomas were for the first and second (primary and advanced) courses, respectively. In order to be ordained to the ministry, one must have completed the second course, which was taught one-on-one by Hopkins. The diploma for the second course stated, "From this Course of Study to the Perfect Ministry you are ordained in the name of the Father, Son and Holy Spirit." The Holy Spirit was the Mother Principle or Mother Comforter. There is a statement just prior to this one that declared: "We have not shown that we are in full fellowship with pure Christian Doctrine till we have preached salvation from sin and death as well as sickness."

Before Hopkins closed the doors of the seminary, at least 350 people were graduates of the "first twelve lessons of Christian Science" and another 111 were ordained after completing the advanced course.

The year 1893 is the only year that a catalog existed for the seminary. The statement of purpose includes:

> The Christian Science Theological Seminary is supported by the C.S.T.S. Church. It is founded to hold daily sessions for the free expression of the extreme conclusions to which Scripture propositions lead.
>
> The Bibles of all times and nations are compared: Their miracles are shown to be the results of one order of reasoning, and the absence of miracles shown to be the result of another order of reasoning.
>
> At this Seminary the teachings of inspired writers are proved to be identical with the native inspirations of all minds in common.
>
> We perceive that inherently there is one judgment in all mankind alike. It is restored by the theology taught here. With its restoration we find health, protection, wisdom, strength, prosperity.
>
> "At the same time my reason returned unto me, and for the glory of my kingdom, mine honor and brightness returned unto me."
>
> Ministers of all denominations, professors of every department of thought, teachers of every science, artisans, home keepers, are warmly urged to attend our twelve o'clock daily services, and see for themselves what is in the divine Truth freely expressed.[66]

Hopkins Taught, Ordained, and Mentored the Fillmores

The largest New Thought group today is the Unity School of Christianity at Unity Village, Missouri. Myrtle Fillmore and Charles Fillmore, of Kansas City, the founders of Unity, studied with Hopkins in Chicago and were ordained by her on June 1, 1891.[67] James D. Freeman wrote *The Household of Faith*, published by Unity in 1951, three years after Charles's death. He spoke of the importance of Hopkins's theological seminary and said, "It was probably the most influential school of its kind of its time."

He lists the people who had been taught by her: Charles Fillmore and Myrtle Fillmore, who were ordained by Hopkins and "became her fast friends" (she frequently called on them to pray for difficult cases in healing);[68] Charles Barton and Josephine Barton, publishers of the *Life* magazine in Kansas City and Truth teachers themselves; Malinda Cramer, the first president of the International Divine Science Association (now a New Thought ministry); Helen Wilmans, suffragist and editor of "Wilmans Express" (a newsletter of the time), also a New Thought teacher; D. L. Sullivan, one of the movement's teachers in Kansas City and St. Louis; the popular writer and poet Ella Wheeler Wilcox; Annie Rix Militz and Paul Militz, who founded the Homes of Truth in the West (it was their student Eleanor Mel, from the Home of Truth in Boston, who was reported to be with Hopkins the day she died in 1925); Kate Bingham, who taught Nona Brooks, with whom she founded Divine Science in Denver; C. E. Burnell; and H. Emilie Cady, a physician and writer whose work remains prominent today at Unity and in New Thought circles.[69]

Freeman says that Hopkins came to Kansas City to teach on several occasions. He describes her as "tall, slender, and good looking, wearing a big picture hat while she spoke, she was a dynamic and eloquent teacher."[70] At one class, there were 87 students in attendance. This attendance broke a record for Kansas City at that time (this class may be the one advertised in *Modern Thought,* the one that would have to change to a larger room because of interest).

Whereas Hopkins traveled to Kansas City as part of her outreach missionary program, the Fillmores sometimes joined her in Chicago. In 1890, the Fillmores traveled to Chicago to attend a review class for more than 120 students. Myrtle Fillmore wrote a detailed letter on the significance of that event: "We met all . . . those whose names are so familiar in literature: Ida Nichols, Nellie Anderson, Julia Twinchester. . . . A finer set of people I never met." The spacious home that Hopkins had purchased in December 1887 was large enough to accommodate many of the guests. Myrtle said, "We were fortunate enough to have a room under Mrs. Hopkins's roof. She is just lovely to be with. . . . It was the happiest, most harmonious family meeting on earth."[71] It was during this time in Chicago at the festivities for the seminary that the Fillmores chose the name for their youngest son. Since his birth, he had been called "Baby." At a party hosted by C. I. Thacher, Charles and Myrtle named their baby Royal. His name came to them because the celebration was held in "an elegant home with things all served up in grand style."[72] There were three servants and a band for the guests' needs and entertainment.

The Fillmores obviously considered Hopkins a mentor. She encouraged them to expand their work and "intimated that the [Kansas City area] might be the site of a great temple," which should heal of "sin and sickness all who step over its threshold." Today, Unity, not far from Kansas City, is the largest and most influential of the New Thought ministries. As noted by Dell deChant in "Myrtle Fillmore and Her Daughters," the mind-cure message was a significant aspect of the ideology of Myrtle Fillmore's life, and Hopkins was "the single greatest personal influence on the Fillmores and their early religious activities."[73]

Hopkins considered the Fillmores good friends and colleagues, frequently addressing them as "My two blessed friends" in her letters to them. To Myrtle alone she used the designations "My blessed friend" and "Dear Heart." In a letter dated November 8, 1890, Hopkins wrote to Myrtle on seminary stationary. Hopkins said that in one of the lessons "before the review," she expected to call on Myrtle. Financial constraints must have made it difficult for Myrtle to think of traveling from Kansas City to Chicago for the event. Hopkins wrote to her: "Do not think of money in connection with the occasion because here you will learn that attitude of mind which brings success. It would add to your storehouse to come more than all the self denial you could practice in a year." To assure Myrtle that the trip would be affordable, Hopkins told her, "you will be the free guest of the Seminary and if ordained will go home for half price."[74] Prosperity is so much an integral component of Hopkins's work that she does not single it out, but interweaves the concepts of abundance and supply with her theology. The letter is signed, "Lovingly your good friend Emma Curtis Hopkins."

It had been seven years since Hopkins requested Eddy's financial assistance in order to attend her classes. She had experienced both financial difficulties and prosperity and could now teach others the way. Four years later, in 1894, Hopkins told the Fillmores, "God is pouring great prosperity through you all the time." Between the time that Hopkins helped the Fillmores financially in their quest to study with her and to be ordained by her and this letter, the Fillmores entered a success covenant with God. The covenant is dated almost a year and a half after their ordination by Hopkins in Chicago. Braden says the covenant was found among Myrtle's possessions after her death.[75]

Hopkins trusted Myrtle with personal insights. Her letters to Myrtle reveal the stress that Hopkins endured when launching her ministry. In a letter dated October 19, 1894, Hopkins, after returning home to the seminary in Chicago from an out-of-town journey, stated: "As you can imagine I am come at from every quarter instantly. There is no describing my life. . . . I need rest." She related that when she was the guest of "people in affluence," they wanted her to remain up late at night, "talking and smiling." She said if she could find the time and place to rest, she "would never see a human being—never speak a public sentence."

Almost a month later, in November 1894, Hopkins wrote the Fillmores from New York's Murray Hill Hotel. She said, "I came here to be alone." She had been caught between "crossfires and have such personal weights to attend to." Apparently, the Burnells had developed "great opposition to Miss Martin" (secretary of the seminary). She was sick of the infighting and what may have been an expression of sibling rivalry. She spoke to the Fillmores as peers in this letter. She was sure that if she could be alone to recharge, she could "easily coalesce all of them someday." At this point, due to her intense fatigue, she stated, "I would put each one into some independent field and be alone in my home as I once was before conferring with others."

The next-to-last letter between Hopkins and the Fillmores was dated January 20, 1923, and written from the Iroquois Hotel in New York City. Hopkins thanked the Fillmores for twenty-five dollars they had sent her. She enclosed a card with a new address announcing "her removal to 218 West 59th Street, New York." It is not clear whether the twenty-five dollars was for treatments that Hopkins performed at the request of Myrtle Fillmore or if it was a gift.

The last recorded correspondence between Hopkins and Myrtle Fillmore occurred May 2, 1923. Hopkins apologized for not being able to come to her as Myrtle had requested. She said, "I have to be in New York with unutterable steadiness and attending to unescapable obligations. . . . I cannot get to Kansas City though I wish I could." This letter indicated that Hopkins had withdrawn from giving lectures. She said, "I am not in the public eye anymore . . . though that will not prevent me coming to you when the moment is ripe." Hopkins had responded to the initial request from Myrtle by sending a telegram on "4–12–23 at 8–35-am" from New York. She said, "Your beautiful letter of invitation just reached me." She refused the summons by saying, "Ask me later on and try me." In the May letter she told Myrtle, "I am so glad in your great success and world wide influence. Everywhere the newer ways are gaining converts. Each pronounced teacher is over crowded with eager listeners."

Hopkins, as an elderly lady, was still concerned with the missionary success of "the newer ways." Thirty-three years after ordaining her, Hopkins told Myrtle Fillmore of her own hectic schedule. "I have my hours laden with applicants for private lessons. . . . Nothing will keep me back from you two when I see with my own eyes to go." There is no documented evidence that Hopkins saw with her "own eyes" to make that trip to Unity. Her approaching death was two years away, and quickly her health was to fail. There is no doubt from the cordiality of the communication that Hopkins reveled in the success of the Fillmores as teachers of Truth and considered them part of an inner circle of people whom she had mentored and ordained, and with whom she had developed spiritual bonds.

Hopkins and Prosperity

The question of poverty and how New Thought came to acquire a focus on prosperity as a tenet is frequently raised. Healing was the original primary focus of the ministry, and the pains of poverty were included. Hopkins addressed the issue early in her writings and speeches. She believed in the power of the word and in decreeing what one wished to have in one's life: "We have no business to have sickness or pain or poverty of unhappiness . . . [W]hen Christians are poor do they talk as if they had chosen poverty? . . . [T]hey are poor because they can't help it and their whining is pretty good evidence. . . . Do not allow yourselves to believe in misery. . . . [D]ecree against it. . . . There shall nevermore be any poverty known among us."[76]

In an article hostile to New Thought called "Mind Power: A History and Analysis of the New Thought Movement," Dean Halverson reports on the premises of New Thought in order to repudiate them. He says Hopkins was a defector of Eddy who founded a seminary and New Thought organization. He connects the "age of Mental Healing" with "the age of women's suffrage." When he discusses the emergence of prosperity in the movement, however, he states that Prentice Mulford may have published the first pamphlets using affirmation for positive effects in life, "including financial well being." He says, "Sometime between 1890 and 1900 the theme of prosperity was added to that of healing."[77]

The August 1889 issue of *Christian Science* had a list of books for sale at the publishing house owned by Ida Nichols. She had an extensive listing for Prentice Mulford, no less than thirty-nine pamphlets for sale. Out of thirty-nine titles, only two related to prosperity: "Use for Riches" and "The Necessity of Riches." Hopkins had routinely addressed prosperity throughout her writing, and she had demonstrated her personal talent for prosperity during the terrible financial crisis of 1888 when she had successfully "turned around" her ministry. Halverson says, "The first source of the teaching is impossible to trace"; I say the source is not impossible to trace if one examines Hopkins's writings. In "Faith," an article that she wrote for the *Christian Metaphysician* in January 1887, Hopkins said, "Whatsoever things ye desire when ye pray believe that ye receive them and ye shall have them."

In July 1888, Hopkins wrote an article for the *International Magazine of Christian Science* titled "The New Religion." On the first page, Hopkins said that "all material things and transactions . . . have underlying spiritual meanings." She said that few people know how to find the spiritual or metaphysical meaning, but she mentioned the Swedenborgians as the ones who had come closest: "No religious people are so happy as the Swedenborgians who search for spiritual meaning to all things and make all things render up to them food for daily living." Hopkins used the story of Jesus and the fishes to demonstrate the value of symbols and signs (Mark 8:1–21). What a person has externally is a direct reflection of where that person is spiritually. She used Jesus as an example of the prosperous world of spirit and bemoaned "that interpretation of [Jesus'] life and teachings which keeps man in poverty and deprivation against his choice, while he is whining at what he suffers and bewailing his poverty and crying of cold and hunger." Hopkins said all limitations could be overcome if one knew what Jesus meant and applied his teaching correctly. For Hopkins, Jesus was the first prosperity teacher; to elaborate on the theme of prosperity was to paraphrase his words. She said, "You must not be sick if you are a believer in the new religion. You must not be poor. You must not cry. . . . If you are any one of these you are not yet a member of the new church." [78]

In *Scientific Christian Mental Practice,* one of her earliest books, she spoke of "prosperity [being] the acknowledgment, either consciously or unconsciously, of the presence of God. He who is prosperous has eliminated from his mind some idea which the one who is seemingly not prosperous still holds." Hopkins used the liar as an example. Liars are prosperous because "they have eliminated a belief in absence" so that their good can "rush to them." She said, "Some liars make good healers on the same plan," because "they have dropped the one belief in the absence of Good which the poor healer holds onto." [79] In this book, she gave the formula for using denials and then affirmations to prepare the way for prosperity.

The first universal affirmation Hopkins made was: "My Good is my God. My God is Life, Truth, Love, Substance, Intelligence—omniscient, omnipotent, omnipresent." She said if one used affirmations to eliminate the old thoughts of lack, then good could come to one: "You will soon be more prosperous." One example that Hopkins used was a little beggar child who looked through "an open gateway into a beautiful garden . . . forgetting his misery for a moment. . . . [He] has given his own character a new vigor of goodness and has increased the strength of his life in some metaphysical relation to life. He has unwittingly given himself a treatment for prosperity." Toward the latter part of the book, Hopkins said, "Complaining and whining are only exhibitions of great desert spots in your character. You must fill up deserts with rain and fertilizer." She advised instead to talk of the "good in the universe."[80]

Hopkins wove the concepts of prosperity into her lessons on life, as demonstrated above. However, the first New Thought writer to seize on the doctrine of prosperity and add her own personal touch to the ideas of abundance was Frances Lord, in *Christian Science Healing*. Braden states that Quimby and Warren Felt Evans placed no emphasis on prosperity. He cites Frances Lord as having "some five pages . . . devoted to the treatment" of prosperity. The work of Prentice Mulford seems to be predated by the work of Lord, who was the first to integrate the teaching. She devoted chapter 9 of her book to "Circumstances," with subheadings "Competition and Poverty" and "Christ's Teaching on Poverty and the Stewardship of Life." Braden asks, "Where did Frances Lord get the idea in 1887? If Emma Curtis Hopkins taught [prosperity] it was certainly not attributed to her by any of her pupils."[81] As we have seen, Hopkins's works were subtly permeated with the prosperity principle. It would be Frances Lord, Hopkins's student, who would single out, integrate, and promote prosperity as a pivotal principle that New Thought has grown to accommodate.

Hopkins as Feminist

Apparently, the concept of Father-Mother God began in the United States with the Shakers and was appropriated by Eddy for use in Christian Science. "Feminism" in the Shaker tradition included both genders in the Godhead and accepted both sexes as elders of the community. Communal celibacy replaced ideas of traditional matrimony. The elevation of women to elder status was a "contrast to traditional male leadership."[82] Although it is beyond the scope of this book to go into details of Shakerism, it will be helpful to look at some of the salient features with feminist overtones. Ruether defines three issues inherent in Shaker thinking: "leadership, marriage and the nature of God." She makes it clear that although "a dual or androgynous concept of God does not automatically empower women, . . .'only in female founded communities, particularly the Shakers and the Christian Scientists, is the promotion of the female divine figure used to promote the equality of women.' "[83] It is this theme that Hopkins used to empower women in a patriarchal culture.

There is no concrete evidence that Hopkins was familiar with Shaker doctrine, yet as widely read as she was it seems more than plausible that she knew something of their ideology. The most significant feature of Eddy's work that Hopkins adopted was Eddy's concept of Father-Mother God, which Eddy seems to have appropriated from the Shakers, but rarely used herself. Under the Shakers and Eddy, this theology was radical; Hopkins, however, developed innovative concepts that gave a new twist to the idea of a feminine principle in the Godhead.[84]

Inclusion in divinity elevated women to a position that had been denied them in patriarchal religions. Classical dualism promoted males as superior and divine, and females as inferior and carnal. The concept of male-female equality took root and flourished among the men and women who were Hopkins's students. This premise of coequality may have been one of the reasons for Hopkins's immediate success in a culture that had previously promoted a two-tiered religious system that deprived women of a place within the sacred. Women now had divine sanction and could found new religious movements with an authority legitimated by a God who was both male and female. Ruether and Keller conclude that there had to be a "definite theory of female empowerment in the ideology and structure" for a group to continue to sponsor a female leader.[85]

The second Shaker tenet, on the establishment of communal celibacy, was never suggested by Hopkins. Although Hopkins did leave her own marriage for personal celibacy, she never recommended it for others. Though a mystic, she was not an ascetic.

Hopkins did institute a new system of religious hierarchy similar in concept to the Shakers in which women were leaders; however, the Shakers had divisions of labor based on gender. Hopkins moved beyond this belief by teaching, training, and ordaining some men but more women as ministers. Hopkins's most able lieutenants were women who became publishers, lecturers, and social activists. All these events happened in a time when it was atypical for a woman to have a career. Now both sexes could support themselves economically as lecturers, healing practitioners, and pastors. In Hopkins's view, the healing ministry was not to be monopolized by men as the medical profession was. She provided equal access for all. I have never come across a charge against her of reverse discrimination against men. In fact, the men in the movement seemed supportive of the women and by their acceptance validated Hopkins's claim of equality. Hopkins had issues not with specific men, but with a dualistic culture that characterized the female as weak, carnal, or evil.

The first class to graduate from Hopkins's theological seminary in Chicago held commencement exercises on January 10, 1889. Louise Southworth was the guest speaker. Southworth was a suffragist who held office in National Women's Suffrage and was a contributor to and interpreter for the *Women's Bible,* edited by Elizabeth Cady Stanton. The Bible was central to Hopkins's teaching. She used biblical stories to illustrate her progressive position and gave them an interpretation that was geared to the equality of women. Southworth demonstrated this stance when in a forthright manner she stated, "Divine Truth has come at last to give woman her proper status in the world." Also speaking was the women's editor for the *Chicago Inter-Ocean* newspaper, Elizabeth Boynton Harbert. "[This] distinguished philanthropist and lecturer welcomed the young ministry to the ranks of public workers." She said that "when it seemed impossible that our desire to preach . . . could ever be fulfilled . . . woman goes forth." The ability of a woman to ordain other women led Southworth to say, "It was my privilege to be present at the Ceremony of the New Era, the ordaining of women by a woman." [86]

Hopkins spoke "against the old dispensation and with one voice declared for a new and a true, wherein the poor may be taught and befriended, women walk fearless and glad, and childhood be safe and free." [87] In a goodwill gesture, the pastors of the graduates' home churches were also invited to these "most impressive" ceremonies. Hopkins's teaching of the male-female components in the Godhead left no doubt in anyone's mind that women were divinely empowered by God to assume primary responsibility in the development of New Thought ministries. Both Southworth and Boynton Harbert recognized the uniqueness of Hopkins's "young ministry" and saluted the revolutionary doctrine that would send "public workers" out into the world for social reform.

Hopkins by example empowered women to seek positions of authority in New Thought. As Ward says, "The sheer volume of women holding positions of leadership, dominating the magazines, founding and running healing colleges, writing books, etc.," was monumental. Ward has compiled an extensive list demonstrating the inclusion of women in early New Thought. He lists seven prominent schools in major metropolitan areas founded by women: Mrs. H. A. Heathwood was president and chief instructor at the new Chicago branch of Choate Metaphysical College; Emma Curtis Hopkins founded the College of Christian Science in Chicago, with Mary Plunkett as president (later Hopkins was president); Eliza Barton Lyman founded the Hopkins School of Christian Science in Milwaukee, and remained as principal; Adelle M. Harper was president and founder of the Hopkins College of Christian Science in St. Paul; Mary J. Butler was president of the Hopkins School of Christian Science in Denver; Angela Crippen-Davis was president of the Louisville College of Christian Science; and Mrs. Gorie and Annie Rix, using only female leadership, founded the Christian Science Home College in San Francisco. Women were also the officers and leaders of the various local metaphysical societies. Ward also states that "the owners and publishers of early New Thought journals were, to a large degree, women." He says, "The list of women who founded New Thought schools is staggering."[88] *Christian Science, Universal Truth, Truth,* and *Harmony* were all periodicals founded between 1888 and 1890 with women editors and publishers. In November 1887, Mary H. Plunkett started *Truth* magazine, which became the organ for the international Christian Science group. Ida Nichols was publisher and editor of *Christian Science* from 1888 to 1891, when it was taken over by Fanny Harley. Later, the name of the magazine changed to *Universal Truth,* still run by Fanny Harley, who by then had her own publishing company.

In the January 1889 volume of *Christian Science,* Hopkins concluded her lesson on the Trinity that was mentioned earlier. She spoke of "the Silent Truth-Principle which when spoken sets all things true." It is this Truth-Principle that "heals the sick and comforts the distressed." This

Truth-Principle can be called by other names, such as "the Mother-Principle" or "Cosmic Substance" out of which all things are made. Hopkins taught by analogy in this particular lecture. She said that through weighing labels and terms and comparing them, one could draw the conclusion that they are speaking of the same thing, and one may call this thing "God." Hopkins demonstrated her eclecticism by saying that "the ancients called it the Mother of all things. . . . [T]he Kabalists called it Shekinah. . . . [I]ts symbol is mother-life."

She further elaborated on the "Mind-Principle" as the "Fatherhood of the Trinity." The "Sonship" symbolizes the children who are "creations of mind." The Holy Ghost is the Mother-Life.

Hopkins acknowledged the passive role that women have been given in society as a result of the normative patriarchal ethos: "We have kept the mother-voice and the sacred mother-power inactive in the world." She held onto the hope that the prevailing time period would be one where woman could be heard "and her prayers for salvation from bondage and suffering [come] back answered." She wrote of the male philosopher who engaged in thoughtful analysis of the ebb and flow of life; her character states that "woman's hour has come": women are working in world affairs and woman is not "what she was and has been." The "special women," the ones who "stand the heat of battle . . . of the Life Principle, shall see only victory and mastery."[89]

Hopkins's achievements are noteworthy. She was the first religious teacher of her time to break away from the dominant Protestantism of the nineteenth century, create an alternative feminist theology, and attract a sizable following for this new theology.

Hopkins developed an ordained ministry for the New Thought movement. Her feminist theology, though discarded by the second generation of the movement, had given women a secure-enough position that its loss did not demoralize them or deprive them of individual or collective power. Many New Thought centers and churches have been bastions of female leadership since the 1880s. As Hopkins's pioneering role in the empowerment of women becomes clearer through recent research, she has the propensity to become a far more significant figure in U.S. religious history than many of her more currently celebrated contemporaries.

Hopkins as Social Reformer

The August 1889 issue of *Christian Science* reports Hopkins's annual address, which voiced her regret (because of the heavy duties imposed by the position) at having been chosen president of the Hopkins Metaphysical Association for another year. With a sense of placing her mission above her personal feelings, Hopkins said, "It was . . . best for the advancement of the work to hold to the cares of President for another year." Hopkins was zealously dedicated to the development of independent Christian Science as a missionary movement that, for the time being, needed her careful direction and spiritual guidance. In her address, she paid particular attention to members of the association who had served this missionary purpose. For instance, she noticed Clara D. Stacy, who had served "for several months in the Southern states, an ardent and brave worker." She then generalized and said, "From among our number there have arisen missionaries, preachers, teachers, authors, powerful minds for the right." She further stated that she hoped "there would be a fund . . . for the use of missionaries . . . similar to that belonging to the alumni of the Theological Seminary"; however, despite the current financial limitations for those people engaged in missionary service, she could rejoice "at the prosperity and good works." [90]

Social reform was a key area to which Hopkins responded. She brought the idea of social activism out of theory and linked it to practicality. In November 1888, the Woman's Federal Labor Union asked Hopkins for help in "assisting the working girls of Chicago." In December 1888, the minutes of the Hopkins Association, prepared by Ida Nichols and published the next month, state that "Mrs. Brady reported in regard to the meeting of The Ladies Federal Labor Union. . . . Three delegates were elected to represent the Association in the work of the Union: Miss J. M. Brady, Mrs. F. M. Harley and Mrs. N. V. Anderson." [91] The union was instrumental in forcing reform in the sweatshops and improving relationships between working girls and the school system.

There were other groups that sought assistance from Hopkins. In May 1889, *Christian Science* reported on the Hopkins Metaphysical Association meeting. J. M. Brady, the delegate of the association to the Woman's

Alliance, stated that twenty-five organizations were represented by the alliance. The recent focus of their efforts had been the issue of compulsory education for children and the legal ramifications of violation of this law. The alliance had been successful in lobbying for truant officers to enforce the law. A substantial portion of the report for May concerned missionary activity. Van Anderson "told of the need of the science everywhere and its eager acceptance" in Tecumseh, Michigan; and Bryan and New Philadelphia, Ohio. Van Anderson further reported that missionary activity was not as readily accepted in some other areas, because people were afraid of Christian Science due to "the warning of ministers" in orthodox denominations. Despite this slight drawback, the personal-mention column of the periodical named thirteen women practitioners who were successfully maintaining practices from coast to coast.

Hopkins had a mystical belief based on the law of cause and effect that she called "rebound." She stated that it would be the voice of woman that would strike at the heart of evil in the world. The "Silent Spirit" would speak through "the mothers of the hour . . . and teach the sacredness of marriage and the Home—great symbol of the Divine Trinity." Children, she taught, should be "rightly born and loved and tended by mother-father care."

In the January 1889 issue of *Christian Science*, there was a report from the Hopkins Metaphysical Association. Hopkins revealed to the group her idea of the sacredness of their mission. She stated, "We are a faithful band of workers to speed the cause of Spirit on earth—which means that the kingdom of God is being hastened by our work."

In the same report, advances of missionary activity were given by Nina Hughes, who was ministering in Dayton, Oklahoma; Sedalia, Missouri; and Olney, Illinois. Angela Crippen-Davis, president of the Louisville College of Christian Science, also gave a positive report. May D. Fisk of Denver, Colorado, gave a good report of her healing work, and Caroline L. Parker, a converted medical doctor, commented on a fine healing done by F. O. Cross of Irving Park, Illinois. There were reports of two new metaphysical associations being established in Madison, Wisconsin; and Sedalia, Missouri. In the October 1888 issue of *Christian Science*, Ida

Nichols said, "Mrs. Hopkins spoke of the necessity of missionary work to be done, especially in large cities." This statement by Hopkins came when she "turned around" the active ministry and wished to show others the "Science." In the February 1889 issue of *Christian Science,* the minutes of the Hopkins Association for December 26, 1888, are recorded: "The Denver Association now meets in the parlors of the Congregational Church. Mrs. Myron Reed, wife of the pastor . . . [is] an active worker in the Association." It is also in this issue that Hopkins made one of her rare autobiographical comments. She closed the meeting with these words: "Five years ago . . . I left my home . . . reaching Boston . . . to enter the class in Christian Science, opening at 10 o'clock. . . . How changed the world looked to me after the lessons . . . to plant definite words . . . to help the poor."[92] Thus, it was her own experience that she used to encourage others to take up the missionary path.

Hopkins's goals for missionary activity among her students were realized: in one area, she managed to establish their equality with existing mainstream clergy. The women working as missionaries were traveling a great deal; passing through Chicago to report for meetings with the Hopkins Metaphysical Association seems to have been a routine practice. According to Melton, Hopkins secured for those ministers whom she ordained a railway discount pass given only to members of the clergy. There were so few women ministers in any denomination in the late 1880s that the railways probably had few, if any, requests from women pastors before the time Hopkins obtained them. However, there is an unsubstantiated report that some liberal Protestant clergymen were allowing their wives to become licensed ministers so that they could travel on passes. The women, however, did not function as clergy.

In the *Christian Science* issue of December 30, 1888, support for temperance was given by Hopkins as part of her "International Bible Lessons." She used Num. 6:1–4 as her guide. Hopkins admitted that Jesus drank wine, but stated that a great example is set by those people who are against "vice and sensuality" and that we may thank the ones "strictly abstaining for all the moral status of society." She said that the "partially temperate cannot be credited with the growing sentiment against tobacco, alcohol and other equally vicious temptations to wrong living." She considered Jesus an exception to the rule, because he was "spiritually minded" and did not partake of alcohol "for the purpose of gratifying a sensual and unspirited body craving an appetizing drink." She said that "the true Christian Scientist grows farther, farther from sense gratifications." In the March 21, 1889, Bible lesson, Hopkins interpreted as follows: "The appetite for wine is a sign of thirst for righteousness and idleness is a sign of longing for right words."

Theology as Feminist Foundation

Hopkins explained the theology that provided the foundation of her feminist statements. The God or Governing Force of the world is a "threefold principle." This "principle" has come to be expressed as three periods of history. The patriarchal ethos is the earliest time in history, when the stronger ruled the weaker; this period symbolizes "The Fatherhood of Deity." The next stage is spoken of as a "Sonship reign," which began about the time of Jesus "and has slowly progressed." Hopkins believed that at the time when each of these two periods was the sociopolitical reality in a given culture, there was in the hearts and minds of the people "an ideal of something better." This "something better" she called the "Holy Ghost—the Third Being of Trinity." And she proclaimed that the Holy Ghost was "the Shekinah of the Hebrew Scriptures and the Holy Spirit of the New Testament." It was the feminine principle and sign of the future.[93]

Specifically addressing the role of the "Holy Mother," Hopkins wrote an undated article of seventeen pages, which she called "The Ministry of the Holy Mother" and published in booklet form. She spoke of prayer as being the preferred tool for the achievement of great things. She said, "The Spirit is only wooed by praises. She only moves down on the hosts embattled against us when we unlock the filmy gates between us by the keys the truth in our hearts tells." Hopkins criticized the Hindu Brahmins, who knew "her white robes of healing . . . then . . . refused that those born in lowliness and those born as women should feel the touch of her seamless robe of healing." Lest the reader be in doubt, Hopkins stated clearly that "the ministry of God is the Spirit of God, the Mother." Yet, Hopkins's postulations on the composition of deity did not eliminate the male role. In fact, "God the Father" was said to be "careful" that the "Holy Spirit [should] not be found where . . . censure . . . scolding . . . or maligning" was going on. The "Omnipotent Father protects Her and allows Her to hear properly spoken pleas for help." Hopkins thus gave the masculine additional support in her quest to unite the Holy Mother with God the Father; it was a question of joint rulership. Hopkins made a special place in divinity for the female without eliminating the significant aspect of male divinity.

Hopkins as a feminist had no quarrels with males per se, and throughout her writings displays a warm tenderness for the ideal male. No doubt her own father and husband had given her the inspiration for the role she assigned to men. She did have grave concern for the greed that seemed to precipitate violence and war as instruments of a patriarchal ethos. For the elimination of war and territorial expansion based on military conquest, she advocated prayer coupled with "metaphysical processes," not material ones. Hopkins worked with Christian texts and attempted to integrate what she believed to be overlooked principles. The *Chicago Inter-Ocean* newspaper carried her metaphysical Bible lessons for almost ten years. Males within her movement embraced her ideology and supported her doctrines of male-female equality.

At one of the Hopkins Associations meetings, E. B. Weeks was called upon to speak. He said that he wanted to hear more from the "King's Daughters." He paid a "beautiful tribute to the exalted womanhood which is the outgrowth of the influence of Truth upon the lives of the Scientists."[94]

In September 1888, George Burnell wrote an article for *Christian Science*. In what must have been an enlightened consciousness for his day, he wrote, "The Holy Spirit or Mother principle of the deity is just taking hold of the world in this age of women. It is . . . infinitely significant that our civilization is beginning to emphasize the power and purity of motherhood in the science of life."[95]

Feminist Analysis

The purpose of this project has been to define Hopkins's role in New Thought events of the latter part of the nineteenth and early part of the twentieth centuries. That she has remained relatively obscure is true. Gerda Lerner asks the question, "Who are the women missing from history?"[96] The women of the last century who did a radical thing in their time by combining healing and religion are examples of women who have been left out of history. These women were active as healers, teachers, missionaries, and pastors. Several, such as Frances Lord, Mary Plunkett, and Hopkins, went abroad with the message, making metaphysical healing a U.S. export. Lerner observes that when "women make contributions," they are usually judged by standards appropriate to men. "The ways of great women" in feminist awareness are ignored. Certainly, this group has been ignored until recently because they were operating parallel to the religious and medical mainstream that largely denied women legitimate roles within its male-dominated structure.

Women working in Christian Science and New Thought in the 1880s and '90s were definitely a subculture within a dominant male culture. They demonstrated collective effort toward the common goals of healing and spiritual fulfillment. As one reads the minutes of the Hopkins Association meetings, a glimpse of their efforts at communality is seen. These women who pioneered the healing movements developed a way to define themselves and function autonomously in a male-dominated culture. They carved socioeconomic career niches for themselves as teachers, healing practitioners, pastors, and writers from Maine to California.

Lerner said that it is the reflections of men that transmit the past experience of women because women are assessed by a "value system defined by men." To construct a new history requires a reconstruction of old history to include women's history. Hansen says, in "Women's Hour," "Women's historian Gerda Lerner calls Eddy one of the three important pioneers of women's emancipation outside the women's rights movement" (the other two are Charlotte Perkins Gilman and Margaret Sanger). Hansen says Eddy was important because she defied convention and achieved "both wealth and institutional power."[97]

The Hopkins Metaphysical Association, the Emma Curtis Hopkins College of Christian Science, and the Christian Science Theological Seminary show patterns of activity following Lerner's paradigm. "Historically," Lerner says, women extended "their concerns from home and family to the larger community." Then they began to be "woman oriented" by becoming involved in activities outside the home where women could meet in groups. It was out of this "communality" that "feminist consciousness" emerged. This "feminist consciousness . . . challenged patriarchal values . . . and attempted to substitute . . . a feminist system."[98]

Lerner states that the "advanced conceptual level" for defining "women's history" includes past "women's rights" issues but can be best described as the "quest for autonomy." This statement means moving into a world where one is free to choose and act, "free to shape one's future." Lerner writes, "The true history of women is the history of their ongoing functioning in that male defined world *on their own terms*." She says, "Women have always made history . . . not 'contributed' to it . . . and had no tools to interpret their own experience."[99]

If one uses Lerner's paradigm to evaluate the achievements and accomplishments of Hopkins, then one can see her as a vital catalyst and charismatic leader orchestrating an emerging religious movement. Theologically, in her interpretation of the Holy Trinity, she sanctified the specific nurturing skills of women. She did not sneak women in through the back door of organized churches as unpaid workers subservient to male clergy and male-dominated church boards. By ordaining women as ministers, she brought them up front to the pulpits of power and prestige, securing for these women an autonomy rarely known in a patriarchal culture. Even Eddy did not ordain women. Preferring to hold control close to her and her authority, Eddy gave certificates for instruction and said her only ordination was of the Bible and *Science and Health*.[100] Hopkins preferred to disperse authority. She ordained her advanced graduates, empowering them as peers to both herself and their counterparts in mainline church leadership. In this respect, she is an anomaly compared with women leaders in Shakerism, Spiritualism, Christian Science, and Theosophy.

Mary Farrell Bednarowski notes, in "Outside the Mainstream:

Women's Religion and Women Religious Leaders in Nineteenth-Century America," that four ideas need to be supported in a religion for women to assume leadership. In brief, they are: concepts of an impersonal deity, modification or elimination of the fall of humankind, dismissal of the necessity for ordained clergy, and views of marriage and motherhood that were not traditional.[101] Hopkins and her theology reflect these innovative twists circumventing the norms of the mainstream religious traditions; however, she did ordain clergy. She offered ordination to ensure the sterling quality of her advanced graduates. She also supported the values of marriage and motherhood.

When Hopkins heard Eddy speak in 1883 in Manchester, New Hampshire, and realized she wished to know more, she set about to find a way that would work for her. She already had a solid education. It was exposure to the atypical in Eddy's theology that provided a viable way for Hopkins to explore and grow beyond the confines of conventional religious culture. It is beyond the scope of this work to ferret out Eddy's particular doctrines in detail. Yet, from Ward's paper one can understand Eddy's theology in such a way as to shed light on Hopkins's development. Ward's conclusion is that Eddy "presents us with an ambiguous feminist reading. . . . She gathered many capable women . . . empowered them . . . was a strong symbol of female leadership." It was this symbol of "strong . . . female leadership" that promoted for Hopkins and the other apostates a clear image of a woman using power to create. Ward says that Eddy's theology was only "vaguely . . . connected to a feminist consciousness," but this "incipient feminism served as a catalyst for the much stronger feminism of early New Thought." Support for Ward's statement is found in Hansen's work. Hansen says she is analyzing part of Christian Science as a chapter in women's history. Of particular importance was Eddy's concept of womanhood. She says, "Although it was certainly not feminism as we know it, there was nonetheless a sense of feminine worthiness embedded in the heart of her doctrine."[102] Whereas Eddy was only "vaguely . . . connected to a feminist consciousness," it was this sense of the "worthiness" of woman that Hopkins was able to use to develop her own theological doctrines.

There was no "ambiguous feminist reading" in Hopkins's theology or practice. The great leap from theory to practice was made in the first bac-calaureate address at the Hopkins Theological Seminary in Chicago on January 10, 1889. Louise Southworth declared, "Christian Science [or New Thought] . . . is frequently termed a woman's religion." Not long afterward, in 1890, Helen Wilmans, a suffragist, wrote, "It is a noticeable fact that the Mental or Christian Science movement is a woman's move-ment. . . . [I]n this . . . woman's 'real' voice has been heard for the first time in the history of the race." [103]

Hopkins's support for women's issues is first documented when, work-ing for Eddy as editor of the *Christian Science Journal,* she included arti-cles from the *Springfield Republican* called "The Ideal of Woman." Two months later, she supported the blacks, the disfranchised, and women who did not have a voice in political decision making. In the July 1885 issue, news was included from *Woman's World* (a magazine created by Helen Wilmans to address suffragist issues) that indicated the topic of equality for women was gaining minimal acceptance by the general population. In August, there was an article called "NWCTU," praising the temperance movement for its valiant efforts in moral and social reform. [104]

In less than four years, Hopkins would be more than supporting women's issues. She would be a staunch advocate of women's spiritual and natural goodness. In *Christian Science* of February 1889, the lesson for February 17 is particularly feminist. Hopkins told the lesson of the sick woman in the New Testament who dared to touch the hem of the garment of Jesus. She prefaced her story, "Women were greatly despised . . . in those days, and then to be so extra unfortunate as to have a mysterious af-fliction." This pitiful lady is healed through her faith. Hopkins said, "the great teacher [Jesus] called upon her to face the multitude and testify" be-cause "public testimony will command the respect of those who despised her. . . . He wants to show them that the healing God loves the daughters as well as sons of His universe." She promoted the ministry of Jesus by say-ing that of all the great or good teachers the world has experienced, only "one of them all was good and true to woman!" She clearly recognized and said of women in general that they are thought "inferior because of [their] sex or attractive . . . or serviceable because of sex."

To demonstrate her position for the primacy of Jesus as an egalitarian, she specifically singled out Paul as the one who commanded "willing mothers to stay at home to learn of their cowardly husbands." She attacked Peter's cowardliness in denying "the Lord," when the "women boldly followed him to the foot of the cross." She switched to modern life to say that a lecturer employed at the New England Conservatory of Music who was considered rather good by his audiences "showed the mark of the same beast that all great teachers have shown by one little contemptuous sneer at poor Annie Hathaway, for being older than her husband!"

Conclusions of Hopkins's Ministry

Hopkins spent the years 1886 to 1894 as organizational founder and chief of a global ministry. Off to a strong beginning, Hopkins's precepts provided a metaphysical education to students from all over the United States. She later expanded her ministry to include Europe, particularly England.

Change meant new directions. Ida Nichols, whose inheritance started the magazine *Christian Science,* retired, and Fanny Harley took over editorship. Under Harley, it was renamed *Universal Truth* and continued publication until the turn of the century, when she sold it to Charles Brodie Patterson; he merged it into his enterprise called *Mind.* Annie Rix, who had been the right hand to Hopkins in administrative duties, would later marry another graduate of the seminary, Paul Militz. She became the vice president of the student association. Later, she and her husband would found Homes of Truth, on the West Coast.

Hopkins's "International Bible Lessons," which ran weekly in the *Chicago Inter-Ocean* newspaper from 1889 to 1898, kept her writing on a consistently busy schedule. People not involved in Christian Science or New Thought still read the metaphysical interpretations. Hopkins continued to write for the *Chicago Inter-Ocean* even after relocating to New York in the mid-nineties.

In 1891, Hopkins published a book called *Drops of Gold.* It contained a meditative thought for each day of the year. She also authored shorter works in pamphlets and booklet form.

Hopkins's energetic focus on administration paid off. By 1893, the large house Hopkins had purchased on Indiana Avenue was no longer needed. The seminary changed locations and moved closer to the Loop, to the Auditorium Building. Strong lieutenants had emerged in the Hopkins Metaphysical Association; Militz and Harley could be left to direct it. After Hopkins withdrew from active leadership, the organization was renamed the Truth Students Association.

Hopkins, in 1893, went to England (probably as a guest of Frances Lord). Consequently, she was not in Chicago in the summer of 1893 for the World's Parliament of Religions, which was linked with the Chicago Exposition. Nonetheless, Hopkins housed her association in the Women's Building, where she had engineered the association's affiliation with the Queen Isabella Association as one more link with the feminist network.[105] Eddy's Christian Science group, in contrast, was housed in the religion section.

By 1895, Hopkins was weary. In less than a decade, she had launched an international ministry. Having trained Truth teachers from coast to coast for nine years, she could take time for herself. In 1895, she formally closed the seminary. She temporarily withdrew from teaching large classes and thus was able to "be alone . . . as I once was before conferring with others." Hopkins, the founder and leader of New Thought, would become Hopkins the mystic, taking her ministry to New York and using another method for religious expression and social reform that would allow her to focus on teaching individually. By the early twentieth century, men had seized the reins of power in New Thought as editors, speakers, and leaders of new centers. Hopkins's clear-cut idea on the Spirit dispensation that elevated the feminine to the Godhead had been dropped. Yet, according to Melton, this idea had already altered the movement in at least one vital aspect: it had provided the infrastructure "for the transformation of New Thought from a lay healing movement . . . or heretical Christian Science, into a more church-oriented movement, with ordained clergy."[106]

Hopkins was not one for self-promotion. She was a committed metaphysical healer who trained key leaders and developed organizations that ensured the growth of the movement into the next generation and encouraged its perpetuation in the coming decades of the new century. Although there were many noteworthy people who influenced the movement as precursors—Emanuel Swedenborg, F. A. Mesmer, Ralph Waldo Emerson, Phineas Parkhurst Quimby, and Warren Felt Evans—Hopkins's contributions clearly established her as the primary founder of the New Thought movement. Today, every New Thought organization of major consequence can be traced to Hopkins's influence.

Because Hopkins released the reins of power in New Thought to the students she had trained and adopted a semireclusive lifestyle, her accomplishments have been somewhat unappreciated. Today, her legacy lives on in sacred and secular forms because the membership of the groups that sprang from Hopkins's missionary activity numbers in the millions. Hopkins provided the building blocks of a feminist theology that transformed the New Thought movement permanently. Despite the earlier encroachment by men who took over the reins of power in the early twentieth century, there is a current resurgence of interest. Women today are emphasizing interpretations that Hopkins championed. The connection of Holy Spirit with the feminine aspect of God is one such emphasis.

Conclusion

In her Chicago ministries, Hopkins fulfilled the dreams of her early life, though in ways that modified the original vision. As a young child growing up in the security of her parents' farm, she had a dream of founding a "hospital for sick, destitute children." The encounter with Eddy in 1883 reawakened these early visions. Sometime between 1885 and 1888, Hopkins shifted her visionary focus from the particular plan of her youth to the New Thought cause of her maturity. The world became an extension of her parents' farm and its inhabitants, the "sick, destitute children." Her hospitals became the lecture halls in which she conveyed her message. New Thought (generic of independent Christian Science) emerged as the crucial therapy administered by minister-physicians who healed in silent communion.

It was a long journey from Manchester, New Hampshire, to Chicago. From the time Hopkins arrived in Chicago until her departure nine years later, she was the central figure of New Thought religion. She was not the same person when she left Chicago. After her difficult but successful Chicago ministry, she understood herself as a transformed person.

In a letter dated December 5, 1894, Hopkins wrote to Myrtle Fillmore and Charles Fillmore of her increasing fatigue and need for rest away from the vexations of running a seminary. No matter how exhausted she was with ministering, she noticed, "Sometimes my dauntless divinity shines even though my bones and skin are like glass, as if the sea of glass mingled with fire were taking place in my body."

This letter was the mystic speaking. The glassy fire she spoke of "taking place" in her body externally radiated the internal transformation. She had, through her national network and international connections, strategically launched a ministry that she believed to be the Second Coming of Christ on earth. Always a private person, the remainder of Hopkins's life would be spent teaching or focusing the future direction of her ministry through private practice. She then left Chicago for New York, as a mode of mystical retreat. She no longer needed to administratively manage the seminary and mediate the temperamental egos of her ambitious students. Their assertive, competitive natures and independent spirits would ensure the future success of the movement. After nearly a decade of nurturing New Thought, she could for a time enjoy her earned solitude and be as she was "before conferring with others."

3

THE NEW YORK YEARS

*E*xactly why Emma Curtis Hopkins chose New York as the place to spend her last years is not clear. She traveled to Europe and England and continued to give public lectures; however, New York remained her home base. The 1900 Census showed Hopkins living in the borough of Manhattan. She gave her true age and marital status on the *Census Report*.[1] It was later in this first year of the new century that Hopkins was divorced by her husband.

Hopkins's reclusive tendencies became more pronounced in New York. She still lectured on New Thought, but also developed a private ministry where she could see people in her suite of rooms, on a one-on-one basis. It was through her private practice that she reached the most impressive clientele of her ministry. In her memoirs, Mabel Dodge Luhan included Hopkins in the book called *Movers and Shakers*.[2] Because the New York literati associated with Hopkins through her practice, she became the grand dame in metaphysical healing and the New Thought movement in New York. Her busy schedule was frequently mentioned; in one of her letters, she said there were four people vying for every one appointment she could offer during the day or evening hours.

Letters to Luhan

The richest source of autobiographical material on Hopkins for the New York years is the letters she wrote to Mabel Dodge Luhan.[3] In 1962, the letters found their way into the Yale Collection of American Literature, Beinecke Rare Book and Manuscript Library at Yale University. They were a part of the sixteen hundred pounds of paper that socialite Luhan deposited there prior to her death. They have been shared with me through the courtesy of the Beinecke Library. (Luhan will be called by her first name in order to not confuse her later with her husband, Tony.) Hopkins apparently encouraged Mabel to write, and it was through Mabel's eyes that Hopkins came to life for the present generation. Mabel dealt with many of the famous persons of her era in a vivid manner. It is largely from her writings and the various biographies of Mabel and Hopkins's letters to her that most of this material about Hopkins was taken.[4]

Mabel Dodge Luhan was born in 1879 to a wealthy Buffalo family. She was the only child of a loveless marriage that had been engineered to bring together two prominent banking families. Her first marriage ended shortly after the birth of her only son, when her husband was accidentally killed in a hunting accident. Mabel then married Edwin Dodge and lived in Florence, Italy, restoring the Villa Curonia and holding a salon for artists Gertrude Stein and Leo Stein, Paul and Muriel Draper, Eleanor Duse, and Bernard Berenson, among other members of the European intellectual community. In 1912, Mabel returned to the United States and set up shop in Greenwich Village. Her apartment at 23 Fifth Avenue became internationally known as a gathering spot of people who were socially and politically active during the pre-World War I era. Notables who attended her New York salon included: A. A. Brill, Walter Lippmann, Max Eastman, Lincoln Steffens, Margaret Sanger, Hutchins Hapgood, Emma Goldman, Jack Reed, Neith Boyce,[5] Robert Edmond Jones, Alfred Steiglitz, Carl Van Vechten, and other radical or avant-garde personages. For several years, Mabel devoted her time and energies to the revolutionary ideas of the radical element. She and Dodge were separated and eventually divorced. Mabel, some years his senior, became the older lover of Jack Reed.[6]

Mabel also affiliated with the Heterodoxy Club of Greenwich Village.[7] The women's club members were devoted to suffrage as well as other political causes. The Heterodoxy Club was a club for unorthodox women "who did things and did them openly," such as Jenny Marie Howe, Charlotte Perkins Gilman, Mary Fels, Inez Haynes Irwin, and Fola La Follette.[8] The ideas of New Thought could not have been foreign to this group. Mabel knew of Hopkins's work and had been taught metaphysical healing by her as had members of her peer group. New Thought ideas also came through Charlotte Perkins Gilman, who embraced many New Thought tenets but stopped short of formal affiliation. Another possible avenue of New Thought influence for the Heterodoxy Club was through Florence Woolston Guy, editor of *Woman Voter.* Guy was an ardent suffragist who supported labor and settlement-house projects. Her spouse, David Seabury (who used his mother's maiden name in order to establish his career autonomously as a psychologist), was the younger son of Julius Dresser and Annetta Seabury Dresser, and brother of Horatio, who wrote the *History of the New Thought Movement,* published by Crowell in 1919.

Mabel heard of Hopkins and became interested in New Thought while in psychotherapy with Smith Ely Jeliffe around 1915–1916.[9] She had also investigated the writings of the Unity School of Christianity. Lois Rudnick, a biographer of Mabel, said that while Mabel was seeing Jeliffe, she also saw Nina Bull, her childhood friend from Buffalo who practiced Divine Science. Hopkins had been Bull's teacher and also had taught the founders of Unity. Rudnick said Hopkins promised to handle Mabel's issues through "the effortless way." In 1917, Mabel switched psychiatrists and began to see the famous disciple of Freud A. A. Brill for psychoanalysis. She also saw Hopkins as a student in her private practice. Mabel apparently never told either Brill or Hopkins of her involvement with the other. Rudnick said that "Hopkins's healing derived much more from her presence than from her philosophy." She gives a technique that Hopkins was supposed to have used in her private practice that is not documented anywhere but in her writing. She stated Hopkins had the persons whom she saw in her private practice lie quietly in a darkened room while she spoke to them gently in a soothing tone of voice. Mabel saw Hopkins three times a week and felt refreshed after each session with her. She referred many friends to Hopkins for treatment, including Maurice Sterne, Andrew Dasburg, Elizabeth Duncan, and Bobby Jones. These members of the intelligentsia found solace in her treatment. It was during this time that Hopkins and Mabel began to write to each other.

The first of these letters indicates that Mabel was involved in an upsetting affair with Maurice Sterne (a Russian artist who had painted for a year in Bali). On June 12, 1917, Hopkins wrote to her, "Fetch your Maurice Sterne along with you on Thursday and let me see him first and you afterwards." Hopkins seemed to think that the liaison between the two was "a new step to take to some richer life." She signed the letter, "Your devoted E. C. Hopkins."[10]

On June 26, 1917, Hopkins wrote to Mabel, "Dear girl, I am not going to see M.S. [Maurice Sterne] on Wednesday. I haven't a single minutes [sic] time." She said she would send a note when she had space for him, and in the meantime she stated, "His genius seems to be stirring— my work goes on absently," meaning absent healing treatments that she performed away from the recipient.

In a letter dated July 13, 1917, Hopkins mentioned to Mabel that Elizabeth Duncan (Isadora's sister) "wishes to take lessons with me. . . . I was greatly sure of her greatness."[11] At this time, she totaled up Mabel's bill (apparently, Mabel paid the bill for some of the friends she had referred). The bill was "fifty dollars" for Mrs. Royce, and Elizabeth's would be "another fifty." Then Hopkins told Mabel, "Do not think you have to pay the 100.00 [sic] this minute."

Mabel's problems with Maurice did not yield easily to treatment. Sister Beatrix, a lay Episcopalian sister and a neighbor at Finney Farm (Mabel's country place), called upon Mabel to bring her relationship with Maurice into a more socially acceptable form.[12] (Sister Beatrix was also involved with Hopkins and referred one of her teachers to Hopkins for "lessons" later.) The advice Sister Beatrix gave to Mabel was apparently followed. Rudnick said, "[h]oping marriage" would resolve the relationship issues, Mabel married Maurice on August 23, 1917. She was reported to have "repeated her marriage vows in a cold, tight voice." Irritated that she had yielded to being tied down again, Mabel submitted to the rhetoric of the president of the Heterodoxy Club, suffragist Jenny Marie Howe, who fussed at Mabel "for her betrayal of the cause of women."[13] Caught between the warring factions of conservatism, which required the legitimation of marriage for a relationship between a man and a woman, and radicalism, which supported living together without benefit of religious, legal, or social sanction, Mabel had acquiesced and, despite intuitive misgivings, taken the conservative path.

News must have traveled fast on the New York grapevine, for Hopkins (on the day of Mabel's marriage, August 23, 1917) wrote to Mabel, "Congratulations . . . you have done the beautiful thing! You have married a great man and he . . . has married one of the sweetest and noblest of women." Mabel did not share her enthusiasm; she was not thrilled with her decision to marry, and "sent Maurice off on a honeymoon by himself out West."[14] It seems that even Elizabeth Duncan spoke out against the inappropriateness of the marriage. Mabel, the morning after her marriage, went for an appointment with Brill, who also chastised her for the quick decision to marry without consulting him. However, after careful thought, he gave his blessing to the marriage via a personal letter to Mabel.[15] Hopkins did not write Mabel again until September 20, and most of that letter is about appointment schedules.

One month later, on October 26, 1917, Hopkins spoke of conflict within Mabel's social circle. Hopkins tried to soothe the breach created when "Hutch [Hutchins Hapgood] spoke heatedly to Maurice." Hopkins pragmatically advised "not taking life quite so hard." Then she told Mabel if she "must have it out with 'Hutch' explain *what he has said* so he cannot mistake it." The issue in question seems to have been a caustic remark that Hutch made about the marriage of Maurice and Mabel. Maurice was sensitive and quick to pick up the disapproval of others, and he sensed that Hutch was not a champion of his marriage to Mabel.

It was in this letter of October 26 about relational conflicts that one gets a rare glimpse of Hopkins's personal feelings about her husband, from whom she had been divorced for seventeen years. She must have trusted Mabel in order to reveal such an intimate detail from her younger years. She said, "My darling lamb went insane. He used to strike me. He did not know it. He had been always the soul of chivalry and loving kindness." From the tone of this letter it may be that George did not develop this "insanity" until after Hopkins had told him of her plans to go to Boston and had achieved a measure of success with her career in Chicago. While she was a homemaker, he might have been "the soul of chivalry and loving kindness." This statement is one of the few clues to Hopkins's refusal to return to George after her success in Chicago, although it probably represents only one of several factors in Hopkins's "abandonment" of him. After all these years, he was still her "darling lamb." Hopkins, perhaps in her compassion for George, never initiated divorce proceedings against him. It was George who finally had to break the marriage contract. Hopkins never openly criticized her former husband.

Hopkins's practice at that time was located in her suite of rooms at the Warrington Hotel at 161 Madison Avenue in New York. Appointments were difficult to get. She wrote Mabel that she would juggle times to accommodate her. She would add a new student, but it must be on "Friday at 7 o'clock. All other hours taken." This letter was dated November 5, 1917. On November 7, she wrote Mabel again that "it will be a pleasure to meet anyone you fetch along." Hopkins let Mabel know she planned to take the week after her visit to go to the country.

It was after Maurice left to go out west on his solitary honeymoon that Elizabeth Duncan came to visit Mabel and spent the night with her somewhat in the spirit of a spend-the-night party. On one of those nights, Mabel fitfully awakened and related to Elizabeth, sleeping across from her, a dream of seeing the face of an Indian "in some green leaves."[16] The dream left a permanent impression on Mabel.

Maurice wrote Mabel from Santa Fe on November 30, 1917. He encouraged her to develop a project of helping "save the Indians, their art culture." He would like for her to do what "Emilie Hapgood and others are doing for the Negroes."[17] While Maurice was gone, Mabel developed a respiratory illness and was bedridden. Hopkins, the nurturer, told her in a December 3, 1917, letter, "Don't go to your husband till you are well and strong again." Hopkins signed this particular letter, "Your best friend, E.C.H."

During 1918, the *New Thought Bulletin* printed a letter from Hopkins about war. This letter was republished in the bulletin during the summer of 1945 (probably to coincide with the ending of World War II). Hopkins was not for war, but realized the world operated on various consciousness levels. She believed people behave on the basis of their own level of understanding. She said, "If anybody were on the Christ plane, he could stop the enemy from willing war. Let the world do it its own way, till it is god-filled to overflowing, then war will be no more."[18]

In 1918, Hopkins was voted honorary president of the International

New Thought Alliance. This group was composed of individual ministries and the more secular factions of New Thought. The *New Thought Bulletin* was the publishing organ for the alliance.[19] Hopkins did not mention this honor at all when writing to Luhan during the year's correspondence. I can find no evidence in her writing that she considered herself a celebrity.

In a January 7, 1918, letter to Maurice and Mabel, Hopkins addressed them as "Dearest Two of You." She gave them a pep talk on keeping "close together" and "never mind idiosyncrasies." It is a brief one-page letter. After Mabel had recovered from the respiratory illness, she joined Maurice in New Mexico. Rudnick said Mabel "reached New Mexico at exactly the right moment to serve as an apostle for the Anglo artists and activists." She enlisted the aid of John Collier, D. H. Lawrence, Willa Cather, Georgia O'Keeffe, and other members of the artist community to help preach the "healing qualities of the land and its peoples."[20] Mabel chose Taos and the Pueblo Indians as her special project. The rights of Native Americans and the protection and preservation of their culture became a central focus for her for the rest of her life.

On April 19, 1918, Hopkins wrote Mabel and Maurice on the subject of the "survival of conscious personality." In this letter, she also spoke of her worry for Bobby Jones, saying he "begins to look thin again" because of his "inward leanings toward nature" that New York does not honor.[21] She must have been replying to a question or statement from Mabel when she said, "I have never seen *one single* astrological chart come out as the modern astrologers averred. Old Astrology (Egyptian) got it right, and we may hit it someday."

Mabel sent Hopkins a blanket from New Mexico, and Hopkins wrote her on January 24, 1918. She noted, "How wise you were to go to Maurice! Be his woman forever—His woman! The play called 'Tiger Rose' draws crowded houses of young people, for they love to hear about *my man!* My woman!" With the gift of the blanket, Mabel must have asked Hopkins to journey out for a visit. Hopkins said, "I have just set out to see if Nina won't go to New Mexico. She seems to be a little off with McKenzie not as entranced. She needs just what you are getting."

On May 17, 1918, Hopkins wrote in response to a letter from Mabel:

"Bobby Jones is going to see you as soon as his series of plays is finished in the west. . . . Nina . . . is going later to visit you." This particular letter is full of gossipy news. Hopkins spoke of Sister Beatrix and said, "I never see Elizabeth Duncan these days. I hope she is on the upward watch."

In the next letter, on July 26, 1918, Hopkins spoke of Bobby Jones and Emilie Hapgood. A bit of personal sentiment came through when Hopkins said, "The success of Bobby fills me with joy. The success of my students is my joy. Like [a] mother their uplifts hit me harder than my own." Hopkins's unconditional love for Bobby was noticeable throughout her letters. Mabel said of the special relationship between Hopkins and Bobby that Bobby "was practically supported in the upper ether by Emma Curtis Hopkins for years."[22]

Hopkins's next letter, on August 20, 1918, told Mabel she wanted to come to Taos to see her, but it would be later, as she was traveling through the Northeast. She was concerned for her mother's health, as her mother was "getting feebler as days go on" (Lydia Curtis was then ninety years old). Hopkins was going "to give some lectures in Boston about 60 miles from her so as to run down to her country place easily." This letter also gives a glimpse of Hopkins's humor, telling Mabel that when she does come to New Mexico, she "shall stay a long time when I go so as to recoup the years that the caterpillar has wasted by keeping me talking night and day for twenty years." When Hopkins orchestrated the New Thought movement in Chicago, there were times between classes when she could recoup. In New York, her private sessions started early in the day and continued to early evening, leaving slight respite for energizing.

All was not well with Maurice and Mabel in Taos. Mabel had met the Native American she had seen in her dream. His name was Antonio Lujan (Tony Luhan), and he was "a majestically handsome Tiwa who Maurice soon sensed was a rival." Hopkins wrote Mabel on September 27, 1918, in response to three letters that Mabel had written to her. Hopkins told Mabel that Maurice had come to see her in New York twice, "once to call and once for a lesson. He is a good deal hurt by having to leave Mabel [actually, Mabel forced him to leave] and terribly hurt by the destruction of his Indian maiden in wax."[23] In this letter, Hopkins spoke again of how busy she was: "Many are wanting lessons, many are needing treatments." Hopkins was now sixty-eight years old and pushing herself to keep up with the demands of her rigorous, unique ministry.

On November 8, 1918, Hopkins wrote Mabel, "Nina is coming to Taos with me for February and March." In speaking of a photo that Mabel had sent her, she said, "Maybe it is too Atlantian for my type." Then as another topic, she said Maurice had no thought of "returning to Taos" (in other words, he was adjusting to the separation from Mabel).

Mabel's affair with Tony Luhan caused problems for Maurice, Candelaria (Tony's wife), and everyone in Taos. As an artist, Maurice had become financially dependent on Mabel. It is obvious from Hopkins's letters that she knew the marriage between Maurice and Mabel was over. She helped Maurice get over the pain of separation from Mabel. Maurice and Mabel, each in their respective books, tell a slightly different version of the beginning of Mabel's involvement with Tony. "Mabel claimed that she and Tony did not become lovers until Maurice left to go back East." [24] Maurice believed differently, and said so in his book. If Hopkins knew the truth, she never revealed it, but soothed each in turn. In a letter of October 10, 1918, Hopkins had said Maurice "likes to be at the Duncan [S]chool," referring to Elizabeth Duncan's progressive school. Maurice would tell in *Shadow and Light* of meeting a beautiful, young girl named Vera at the Duncan School when he was on the rebound from Mabel. As an adult, some years later, Vera became for Maurice "the woman with whom I have lived so happily ever after." [25]

On November 21, 1918, Hopkins wrote to Mabel that she and Nina planned to go to Taos. She said there had been no rebuke in her earlier letter to Mabel. Hopkins stated clearly:

> As to Maurice—a woman cannot live with a man in these days if she can't. Women are free. I am the last one to urge it. You are my brilliant and beautiful girl and what your free spirit chooses gratify.
>
> You may imagine notes of change in other people, but never in me. For I never change and if I have anything to say am daring and bold to say it without an undertone.
>
> Your devoted E.C. Hopkins

Hopkins's equanimity was never shaken through association with the most radical and freethinking socialites and artists. A large portion of time in her private practice seemed to focus on helping bright bohemians adjust to changing roles in a new world of their own choosing. When Hopkins left Chicago, she moved from a highly visible frontline position in a revolutionary new religious movement to a quieter and more comfortable position in her career. She became a trusted mentor and spiritual teacher to a number of the literati who were instituting innovative developments in art, music, drama, and social-justice arenas.

Perhaps because she had worked with such large groups in Chicago, Hopkins wanted to continue to heal and teach, but on a one-on-one basis or through absent treatments where she meditated for the person's healing without being in their presence. There is no doubt that her associations with the artistic community helped extend New Thought and metaphysical tenets into new avenues of U.S. society. Many of the people she influenced were of significant influence in social reform. As confidante, mentor, and healer, Hopkins's influence permeated society through the very power of the people with whom she was associated, a contrast to the Chicago years when she attracted eager theological students and underwrote social-justice causes with a largely middle-class population.

Hutchins Hapgood, for example, was a literary journalist writing for the *New York Globe* about the masses of suffering humanity. He and Mabel were rebels who embraced an "open-ended commitment to change. . . . They shared what William James had once described to Hutch as a 'mad unbridled lust for the absolute!' " It was Hutch who introduced Mabel to Emma Goldman, whose "obvious activity seemed to be publishing the anarchist magazine *Mother Earth*." [26] Hutch's brother, Norman Hapgood, served as the editor of *Colliers Weekly* and "was also a radical," according to Mabel. Hutch's wife, Neith Boyce, was a noted feminist writer who penned the first play for the Provincetown Players as they laid "the foundations . . . of modern theatre in America." Her play *Constancy* was based on Mabel's love affair with John Reed. [27]

Mabel said at one point in *Movers and Shakers* that Hutch was "the true citizen of the universe. . . . [H]e belongs to *all* individuals." This universality may be a keystone for understanding how he and Hopkins related to each other. Hutch's focus was primarily spiritual in a world committed to materialism and governed by power brokers. Lincoln Steffens, who among other literary trophies edited *McClure's Magazine,* "perhaps the finest magazine this country ever had," was a great friend of Hutch's. Steffens had invented "muckraking," and Hutch resonated to radical social agendas.[28] Hutch also introduced Mabel to Alfred Steiglitz and hence to Georgia O'Keeffe. O'Keeffe was a promising young artist who became a stalwart painter of western scenes, intrepid enough to use the pistils, stamens, and petals of flowers to create sexual symbolism celebrating women's sexual organs.

At the time Mabel met Hopkins, she was set on knowing anyone who was anyone. Mabel's wealth and socialite standing facilitated this need to know people who were the heads of organizations. Because of her curiosity, she aspired to meet Hopkins, for she recognized her contributions to early New Thought and was intrigued by her charisma and mystical lifestyle. It is interesting to note that Mabel recognized Hopkins's prominence as the head of a major organization when in this same year, 1919, Horatio Dresser overlooked her significance when he published *The History of the New Thought Movement.*

In 1919, Hopkins wrote many letters to Mabel. During the New York years, Hopkins also wrote and published prolifically in New Thought circles. Her last book, *High Mysticism,* published first in a series of lessons beginning around 1907, was completed, along with its companion volume, *Résumé.*[29]

In January 1919, Mabel sent Hopkins one hundred dollars for tickets to come to Taos, New Mexico. Hopkins's clientele must have been upset about her proposed absence, for she gleefully told Mabel in her letter, "The howling is terrific about my leaving New York."

On Tuesday, January 15, 1919, Hopkins wrote Mabel that she and Emilie Hapgood would be leaving on the 2:45 train on Saturday, February 1, for Chicago.[30] She said they would make a layover in Chicago for one night and phone Mabel from there. She concluded the itinerary by saying that on February 3, they would leave Chicago for Santa Fe and Taos Junction. There is a gap in the letters for February and early March

1919, when it can be presumed that Hopkins was in New Mexico with Mabel.

On March 12, 1919, Hopkins wrote Mabel a warm, newsy thank-you for the time she had spent in New Mexico. Bobby Jones had been in for his appointment and was eager to go to New Mexico. Hopkins told Mabel, "I will tackle Elizabeth Duncan next." Apparently, Mabel had assigned Tony (still Mabel's lover and not her husband) and Mary Young-Hunter to escort Hopkins part of the way back on the train.[31] Tony had taken Hopkins into his confidence while serving as her escort. He said that he wanted to take Mabel farther "out west" to enhance her experiences about the nature of western culture. He also gave Hopkins his name, saying he would call upon her when he came to New York again. Somehow, the mystical strain in Tony's nature and the mystic in Hopkins must have recognized kindred spirits in each other. Hopkins always spoke positively of Tony and made the return trip home carrying corn and sage grass as souvenirs to remember her trip west. Upon returning north, Hopkins had gone to her mother's farm in Connecticut. She said she had had a hard time convincing her elderly mother "she had been far away."

On March 13, 1919, Hopkins, having returned from Taos, admonished Mabel not to listen to Tony's protest that she did not love him. The tone of the letter suggests that Hopkins had missionary plans for Mabel. She said, "The world's need for your gentle and sunny message is so great that you feel like responding." Also, a note with the date March 13 advises Mabel, "I will be with you by 4:00 A.M. your time every morning." This time was probably set aside for communion with Mabel through the silent process of absent healing.

This letter also revealed Hopkins's genuine pleasure at having been pampered while in New Mexico. She reminded Mabel "that you took care of me as if I had been a baby and that I stayed in bed till noon . . . and ate everything." Hopkins's delight in what was a rare experience for her shines through the letter. Because of the sanctity of her mission, Hopkins devoted as many days as she could to her ministry. This holiday was an extraordinary event for her.

On March 19, 1919, Hopkins sent word to Mabel that Maurice was

not as "unhappy as they make out he is." Then on April 6, Hopkins said
Maurice would not give Mabel a divorce. Maurice was upset and had written to Mabel because he thought "everybody was talking" of their separation and Mabel's extramarital liaison with Tony. Hopkins pleaded for
gentle treatment of Maurice in his agony. She told Mabel, "His heart truly
is bruised." Mabel's affair with Tony caused Elizabeth Duncan not to go
to Taos. One can imagine that with Maurice spending time at the Duncan
School, Elizabeth had been privy to his grief and did not want to be emo-
tionally torn between Mabel and Maurice. Hopkins attempted to mend
the fences between Maurice and Mabel by telling Maurice not to judge
Mabel by standards of other women because Mabel was "from Atlantis in
every fibre." [32]

On May 8, 1919, Hopkins responded to Mabel's letter. The uproar
that was occurring over Mabel's liaison with Tony had caused her to write.
Hopkins assured her that others, too, had their problems. If there was an
immediate flurry, it would be over. Hopkins said, "I think that the Tony
part of the situation will come out all right for your happiness." On May
15, she addressed the issue again: "You have work to accomplish in some
way with Tony—a great work." She encouraged Mabel to "*write*. You are
a writer." [33]

Hopkins astutely recognized in Mabel a latent talent that, once
sparked, could leave future generations a lasting literary legacy. Whether
she meant that Mabel was destined to work with Tony for the good of the
Native American peoples or that Mabel and Tony had karmic soul issues to
work through is not clear. The fact that she knew and loved both Maurice
and Mabel must have made it difficult for her as the counselor of both to
travel to Taos and to meet Tony Luhan. Hopkins was placed not only in a
crucial position as mentor, but also in a delicate one. In *Shadow and Light*,
Maurice confessed that he had "borrowed a huge revolver," but of course
never used it on Mabel or Tony. He said that he had "kept it under my pil-
low in a childish . . . attempt to play cowboy to Tony's Indian." Hopkins
always seemed to know the latest news in this group of artists and writers,
so it may be that she knew of this specific incident and attempted to handle the triangular affair in the most careful manner possible. Although
Maurice never used the "borrowed" revolver, he and Mabel ended up "in

a violent scene." He said of their fight, "we struggled. . . . I pushed her down, off the bed, and onto the floor." [34] Not long after, he left Taos. He and Mabel never reconciled, for by this time Mabel considered her relationship with Tony providential.

At about this time, June 25, 1919, Mabel became involved with an occultist named Lotus Dudley.[35] Several members of Mabel's social circle had gone to see Dudley in Connecticut. Dudley wrote to Mabel that Mary Young-Hunter and another person would be able to give her the news from there. Hopkins did not like Mabel or her friends to associate with Dudley. Perhaps she sensed a rivalry for her authority in the realm of metaphysical healing or felt threatened financially because of their change of allegiance. The news that Dudley gave Mabel was that Mabel had a "cosmic task" to perform. Mabel, unsure of Dudley and her message, wrote to Hopkins because she was concerned about the validity of the message and its importance to her life. Hopkins wrote back and reassured her: "There is no cosmic task to be imposed upon you." Responding to what she must have sensed as fear in Mabel, she said, "I told you to cling up tight to free and fearless *me*," who would advise her without "mercenary sub reasons." Hopkins believed that the previous letter from Mabel, on June 20, 1919, had shown it was time for Mabel to surrender and place her fears on the "spiritual bosom" of Hopkins.

Two of the members of Mabel's circle who had associated closely with Dudley were Mary Young-Hunter and Selena Chamberlain. Hopkins made an assessment of the behaviors of Young-Hunter and Chamberlain: They "act like people obsessed. They do not act or look like themselves." [36] She made the statement that *"money"* was behind the "occult investigations." She excused another member of Mabel's group who was "a sincere seeker" who had been "humbugged" by Dudley. Hopkins took the path of least resistance with this bedazzled group when she said to Mabel: "While a frenzy . . . is raging let the fire engines have the track. So I let them rage, and say nothing, as every one of them knows I am not an occultist. I am in league with the free spirit of God." When it came to human behavior, Hopkins was not naïve. As a mystical teacher, she was never ignorant of practical situations. She said, "I'm subtler than people know."

On June 28, 1919, Hopkins again mentioned to Mabel "the strange coterie." She used her observations of Mary Young-Hunter's actions as an example of their bizarre behavior. She said that Mary had wanted to take the first six lessons from Hopkins over again until she went to Connecticut with the Dudley group and "came back a different person. . . . She did not look like herself at all. . . . Chamberlain has been in . . . looking very strange. They are desperately trying on a wrong trail."

On July 3, 1919, Hopkins gently admonished Mabel for seeing Dudley, and on July 16, Hopkins wrote to Mabel of her concerns for Dudley. Dudley had come to pay a "brief and only call" after Hopkins returned from her visit with Mabel in New Mexico. Dudley told Hopkins she should know what it was like to be "torn to pieces by the unseen forces." Hopkins replied, "No, I know only the sweet and calm defense of the everlasting arms." As a result of her positive answer, the occultist "looked very resentfully" at her. Dudley may have been a college or finishing-school graduate because Hopkins considered her attitude and behavior a waste of "her beautiful education." Hopkins no doubt had her hands full with this peculiar situation. The intensity of the power struggle between mystic and occultist must have escalated, because those people in league with Dudley turned on Hopkins and spoke ill of her to Mabel. Hopkins wrote Mabel on August 5 from Lenox, Massachusetts, where she was staying for several weeks. In answering a letter that Mabel had written, she related: "Tony is pretty shrewd to read under the lines that an unconscious sex feeling is motif—but you *must* notice that they are now off . . . base and have become dangerous. And you must look out now for outward *moves*. . . . [I]t is in the first place insanity to turn against me their very best friend. It is secondly insanity to try to dominate your life domestic or public."

Later that month, the unusual circumstances of Mabel's occult associations again plagued her, and she sought advice from Hopkins. Hopkins wrote in response on July 29, 1919. She believed it ridiculous that the people involved in the occult were going to "*manage* Mabel!" She told Mabel in no uncertain terms to "stick up close to the unmanageable me and fly on tires of strength Studebaker built beyond the ways of the purposes of men." Later in the letter, she told Mabel, "Some of the things that are going on are positively indicative of insanity. Do not be misled. Be sane!"

On August 8, 1919, Hopkins wrote to Mabel about "a diabolical attempt" to harm her. The "strange coterie" had taken tales to Mabel about Hopkins, and Hopkins was irate. She disowned them and told Mabel, "They can form a league and start a new society." Hopkins apparently believed the dabbling in occultism made them heretics, and it would be best for them and her to disassociate.

The next communication from Mabel or members of the coterie must have mentioned more conjecture about Hopkins's character or behavior. Hopkins told Mabel in the July 29 letter, "Some of my powerful friends are deliberating a hundred thousand dollar suit for flagrant misrepresentation with attempt to injure. It is against the law of the land to attempt to injure anybody." Hopkins planned to detect who was slandering her and told Mabel in an August 22 letter that she had planted an idea with someone that Mabel had invited her to go abroad. She was waiting for the story to be misconstrued to see who carried the tale. On August 24, Hopkins reported, "Mrs. Young-Hunter wrote me a vicious letter." Hopkins again threatened legal action to protect her name: "My word of honor is precious to me and must not be jeopardized."

Apparently, Eve, who was staying with Mabel, had been given a rough time by those dabbling in the occult.[37] This group had attempted to turn Mabel against Eve, and Eve wanted to leave. To antagonize Mabel, they told her that Eve followed Tony around. Hopkins defended Eve. She said Eve had "followed Tony . . . due to astonishment and admiration. . . . [S]he had never met such power and full blooded masculinity in all her . . . life before." Tony was for Eve a hero of some mystic realm for which her studies were "fitting her." Hopkins was seventy years of age when she made those remarks about Tony's "power and full blooded masculinity." While maintaining the "upward watch,"[38] Hopkins never lost sight of the sexual ramifications of human behavior and the social repercussions stemming from sexual attractions.

On September 2, 1919, Hopkins wrote of her role in the lives of others in her private practice. She told Mabel, "I am the repository of the profoundest personal secrets of many people's lives. . . . [A]ny kind of a report as coming from me would be panic stricken" (here she seems to mean the people who heard of her reporting would be panic stricken). There was a glimpse in this letter of her mystical mind-set: "I wonder if the sensitives hereabouts catch things . . . or catch thoughts—as if they had been spoken." She used two people as examples of this type of sensitive person: "R. W. Emerson" and "Dr. Weeks."[39]

Hopkins preferred to be mobile, traveling lightly. After she purchased the large house in Chicago as a base for her ministry, she never again seemed interested in ownership. When Hopkins's father, Rufus, died in 1910, he bequeathed portions of his possessions to his five living children. He gave Lydia, his wife, use of all personal property and real estate as long as she lived. Then he divided his other property and his money. There were two daughters who received money alone, with no property. Hopkins received the sum of one thousand dollars, a significant amount of money at the time. His daughter Estelle and son Lewis were executors of his estate. Hopkins's reluctance to own furniture (or any large encumbrance) must have been known to her parents, because she and another sister, who lived out-of-state, received none of the real estate that Rufus had acquired in his long lifetime.

On September 16, 1919, Hopkins wrote to Mabel that she would take "three light rooms with a private family the coming year in order to feel the temptation to write." People kept besieging her to give lectures: "From the ends of the earth they appear and I must not disappoint them." She told Mabel that she must furnish her reception room and asked if Mabel had any furniture in storage that she could rent for that period. Hopkins's disdain for encumbrances was exemplified here: "I do not want to *own furniture*."

By November 1919, what Hopkins perceived as the fierce backbiting and backstabbing of the dabblers in occultism had temporarily ceased. In a letter dated November 20, 1919, Hopkins told Mabel that she had heard that "Mrs. Young-Hunter loves *me* beyond words." Hopkins's blasé response was, "Life is not made up of bric a brac." Mabel had apparently asked Hopkins to relocate to Taos, and Hopkins answered: "Oh I am about a special task. I never leave it. The longest time I have spent away from headquarters was with you. Things are on the monotonous with my work. You couldn't stand monotony. It makes you sick. But life breathed on from the Steadfast God makes me buoyantly strong in monotony. Maybe you will like the same some day. My love to Elizabeth Duncan. Tell her to be head of her great school World without end."[40]

Hopkins viewed herself as someone with a mission, fulfilling a transcendent cause. Her simple but elegant lifestyle allowed her to focus 100 percent of her time and energy on teaching, healing, and writing. The only time Hopkins was not healing or teaching was when she traveled to her mother's farm to see her. In fact, her mother's age and frailty no doubt caused her to work hard even while there.

On December 21, 1919, Hopkins wrote Mabel a ten-page letter full of news and ruminations. It mentioned that Alice Sprague had asked Hopkins to treat Elizabeth Duncan by absent healing.[41] Mabel had written that she and Tony were treating her. Hopkins had deferred to their ministration, saying Elizabeth "will come out all right." Probably, Hopkins had taught Tony her method when she made her trip out to Taos in the preceding spring. She did not say in her letters, but one cannot help but wonder what Tony the Tiwa from the Pueblo thought of this healing modality, and which aspects of it were suggestive of themes in Native American religions.

Hopkins recognized the similarities between metaphysical principles and the cosmological precepts of Native American culture that included interactions between the invisible world and the finite. She accepted the atypical relationship between Mabel and Tony and became their spiritual mentor, creating a bridge between New Thought and Native American spirituality in which the transmission of common holistic religious practices could take place across cultures. These have been two tributaries of the New Age spirituality movement, which coalesced as a vocal, ecologically oriented, holistically expressed metaphysical vehicle in the 1970s. New Age ideas purport that through heterodox thinking, alternative medicine, and mind-body-spirit integration, humans can achieve an earthly nirvana. Hopkin's familiarity with Asian religious scripture also allowed Theosophists to join the Hopkins Metaphysical Association in Chicago. These areas of study are reflected in the New Age belief that the planet has become a pluralistic global village for its inhabitants.[42]

Hopkins certainly prophesied a victory for "the newer ways" and, as a perennial philosopher, the way for the progression of alternative religious and healing modalities. Yet, her everyday ruminations about her lifestyle kept a part of her focused in the present. For example, Hopkins spoke of her tight schedules. She had changed residences in order to lighten her caseload. She wrote to Mabel, "I thought if I went as far north as 59th Street I should have a little time to myself, but I am just as full up with engagements as the hours will hold." She mentioned the occult group and said a member of her clientele had said "I ought to stop them for they are all acting very strangely." Hopkins also mentioned in this letter that her mother was "still living at ninety-one and talks pretty straight for each moment but forgets each last moment." There is an undated note from what can be presumed to be this period. Hopkins wrote to Mabel of the dabblers in the occult, "You do not seem to notice that Dudley-Hunter-Chamberlain have one up their sleeve and are calling you to it." The social tension, coupled with high drama, must have taken a good deal of energy for Hopkins to handle. She probably believed that resolving crisis situations was one of the duties of her social mission. Without a doubt, Hopkins hoped to welcome her renegade students back to the fold of the "upward watch."

On July 8, 1920, after the death of her mother, Hopkins wrote from the Hotel Aspenwall in Lenox, Massachusetts. She told Mabel, "You must have wondered about me. Well I had to go often to see my mother. Then I spent the week of her funeral on the farm." It was a newsy letter, because some time had passed. Hopkins told Mabel she was trying to change her headquarters in New York, "but as N.Y. is crowded to overflowing I do not know that I can." Her mother's sickness and death had taken a lot of Hopkins's strength. She said, "I had worked so hard by the time my mother died that I could hardly stand up with fatigue." She informed Mabel she had heard from a Mrs. Taylor. Taylor, an artist, was going to Santa Fe, but would "not ally herself with Taos people as her work is to do the clay modeling in company with other artists."[43] Hopkins closed the letter with a salutation for Tony and then asked Mabel, "Tell me how it is with you. And if you sense God!"

In August 1920, Hopkins wrote "Dearest Mabel." This salutation was a change; she usually called her "Dearest girl." She said Mabel's letter had reached her in only five days from Taos. Apparently, a letter with a check to Hopkins was lost in the mail. Hopkins told Mabel that Taylor had written her of "Mrs. Young-Hunter's world having been snatched from under her feet. I do not know how Eve is. I have not heard from her since early last June. I told her there was no man . . . worth [unreadable word] her reputation. . . . Men don't stay put anywhere except in rare cases. And some women can't stay *put* either!" These letters indicate an ability to walk in two worlds. Hopkins's solitary lifestyle speaks of her yearning for a semi-cloistered existence, yet she was not naïve and her clients brought all the ramifications of big-city life to her doorstep.

In this same rather lengthy letter, Hopkins spoke of having written Mary Young-Hunter about how "Providence like an over river must be noticed in the days of mystery. . . . Dante speaks of the over hand . . . I believe in an overhand! I could not go on with my own life if I did not! From the throne of Allah to thy destined foot." She also told Mabel that Emilie Hapgood did not like it that Jack Barrymore had married, because it might affect his ability to play a preferred role in one of the upcoming stage productions. Perhaps the ability to speak about spirituality and, in another paragraph, to address the vital concerns and the frivolities of the literati indicates a hard-won balance on her part to dwell as a liaison between two worlds—the world of the spirit and the world of the mundane.

In an undated letter, Hopkins again supported Mabel as a writer. Mabel must have written her about conflict with work, because Hopkins answered her, "As to work—Why you are a writer. So write! Hard or easy, write! Work at it. You know that I am always backing you up."

In yet another undated letter, she spoke of Mary Young-Hunter and sent Mabel a letter. Apparently, John Young-Hunter did not tell her about the issues he discussed with Mabel. This breach might have been the omen that John and Mary would soon separate and divorce.

On September 19, 1920, Hopkins wrote Mabel about a note she had received from her and a check for forty dollars: "It seems as if there were an objection to my having any financial dealing with you in straight for-ward business fashion as this check has been struggling to get from you to me since last July." In this particular letter, Hopkins also explained to Mabel that she believed Mabel's money had caused people to treat her differently. Hopkins explained to Mabel that she had never charged her for treatments, "absent or present," except once when she was "helping Maurice two years ago." [44]

That Hopkins perceived herself as on a mission of divine importance was obvious in another undated letter. She said, "I am to stay hard at my post in New York, except the days I lecture in Boston and Philadelphia." She was sure she had a headquarters and a post to serve with diligence and vigilance. Her delight at being able to go to Taos for a month and sleep late and eat as she chose had indicated that anything so frivolous was not a part of her everyday lifestyle. Despite the upbeat ambiance displayed in her letters, Hopkins's fatigue was beginning to show. She was seventy-one years old. There was no talk of plans for retirement. She had been in the public spotlight for more than thirty years, orchestrating the "newer ways." Despite her fatigue, she remained a centralized theological authority for a diverse movement that had spread to other countries. It is interesting to note that Hopkins used military parlance to denote her chosen mission in helping to usher in the Second Coming of Christ. This one-pointed focus, to reach out and minister to as many people as possible, strained the parameters of her own health.

In a letter dated November 10, 1920, Hopkins wrote to "Dearest girl." This time the letter was about the intricacies of the personal relationships that surrounded Mabel and Hopkins. She spoke of Mary Young-Hunter and asked if she was going to give up her husband. Then she said, "I shouldn't wonder if some lover would hail into her life to take his place. When half gods go, the gods arrive. This is not discounting Mr. Young-Hunter." Hopkins, for all her mystical nature, was a pragmatist. Her letters recognized the irrational methods humans construct to get their personal needs met. Her judgments about the comings and goings and changes of partnerships among the intelligentsia were usually gentle and, above all, realistic for the specific situations.

In Hopkins's next letter to Mabel, on November 15, 1920, she spoke of changes in Eve's countenance. (Eve had left Taos and returned to New York for a stay.) She believed these changes were due to a love affair with

John Young-Hunter, but out of delicacy did not confront Eve: "I am on general principle, shy of love affairs of the sudden and astonishing variety so I do not pry. If the Young-Hunters have been drifting apart for a long time they can't have been very happy together."

Hopkins said she did not understand why people remained in relationships where the other partner did not want them. Perhaps this query is autobiographical, wondering why her own husband waited fourteen years to divorce her when she refused to return to their marriage. In this letter, she encouraged Mabel to visit New York, because "something about you wins my love and everlasting devotion and I like to have you around." She mentioned how busy she was in her ministry "with people who want me to talk to them of the Self existent and the laws thereof."

On January 5, 1921, Hopkins wrote again to "Dear Darling Girl." Mabel had referred her friend Agnes Pelton to Hopkins. Hopkins gave Mabel a progress report on her. She was "sweet as a flower and [was] doing wonderful portraits. She will have her eighth lesson tomorrow." Furthermore, she said, "Eve has been paying for her course of lessons by working . . . one hour every morning, 8:30–9:30. She has been very valuable to me."

Part of the letter contained advice. Referring to a certain "N. B.," she said, "I never interfere with love affairs or with family matters. I may know . . . but I make no reports. My mother taught me to mind my *own* business. I have been greatly astonished . . . but I have not interfered." The initials "N. B." probably referred to Neith Boyce, but they also could have designated Nina Bull.[45] Extramarital liaisons seem to have been a part of the activities of this group of literati, and Hopkins no doubt was privy to them. Why this particular one should have caused her astonishment must have been due to the fact that she had considered the participants unlikely to behave in such a manner. This letter of January 5 was long and detailed. Hopkins had heard that Mabel and Tony were coming to New York and wished to see Tony, as he promised to "see me when he next visits New York. . . . I hope he can breathe better this time near the great ocean." At this time in 1921, Tony and Mabel were still not married. Hopkins wrote Mabel, "Now that you have married Nina off can't you find a splendid one for Mary Y-H? If she has not been loved for years . . . she deserves love now." Despite Hopkins's choice of a celibate lifestyle, she was aware of the needs of noncelibates. In fact, Mary Young-Hunter was the one of the dabblers in the occult who had written her a "vicious letter" sometime previously, but Hopkins, whose spiritual presence radiated unconditional love for her students, was now concerned about Mary, who had "not been loved for years."

In the remainder of the letter, Hopkins made some unusual biographical statements. She said, speaking of Mary Young-Hunter, "Her married life was exactly like mine and ended exactly like mine, but I, you know, wouldn't look at the best man that ever walked the planet. I am married to God."

This letter, written in 1921, is seminal in understanding Hopkins's idea of her place in the world through her marriage "to God." It is vital, too, in understanding the particular issues involved in her marriage. I have attempted to obtain any works by Mary Young-Hunter or John Young-Hunter that would tell the story of their marriage. There was, however, a silence about that time in John's life. He never addressed it in his book, *Reviewing the Years*. Nothing on the subject from Mary's point of view seems to be available either. Mary may possibly have remarried. Considering her association with the occultists and Selena Chamberlain, she may surface someday as part of another artery of the New Thought or metaphysical movement. Hopkins's dedication and her marriage to God may explain one of the reasons she never returned to her husband. She also never divorced him. She forthrightly moved into theological arenas where she could express the vision from her childhood to found "a hospital for sick, destitute children." She devoted 100 percent of her time to laboring for the "newer ways" and healing where she found the need for her presence. Apparently, she had transcended the need for a mortal by the acceptance of the Immortal. She had found her spiritual home, and it was not with George Hopkins.

There was a gap in the letters from January until July 15, 1921. Hopkins may have been abroad. In July, Hopkins received a letter from Mabel dated July 8, forwarded to her in New London, Connecticut. Hopkins then advised Mabel in an undated letter that she was leaving her former address because she had a "divine sense of individual rights and I am making ready to leave . . . because my sacred privacy is perpetually invaded and my belongings too." She planned to move into the Iroquois Hotel in New York in September. She answered some of Mabel's questions in this letter. She said she was sure "Eve would wilt under the ordeal. But they are both intending to be game. . . . John shall have some unseen helpings.[46] I must see him some time when I find my place in N.Y." The Eve mentioned here was the person that Mabel credited with introducing her to Hopkins. Eve assisted Mabel in the running of her spacious hacienda in New Mexico and lived with her in Taos from time to time. Eve was probably acting as a social secretary when staying at Mabel's. (This woman was the same Eve that Hopkins mentioned as working for her from 8:30 to 9:30 in the mornings.)

In this letter, Hopkins told Mabel, "Bobby would not hear of my going away to Philadelphia, Boston, Lenox, New London. . . . I was so overcrowded with people in New York that I ought never to have taken on a single out of town class. . . . I had so little real life that I let myself enter into the outer demands before I realized."[47] Hopkins's reference to "real life" indicates she knew what sacrifices she made to remain at her "post" or travel to give lectures to her devotees. This genteel lady who served as a spiritual touchstone had found her charisma and eloquence could be a two-sided sword where her own health and welfare were concerned. She then told Mabel, "I am sorry for Mary Y-H, but she should have seen in me the best friend she would . . . have." Mary had dissolved her marriage to John and seems to have severed her connection with Hopkins also.

At this time, Hopkins told Mabel clearly that she and Tony had "some pre-historic blood mingling. I told Maurice something to this effect. So I did to Alice Sprague who had heard of the alliance only very lately." Hopkins explained the attraction between Tony and Mabel this way to avoid hurting their respective spouses, but she also believed it herself. Hopkins also told Mabel, "It does not seem as if you could be in 'change of life.' In breath the strength ethers." At this time Mabel was in her early forties.

On November 7, 1921, Hopkins wrote Mabel. She had already established herself at the Iroquois Hotel on West Forty-fourth Street in New York. She answered Mabel's letter of October 31 about her concern for her son, John.[48] She stated, "I can sympathize with you in your dilemma as to John and I will write at once to him and go to him if he likes." Hopkins gave Mabel advice on the parameters of her responsibility as a mother. She was clear where Mabel's duty lay. "It is not for *you* to decide whether he shall leave Yale or stay there. It is up to him entirely! You are not obliged to go to Egypt until the question is settled. Life is peaceful with you . . . now. Let it rest. If you leave it to Providence you will find it straightened out *for you quite soon*. I have you under my devoted wing. Come when you can."

On November 10, 1919, Hopkins wrote to Mabel. "I went to see John yesterday Wed[nesday]. He looked very thin and said he had been blue all day thinking about whether he should resign from Yale for one year . . . or . . . do the extra hard study and stay on. . . . [T]he boy's mind is tired. . . . (He strikes me as a child that *has not* been soul happy)." Hopkins then switched the topic to Mabel's mother and said, "Your mother has not left N.Y. . . . [S]he wishes John to resign for a year."

Hopkins responded to a query from Mabel: "Of course you ought to have your loved ones with you! If we can't, let us put up with it." She sent word that Bobby was "trying to do more cheery things and wants to be with you." Bobby was also maternally attached to Mabel. His reverence for Mabel dated back to a life-and-death situation he had experienced with her. According to Mabel, when Bobby returned from "studying with Reinhardt in Germany," he seemed to be underweight and gaunt and attached himself to Mabel. Together they would spend the night with Neith Boyce and Hutchins Hapgood. One night while visiting, Bobby developed acute appendicitis and was rushed to the hospital. Mabel said she sent her energy "like ribbons of fire" to save his life. Bobby, after recovering consciousness, said to Mabel, "I thought I was dying. . . . [Y]ou . . . saved me."[49] Bobby, already having an attachment to Mabel as a nourishing mother, strengthened his bond to her with this event. If Mabel was his surrogate mother, in his psyche Hopkins must have been his spiritual godmother. There is no doubt he basked in the protective power of these two extraordinary female figures who encouraged and championed his creative ventures in the theater.

On December 30, 1921, Hopkins wrote to Mabel, "Life seems to hang hard on the backs of all the world now that two planets are heavy on their orbits and the moon is 12 miles off her heat." She did not tell how she had arrived at this unusual conclusion. Whether this belief was something she had picked up in her mystical meditations is hard to say. Perhaps she sensed that the cosmological order was changing because of the new year.

In 1922, there were three letters between Hopkins and Mabel. They were dated in the fall of the year. Hopkins may have been abroad for the first nine months of 1922. The first letter was written from the Ritz-Carlton Hotel in Philadelphia. Mabel's letter had reached Hopkins there. The date of the letter was September 12, 1922. Hopkins told Mabel she would be returning on September 13. Mabel had written seeking answers to questions, and Hopkins answered each of them in turn. She told Mabel, "You belong to the *living* influences of the world. . . . [Y]our mother won't stay mad at you! She is too proud of you!" The next issue that Hopkins addressed was Tony. In 1922, Tony and Mabel were living together, but would not marry until 1923. Apparently, Tony had been attracted to another woman, and Mabel was concerned about his continued affection for her. Hopkins replied, "As to Tony! I guess back of it all he has an abiding affection for *you*. Men have a tendency to temptations outside their honest loves. But their honest loves are under currenting all their goings on." As a morale booster, she gave a pep talk to Mabel before closing the letter. "You are brilliant and powerful. All people feel it. Wherever you are you are a winner!"

On September 16, 1922, Hopkins had returned to her "post" at the Iroquois Hotel on West Forty-fourth Street in New York. Hopkins wrote to Mabel of her idea for Mabel to "hostess . . . an Inn Beautiful. Where all the artists and literati might turn in for renewal. And all the world go for conversation as all the world went to the castle of Frederick the Great for conversation." In fact, Mabel's hacienda in Taos had this ambiance. Her salon at 23 Fifth Avenue had fulfilled this idea in New York. The Villa Curonia in Italy had this same reputation during Mabel's years there.

On November 17, 1922, Hopkins wrote a note to Bobby, an apparent response to a note of his. She answered that she could not "receive" him for the day he requested. She thanked him for the two tickets he had sent for her and another person to attend *Hamlet*. She told Bobby, "We were

delighted and astonished last night at the splendor and perfectness of . . .
Hamlet." Who the two of them were she does not specify, but assumed
Bobby knew.

On November 28, 1922, Hopkins said, "It's Thanksgiving week . . .
no Mabel in NYC!" She spoke to Mabel of Bobby and how much Bobby
needed someone to sympathize with him "in the terrific demands laid
upon him and his masterly handling of [a] colossal undertaking." She, of
course, suggested that Mabel was the one to do this task. She told Mabel,
"My heart has been to you like a mother. I suppose your blood mother has
given you the usual allowance by this time. How could she do other when
she loves you and is proud of you?" Mabel had a trust from her grandpar-
ents that gave her about twelve thousand dollars per year. She always over-
spent that amount, and her mother supplied the difference.

Hopkins wrote Mabel on January 13, 1923, a quick one-page letter
that seemed to be a response to a letter from Mabel. She mentioned
Bobby, who would visit Taos soon. On March 16, 1923, Hopkins wrote
Mabel another one-page letter. She said, "Whether you hear from me or
do not hear I am just here as above on the job of blessing you."

On May 28, 1923, Hopkins again wrote Mabel. Apparently, a Mrs.
Shivsky was the one to bring Hopkins the news that Mabel had married
Tony Luhan. Hopkins, elated for Mabel, said, "Well—I congratulate you!
Finding a mate is divine chording." The joy at their marriage was not
shared by everyone involved in this match. Mabel's son, John Evans, was
in London where he was honeymooning with his new bride, Alice Rossin.
It was reported that when John heard of the marriage, he "took to his bed
for two days; and Edwin Dodge [Mabel's second husband] is alleged to
have shaken his head and said, when he heard the news, 'Lo, the poor
Indian!' "[50]

Hopkins, in her newsy letter, said she heard little from Bobby Jones because "he is in Europe quite successfully helping O'Neill with 'The Hairy
Ape.' He thinks O'Neill out of sight in genuine genius." Then Hopkins
relayed news of "Mrs. Hapgood" who "is in Europe on somewhat of the
same sort of errand but not so well accompanied and backed up as Bobby.
She is making a desperate fight to get somewhere."[51]

A part of this letter was directed to telling Mabel that Alice Sprague should go to her for "your normalizing quality. Has been nearly out of her head with psychic things such as Mrs. Dudley . . . delved among. Mrs. Dudley was quite off for a long time. Do let us have common sense!" [52]

On June 10, 1923, Hopkins wrote Mabel about a new artist: "I do hope you can have Clarence E. Thompson the young artist in your own ranch.[53] He is full of the Spirit of the New Age and actually thinks he would prefer an Indian wife to a pale face. He is a young yogi and does not know it." [54]

The remainder of Hopkins's letters to Mabel were not written from the Iroquois Hotel in New York. Beginning August 21, 1923, Hopkins wrote from her sister's home in Killingly, Connecticut, where she was recovering from a sudden heart attack. She addressed the letter to "Dearest Mabel Luhan"; acknowledging Mabel's marriage was her intention. Mabel had sent her a shipment of fur pelts. Hopkins read the letter from Mabel dated July 28. Hopkins wrote to her, "I did not read letters while my heart failure was holding me breathless and voiceless. . . . I am answering gradually day by day." She thanked Mabel for the furs, which had just been forwarded from her New York address. She told Mabel why she was at her sister's house in Connecticut. Mabel had wired her, and Hopkins was having her sister send a wire back. She said, "Mrs. Darrow does more than everything." [55] Hopkins again mentioned the artist Clarence, who had written her glowing reports about Mabel. She ended the letter by saying she would think of what she wanted to do with the furs. Then there was a postscript in shaky handwriting: "The Indian boys did their work like Masters of Art!" She signed her letter in "care [of] Darrow Killingly Connecticut." Her handwriting was smaller, and in some places it looked as if her hand was trembling as she wrote.

On August 28, 1923, Hopkins wrote from Killingly: "It is true, I am getting better day by day in a [word unclear; looks like *slim* or *dear*] fashion because I was not a sick person but one stricken suddenly with the touch of death—as if I had finished my career." She then added in the next paragraph, "But I rallied, against all diagnosis and am now with my sister who takes divine care of me." Hopkins had decided to make the furs sent by Mabel and Tony into lap robes so they would "never wear out either in my life time or yours." She was next concerned about Tony, who "was feeling keenly the way people treated him because of his marriage to" Mabel. Hopkins seemed to be one of the few supporters of the interracial marriage. She was no doubt sure that Mabel and Tony would support politically and financially the rights of Native Americans. In fact, Tony and Mabel were instrumental in getting an ally of Mabel, who was sensitive to Native American culture, appointed as director of the Bureau of Indian Affairs.

Mabel, ultimately of course, wanted to create a bridge between U.S. and Native American cultures not only to foster her relationship with Tony, but also to establish Taos as a center of enlightened activity. This ambition was compatible with her original desire to create an artist community, a sort of spiritual mecca for the avant-garde, not unlike Hopkins's ideas of the Inn Beautiful with Mabel as hostess. Mabel wrote Arthur Brisbane about her discovery of New Mexico because of his power to proselytize with the press, but he refused to be drawn into the promotion. It turned out that if anyone "put Taos on the map," it would be Mabel. Mabel was able to attract artists and writers who appreciated the clear, cool beauty and the propensity for spiritual and emotional refreshment that the desert region offered.[56]

Toward the end of the August 28 letter, Hopkins wrote of an article that Mary Austin had published: "It was on the vicarious principle although the word vicarious appears no where in the article. Salute her for me."[57] The article was meaningful enough for Hopkins to save with other "things worth while." She thanked Mabel for "the little pictures [that] are good to see." This writing was the last bit that Hopkins sent to Luhan. It was about a year and a half before Hopkins's death. Whether Hopkins is mentioned further in the Luhan Papers is unknown.

Hopkins as Seen by Others

Hopkins's portrait viewed through her letters reveals a slightly different character from portraits of her painted by others. Two people who wrote about her as she appeared in the last decade of her life are Mabel Dodge Luhan and Ernest Holmes. Seeing Hopkins through their eyes adds another dimension of who and what this enigmatic mystic was.

Mabel said she had been seeing Smith Ely Jeliffe for psychoanalysis, "and the old . . . depression came back." Then, she said, "someone . . . introduced me to Emma Curtis Hopkins and she . . . soothed me into 'the effortless way.' " During the last nine years of Hopkins's life, when she was an elderly lady, Mabel went to see her regularly. She said that when she traveled to see her in the Iroquois Hotel, and Hopkins was "clothed in an exquisite gown all soft black lace and silk, a large brimmed lace hat on her soft white hair, and she smoothed and relaxed one so that at the end of one's hour one was renewed and reassured." Mabel says she went to her three times a week when she was in New York and sat "in a comfortable armchair. . . . Her violet eyes held mine as she—inspired . . . [t]he effort-less way [to] . . . 'Be still and know that I am God.' "⁵⁸

In her description, Mabel said Hopkins's teachings were "based upon intuition and there was a great deal of truth in it." Mabel called her "an old fashioned New Englander from Boston," who had formulated her doc-trine into "Twelve Lessons in Mysticism." Mabel says about Hopkins, "She stimulated and renewed one. . . . She loved us all . . . and appreci-ated us. I gradually impelled all my entourage to her quiet asylum. Bobby, Maurice, Nina, Elizabeth, Andrew and others—." Mabel said that Hop-kins would in the hour of their appointment "gaze at us . . . with eyes of shining love and tenderness, enhancing in each of us our feeling of worth." Hopkins conveyed love to everyone who would open themselves to her presence. Mabel wrote: "At the end of the hour . . . she would go to the door, and, smiling a little coldly, grown remote . . . show us out, ap-pearing loath to shake the grateful hand or to continue the intimacy. . . . [W]e grew to understand that the love . . . did not . . . extend to the per-son—it was for the hidden self."⁵⁹

Hopkins the pundit saw the hidden self in all of her students. This "Self," as she sometimes wrote it, was the spark or the essence of the Holy within the individual, and her spiritual ministrations were designed to transcend the everyday personae of her clients. That she was aware of and understood their struggles for success was also apparent.

About her friends who saw Hopkins, Mabel said, "Bobby [Jones] she called a Genius. . . . [S]he just suited Elizabeth [Duncan], whose teach-ings coincided with hers." Mabel said she was restless as she drove through the countryside to see Hopkins, but when she saw her "in the dim room among her roses and lilies, her immaculate toilet forever fresh and charming . . . what she gave one was worth all the dusty miles." [60]

Mabel also told the following story about an excursion she took with Hopkins. She had persuaded Hopkins to travel with her to meet a friend who was extremely sick. In her words, she "begged Mrs. Hopkins to go." It was a hot day as Mabel motored out to see her friend, taking Hopkins with her. Hopkins "beamed and blessed," not seeing the dingy road or feeling the oppressive heat. Mabel's woman friend Eva had married a village rector named the Reverend Mr. Royce. He met them in the hall when they arrived. He looked at Hopkins, and "instinctively he smelt heresy and competition in Divinity." Mabel says the rector would have liked to forbid them to see his sickly wife, "but Mrs. Hopkins was such an evident lady, so exquisite, so fashionable, and so smilingly sure of her welcome" that he could not refuse them entry. They went into the darkened sickroom, and Hopkins went straight to the ailing Eva, "bending over poor Eva . . . smiling like an angel." Hopkins gave her short passages to remember, such as "My Word is the Everlasting Life." When asked who she was by Eva, Hopkins replied, "Oh, I am a friend of our dear little Mabel. We came to see you this beautiful summer day." Mabel says Eva's husband did not like this "unorthodox scene." "He felt God and the Scriptures belong in Church and should not be introduced into social situations." Despite the tension, they were invited to stay for the evening meal, and Mabel said dinner was tenable only because of "Hopkins's serenity" and "her apparent ignorance of" Royce's distaste for them both. On the one hand, he had never liked Mabel because she wore "such queer clothes." Hopkins, on the other hand, "smiled and praised and enjoyed herself so much that he melted with the coffee and found himself giving her an account of his work in the parish." [61]

Mabel's writing has enriched what was known about Hopkins and many people of the times. How accurate are Mabel's reports? Several reliable sources support the quality of the writing that Mabel left behind. Winifred Frazer, Mabel's most recent biographer, says, "Mabel herself and her autobiographical volumes are . . . remarkable products." Frazer says Mabel "drew an accurate picture of her life and times." How valuable her contributions are to U.S. history may not be clearly recognized until all of her papers are released for study. Donald Gallup of Yale University says that when the sum total of her work is made available, it will "constitute an invaluable record of the period as seen by a woman of a superior order of intelligence and understanding, gifted with an extraordinary memory and a natural talent for self-expression." [62]

Luhan as Seen by Hopkins and Lasch

Conversely, it was in part through Hopkins's letters that Mabel was recorded for posterity. Hopkins saw Mabel as a modern-day Margaret Fuller, Hopkins's girlhood hero whom she never stopped admiring. Christopher Lasch was rather critical of Mabel. He juxtaposed her with a more saintly, but rebellious, Jane Addams, and said, "Life in respectable families no longer seemed merely boring and pointless; it gave off an atmosphere of actual decay." He cited "the decline of patriarchal authority" as a factor in Mabel's development and then generalized that this problem was the reason for the degeneration of U.S. culture. Lasch used Mabel and her peer group to demonstrate this decay.[63] According to Mabel's vividly graphic descriptions of these achievement-oriented people, there was no atmosphere of "decay." If, by the decline of "patriarchal authority," he meant that some men were losing the behavioral control of the women in their specific domain, then Mabel, Hopkins, and other women of that time, such as the members of the Heterodoxy Club, were examples of this paradigm shift toward more egalitarian roles for women. The restructuring of patriarchal authority was exactly what this noted group of intelligentsia was all about. *Decay* implies a process toward atrophy or stagnant nongrowth. Mabel's entourage, who also were students of Hopkins, were people who supported suffrage, equal rights for Native Americans and African Americans, and the emancipation of women and minority groups. Mabel's radical ways of thinking and living supported positive changes in the status quo and underwrote an acceptance of progressive thought that would move culture forward. It was fortunate that Mabel was preserved through the eyes of people who knew her well, persons such as Hutchins Hapgood and Hopkins.

Ernest Holmes Studies with Emma Curtis Hopkins

The final picture of Hopkins was drawn by Ernest Holmes, who studied with her in 1924, shortly before he published *Science of Mind* (1926). Holmes was the founder of the youngest New Thought group called Religious Science. He tape-recorded his recollections of Hopkins before his death, and his vignettes encapsulate her distinctive charisma as the enigmatic sovereign of her unique mystical path. He said she was "a very stately woman who wore long dress and a hat at all times."[64] The first three or four times Ernest went to see her, he did not know if she even knew his name. Finally, he took her a "bouquet of roses." She was delighted to have them for a funeral she would attend the next day. Ernest said he had to accept that theirs was a "teacher-student relationship." The roses, however, seemed to unbend her formality, and Ernest used to stay and have long conversations with her. He said she was "witty, cheerful and loveable." She told him of a convention in Chicago where an absolutist who believed he was God began to scream, "I am God." Her response was, "There, there George, it is all right for you to play you are God, but don't be so noisy about it."

Ernest said, "She was a very sweet character, and there was something about her that you felt rather than heard." Ernest considered it rare that she combined mysticism with metaphysical healing. He said, "There is a common denominator of mysticism . . . and she was the first and greatest to express it in terms that are applicable to healing." Ernest believed that Hopkins experienced Being and had "the consciousness of the mystic," which she could concomitantly awaken in her students. Ernest said none of her students "studied" with her. "What she said was *IT* and . . . like some ancient seeress, dispassionate but not cold, she powered it with a conviction so great that it imparted something . . . a 'psychic breeze' . . . an awe . . . at once personal and impersonal, identified with her and yet something more."

Hopkins taught Ernest to turn away from all events and persons in order to develop the consciousness of a mystic and become "God-conscious . . . as an inner identity." She stressed "realization . . . of the

Perfect Presence, the ONLY Life, . . .in which the elevated consciousness
. . . does the work: God is all there is, there is no other Life."

Hopkins as Mystic

The first documented account of Hopkins's mystical nature was found in
her article "Teachers of Metaphysics." In flowery language, she said her
teacher, Mary Baker Eddy, fostered her first look at "the glorious inheritance of *pure understanding*." She claimed this brief look "face to face"
fixed "forever in [her] mind the sweet consummation." [65] Probably, Hopkins had the mystic's propensity from childhood. This occasion may have
been the first, or at least an important, one to give it fuller sway. To have
her transcendent experience authenticated and validated by her noted
teacher was fortuitous. At this crucial juncture in Hopkins's life, Eddy
helped set the seal of approval upon her mystical nature. Hopkins became
a spiritual soldier pursuing the mystical path in a most extraordinary
manner.

Hopkins was not a Western type of mystic who experienced the "dark
night of the soul" and the spiritual stages of enlightenment in the way
Evelyn Underhill describes them. Hopkins was what W. T. Stace, in *Mysticism and Philosophy*, called an introvertive type of mystic who "gets rid of
the empirical ego" so that the "pure ego, normally hidden, emerges into
the light." *"The undifferentiated unity between the person and the world is
the essence of the introvertive mystical experience."* Stace said that this state
of consciousness is frequently spoken of "as the Void . . . One . . . the Infinite." This type of experience usually does not happen spontaneously, as
the extrovertive type does. Stace quoted from the *Mandukya Upanishad*
to demonstrate: "It is pure unitary consciousness. . . . [I]t is ineffable
peace. It is the Supreme Good. It is One without a second. It is the Self."
Such an experience was ultimately ineffable. Stace said this enlightened
state was more commonly described by the tenets of Oriental mysticism.
Although more common in Eastern culture, however, there are "Christian
examples of the introvertive type of mystical consciousness." He names
Jan van Ruysbroeck (1293–1381) as an individual who personified this

type of mysticism in Western culture: "The God-seeing man . . . can always enter, naked and unencumbered with images, into the inmost part of his spirit. There he finds revealed an Eternal Light. . . . [His spirit] is undifferentiated and without distinction, and therefore it feels nothing but the unity." Stace noted: "Acquired introvertive experiences . . . can as a rule be thereafter induced . . . over long periods of life. . . . He says there are rare cases in which the mystical consciousness is believed to become permanent, running concurrently with, and in some way fused and integrated with, the normal or common consciousness." [66]

This experience is the "spiritual marriage" or "unitive life." It was known technically as "deification" in the Christian worldview.[67] It was this unitive life that Hopkins spoke of when she said she was "married to God" in her letter to Mabel. If Holmes's assessment of Hopkins is correct, then her mystical consciousness was "fused and integrated with" the normal consciousness. Mabel's reports indicate that Hopkins could share and envelop her students in the spiritual presence. This extraordinary consciousness was the tool Hopkins used to awaken the mystical propensities within her students.

William James speaks of mystical states of awareness: "The overcoming of all the usual barriers between the individual and the Absolute is the great mystic achievement." To "become one . . . and become aware of . . . oneness" is the objective. To Hindu or Christian mystics, "the same recurring note" was a central and unifying vision among the various "mystical classics." James also believed that it would be the practitioners of the mind-cure movement who would "reintroduce methodical meditation into our religious life." [68]

The first documented evidence that Hopkins was undergoing a transformational experience is seen in her 1894 letter to Myrtle Fillmore when she spoke of "the fire" and of her "dauntless divinity." It was not long before Hopkins was adept at introvertive mysticism, which is, according to Stace, rare, and "believed by mystics to be the supreme summit of the mystical life." The examples of this type of mysticism that Stace gives are Saint Teresa and the Buddha, who "also reached a permanent enlightenment consciousness." Mabel, acknowledging Hopkins's "living responsiveness to life," recorded how Hopkins the quintessential mystic viewed her spiritual states. Mabel, recognizing Hopkins's hermitlike lifestyle, on one occasion asked Hopkins how she could tolerate her life, "so alone except for all these people who come to you for help." Hopkins told her tenderly, as she beamed at her, "Oh, it is wonderful to be alone and feel your oneness with everything outside you! . . . Sometimes when I am waiting for a student I go in my room and draw the curtains, and I lie down on my bed and draw the blanket over me and I have the most delicious moments." [69]

Erroneous Reports of Hopkins's Death

There was a hearsay report claiming that Eleanor Mel of the Boston Home of Truth was with Hopkins on the day she died. According to the information received from Mel, "Mrs. Hopkins was at her High Watch Farm in Kent, Connecticut, attended by her sisters. Intuitively knowing that her death was near she asked her sister to have Eleanor Mel come to see her." The message was relayed to Mel in Boston at the Home of Truth there, and she "drove at once" to see Hopkins. She was greeted on arrival at the farm, "and [Hopkins] told Mel that she was going to make her transition almost immediately and asked that Miss Mel read to her from metaphysical books." After about an hour, Hopkins told Mel to "open the Bible and read it to me." Mel picked up the Bible and opened it where it fell to "John 17 and read the first verse—These words spake Jesus, and lifted up his eyes to heaven, and said, Father, the hour is come; glorify thy Son, that thy Son also may glorify thee!" Hopkins quietly passed away while this passage was being read to her. According to the source, "Her sister had an Episcopalian Church Service in Boston for Mrs. Hopkins who was buried in Boston. Miss Mel was the only Teacher of the Truth present." This story cannot be substantiated.

There are many conjectures about various aspects of Hopkins's life. However, this story is not supported in other documentation. High Watch Farm, a teaching center and publishing arm for Hopkins's work, was in western Connecticut near Cornwall. Mel would have had to drive for hours to reach that location. Due to Hopkins's precarious condition, it was more likely that she died at the family farm in Dayville in eastern Connecticut, which would have been about a two—to three-hour drive from Boston in those days. In a conversation with Alan Anderson, who had met Mel, I asked him if she would have knowingly distorted the report. He said no.

Official records indicate that Hopkins died on April 8, 1925, and was buried with the Curtis family in the family lot at the cemetery in Dayville, Connecticut. Upon investigation of the site, I found Hopkins to be buried with her parents near the community Congregational church that had been dedicated to service in 1845.[70] The family monument lists her name and date of death. Her personal gravestone simply states "Emma." This marker is consistent with other members of the family who have identical ones bearing their first names. The individual stones of her parents say "Mother" and "Father." Dayville is probably the location of her funeral service also. I cannot guess why Mel would say she had attended the services in Boston, unless there was an additional memorial service there. Certainly, this last report leaves room for conjecture. Someone who knows what actually happened may someday step forth and set the record straight. It is an ironic consistency that these mysterious entanglements blot Hopkins's biography concerning episodes connected with her birth, marriage, and death. The dates of her death are given as June 9, 1925, in the *New Thought Bulletin* (summer 1925), and April 25, 1925, by Braden.[71] All contemporary sources using these older works have quoted erroneous death dates.

Hopkins's death certificate indicates she died of chronic myocarditis on April 8, 1925. The challenges to her health had begun two years before. This information seems accurate. She stated in her letters to Mabel Dodge Luhan that she was always healthy and had been stricken rather suddenly. The dates given were borne out in the letters.

The obituary column for Hopkins stated, "Her husband, dead many years, was a professor at Phillips Exeter Academy."[72] Records indicate that George Hopkins was never employed there. One could presume that the same family member, Estelle, who supplied the information for the death certificate also supplied the obituary to the press. It was reported in the obituary column that Hopkins had been a noted writer who helped develop and establish a "cult"; however, the term *cult* seemed to be used not in a derogatory but in an informative manner. The death certificate erroneously reported Hopkins's birth year and stated that she was divorced from George Hopkins. The newspaper obituary portrayed her as a widow.

George Hopkins did not actually die until February 26, 1935. He outlived his son, John, and his former wife, Emma, by many years. He was eighty-five when he died. At the time of Emma's death, he was alive and had been living in Manchester, New Hampshire, continuously for more than forty years. He had not been "dead many years" as Estelle (or another family member) reported to the newspaper. He also remarried after his divorce from Emma and outlived his second wife, Daisy E. Flanders.[73]

It was unlikely that Estelle did not know her oldest sister's true age, her birth date, her former brother-in-law's place of employment, the status of the marriage, or whether he was dead or alive. The initial confusion was created by Estelle to cover the erroneous birth date she had given Hopkins. Also, for a woman to be divorced in 1900 for "abandonment" was considered scandalous. The white lie to the newspaper about Hopkins being a widow was a cover-up to protect her reputation.

4

THE CONTINUATION OF
HOPKINS'S TEACHINGS

*A*fter the death of Emma Curtis Hopkins on April 8, 1925, her sister Estelle Darrow Carpenter attempted to keep Hopkins's literary work alive. According to Braden in *Spirits in Rebellion,* Eleanor Mel helped Carpenter. Several other persons also were involved. One was Etheldred Folsom, who later married a man named Helling. Folsom, or Sister Frances as she preferred to be called, was reputed to have been a student of Hopkins, and had traveled abroad with her. She had money that she wished to have used for the perpetuation of Hopkins's teachings. She purchased a large farm near Kent, Connecticut, called Joy Farm and distributed Hopkins's writing under the rubric of "The Ministry of the High Watch." Estelle Carpenter and Sister Frances's husband incorporated the business. Later, Helling divorced his wife and moved away. Sister Frances and Estelle continued to support the work of Hopkins, and, though teaching was discontinued at the farm, many people could go there for restful vacations.

Elizabeth C. Bogart, a former secretary to Myrtle Fillmore, became impressed with Hopkins's teachings and associated with the group at Joy Farm.[1] By this time, Charles P. Wade had come to Joy Farm to teach the classes there in Hopkins's methods. Bogart started to collect Hopkins's writings; she journeyed to Chicago and collected the articles and "International Bible Lessons" that Hopkins had written from 1887 to 1898 for the *Chicago Inter-Ocean* newspaper. She purchased a multigraph and began to print and distribute Hopkins's work. Wade was called away from

Connecticut and went to Wisconsin, where he eventually became a Presbyterian minister.

When Estelle Carpenter died, she left the books to a realtor, Leon T. Wilson, who sent material out under the label of the Emma C. Hopkins Publishing Company. In 1951, he wished to sell his interest. Elizabeth Bogart and Harry Bogart purchased the rights and published *The Higher Mysticism,* now called *High Mysticism.* They continued to scout around for other works in manuscript or in old newspapers and magazines. High Watch or Joy Farm was eventually sold. The Bogarts moved a short distance away and continued to sell books through mail order.

High Watch Farm is operational today in Connecticut as a residential treatment program for male alcoholics. It has no association with Hopkins or with the people who followed her, says the town historian at Cornwall. A former post-office employee remembered the mailings from the Bogarts' farm and says they were extensive. A relative remembered his aunt being active and concerned with Hopkins's teachings. She worried that at the time of her death there might be no interested person who would carry on her work. However, the Reverend Marge Flotron wished to create a ministry based on Hopkins's teachings. The copyrights that Elizabeth Bogart held were signed over to Flotron. After Bogart's death, the pamphlets that she had in her possession were boxed and given to Flotron.

Harley B. Jeffery of the Unity School of Christianity taught courses based on Hopkins's work. Braden stated that Jeffery wrote several books: "His *Mysticism* is strikingly like *The Higher Mysticism* of Mrs. Hopkins." [2] Hopkins spoke of Jeffery in a letter, dated October 27, 1916, to "My beloved Myrtle Fillmore." In what must have been a question from Fillmore, she responded, "I have always spoken in the *highest* terms of Mr. H. B. Jeffery. . . . [H]e is one of the greatest healers in this country. . . . [W]hoever has reported anything different has spoken a malicious falsehood (motive unknown)." From the tone of the letter, it looked as if there was internal dissension at Unity that involved Jeffery and as if Hopkins was trying to set the record straight on his behalf with Myrtle Fillmore. After the death of Jeffery, Christ Truth League of Fort Worth acquired the rights to his publications.

Hopkins's premises about spiritual healing have been absorbed into some mainstream religious movements. Stillson Judah reported that the International Order of St. Luke the Physician is an interdenominational group that places primary emphasis on spiritual healing. This order was founded by John Gayner Banks, an Episcopalian priest, in 1946. The census of this healing order in 1961 indicated that "eight thousand people from thirty-eight states of America, ten provinces of Canada, and several foreign countries, were drawn to the conference." [3]

Banks had the progressive idea of integrating the various healing modalities "from the teachings of Jesus, the apostles . . . medical science, psychiatry . . . [and] ideas emanating from the metaphysical movements." He spoke up in favor of the term *metaphysical healing*. He believed the topic of metaphysical healing had been abused and maligned because "it represents an entirely new way of teaching and practicing the elements of Christian healing as given in the Gospels." [4]

Banks was not afraid to give credit to Warren Felt Evans and Emma Curtis Hopkins for their contributions to the subject of metaphysical healing. The "association's study courses entitled *Truth That Heals,* published by the St. Luke's Press" is primarily made up of Hopkins's ideas on spiritual healing. [5]

Robert Peel, in *Mary Baker Eddy: The Years of Trial,* stated that Hopkins taught the young clergyman John Gayner Banks in California and that as late as the 1960s the official organ *Sharing,* which was read by both Anglicans and Episcopal devotees of spiritual healing, ran advertisements for Hopkins's lessons in *High Mysticism.* I recovered a 1947 edition of the *Truth That Heals,* and Hopkins's metaphysical ideas and mystical lessons were acknowledged by Banks and implemented in his teaching manual. It was apparent he revered her as a Truth teacher.

Ministries Using Hopkins's Materials

Clara Stocker, who became a teacher of Hopkins's mature metaphysical teachings, studied with Hopkins in her late New York years. She relocated to the Northwest and divided her time between Cascade, British Columbia; and Spokane, Washington. According to Melton, in "New Thought's

Hidden History," her pamphlet, "Realization Through Concentrated Attention," inspired Albert Grier to found the Church of the Truth. Stocker herself created a Hopkins Memorial Chapel in Cascade.

The Sanctuary of Truth in Alhambra, California, taught the work of Hopkins for many years. The late Reverend Carmelita Trowbridge, who had studied with Ernest Holmes, was at one time affiliated with Religious Science, but left that ministry to found her own. Another of Trowbridge's teachers was Myrtle Cate, who had studied with Hopkins in her New York years. Cate led the Unity Truth Center in Phoenix, Arizona, for a number of years. In 1989, Trowbridge was in her nineties and retired. Her health was reputed to be frail. I placed several phone calls to her ministry, but they were not acknowledged by the current pastor, Mary King.

A pamphlet from the Sanctuary of Truth indicates that "for 25 years in California, [Trowbridge] has taught this work [Hopkins's] to thousands." Trowbridge said that "the glory of [Hopkins's] teaching is that it arouses the hidden creative genius in the student so that he goes forth inspired to accomplish some great work of a unique and inimitable sort by the recognition of his own inherent divinity."[6]

The pamphlet listed books that were available by mail and says, "Through the kindness of an anonymous donor, many of Mrs. Hopkins's books never before in print are being published by the Sanctuary of Truth."[7] This pamphlet was apparently an old one. There was no date of publication, but one assumes because of Trowbridge's advanced age that it must be old.

In November 1989, I attended a service at the Sanctuary of Truth. The service was conducted by the pastor, Mary King. The church sanctuary had no more than fifteen people and all but two were apparently more than sixty years of age. The service seemed to be generally New Thought, but not specifically Hopkins oriented. There was a colored oil portrait of Hopkins in the foyer leading to the book room that was painted from a photograph and placed there during Trowbridge's tenure. However, as late as 1998, advertisements for the ministry mentioned the work of Hopkins being taught there.

Today, the most prominent ministry devoted exclusively to the perpetuation of Hopkins's work is the Ministry of Truth International in

Chicago, Illinois. The Reverend Marge Flotron, a former advertising executive, developed a deep and abiding interest in Hopkins's teachings. She began to teach part-time while retaining her employment in advertising. She eventually resigned from her job and devoted her life and her ministry to a full-time focus on Hopkins's teachings. This ministry is primarily instructional, not congregational. There are outreach study programs affiliated with Flotron. The statement of purpose for the ministry says, "It is dedicated to the teachings in all of the Great Bibles of the World, with emphasis on the Judeo-Christian Bible. . . . [I]t uses the textbooks from the works of Emma Curtis Hopkins."[8]

The newsletter for June 1987 announced a "Metaphysical College" with course work "based on the works of Emma Curtis Hopkins." Such classes were held at the Marriott Hotel in Chicago or through the outreach program. This issue also stated that Flotron taught two seminars in Hopkins's work at Unity of Madison, Wisconsin; and First Church of Religious Science, in St. Louis, Missouri. There were three other future seminars planned in St. Louis, Kansas City, and Long Island.

I attended the Sharing III Seminar on the hundredth anniversary of the writing of Hopkins's *Class Lessons, 1888*. This event was held in Moran, Wyoming, on June 8–12, 1988. The ministry brochure indicated that this seminar was a special one for people "interested in the teachings of Emma Curtis Hopkins, as these teachings require a very definite soul understanding!" Flotron quoted from Hopkins, but did not cite sources: "We are all posited on this planet for the one purpose of accomplishing some great opus of work."

Mention was made of the New Age as "The Age of enlightenment for everyone." Flotron spoke of Hopkins "as having influenced many people in the New Thought Movements. . . . It is said that she ignited their souls and they were so inspired that many went out into the world and did a very great unique individual work for the benefit of all mankind, and the work is still going on."[9]

Flotron selected the site in the Grand Teton Mountains for the seminar because of a comment that Hopkins had made about "a long neglected spot of earth showing people a new way of thinking with Truth!"[10] The program consisted of the material of all twelve chapters of *Class Lessons*,

1888. Each person was allowed the choice of being a teacher for a particular chapter or a student. A minister from the Desert Center of Learning Light in Tucson, Arizona, was scheduled to teach two of the seminal chapters. Volunteers taught the remaining lessons. This writer was graciously allowed to attend the conference as an academic participant-observer. Flotron waived the conference registration fee of fifty dollars. In exchange for the tuition waiver, I volunteered to teach chapter 9 of *Class Lessons, 1888,* and furnish piano music for the event (the person in charge of music could not attend). The song selections were original and had been written from New Thought perspectives.

The program coordinator for the retreat was from Virginia. In an interview, he told me that he had experienced unrelenting prejudice as a black man in a predominately white culture. He was using "Emma's" work because it gave him a spiritual tool and a healthy way to handle his feelings about the prejudice. He assisted Flotron with the taping needs of her ministry.

The activities coordinator of the retreat was from northern California. When interviewed, he said he had come because the beauty of the location drew him there. He also enjoyed the conference participants, but was not a disciple of Hopkins. He cordially served as photographer and was helpful in other areas as well.

Jackie Kryszak served as receptionist and check-in coordinator for the conference. She was from northern California, also. She had been a friend of Flotron for some years and had studied Hopkins as well as several other metaphysical writers. Kryszak had a master's degree in a health-related field and was interested in the holistic health aspects of Hopkins's teaching. She was also interested in the more scholarly comparative method of examining various religious texts.

Eliza Sutherland was in charge of the prayer panel and the book table. She also participates in the silent-healing component of the ministry. Her career background had been in literary editorship, and she frequently handled communication with other participants via letter. Sutherland studied Hopkins because she believed the tenets applicable to life today.

The workshop leader was a minister from Oregon. Her ministry had a chief focus of sending monthly newsletters with various teachings through the mail. She had discovered Hopkins and wished to pursue the teachings. A close relative, also from Oregon, attended the conference, too.

A New Thought minister taught two chapters of *Class Lessons, 1888,* using scientific paradigms when applicable. She recommended a book called *Stalking the Wild Pendulum,* by Ishtak Bentov, for anyone interested in the interface between physics and religion. She is an electromechanical designer by profession and teaches Hopkins's material at her center in Arizona. There were two other people from her center in attendance: Christina Quick, who was a teacher there, and another person, who was senior member of this highly eclectic group. Quick advised me that she had become interested in Hopkins because of the healing aspect of her teachings.

Three retreat participants arrived too late to be formally interviewed by this writer. However, brief conversations with them indicated that they, too, saw material in Hopkins that they could synthesize with other traditions and use today.

Altogether, there were thirteen people besides Flotron and me in attendance at the retreat. The group was eclectic and multiethnic. Two of the participants were originally from Great Britain. Six had roots in the Chicago area, three were from Arizona, two were from Oregon, and two were from California. Four were black. This diverse group seemed to enjoy the exposure to other people who studied Hopkins. Despite variations in occupation and profession, these participants seemed to use Hopkins as the common meeting ground.

Most of the classes were held in seminar rooms at the Jackson Lake Lodge. One particular class was held outdoors, with the awesome beauty of the Grand Tetons as a backdrop. An afternoon had been left free from course work to travel to Yellowstone National Park. People who had flown were offered rides with ones who had driven or rented cars, and everyone went to Yellowstone to observe the geysers and have an informal dinner together.

I found these heterogenous retreat participants positive in their outlook on life. If there was a common thread among their ideas, it was that they believed Hopkins had developed a philosophy and a method of teaching to support the unlimited advancement of individual and collective spiritual growth. They believed the work as relevant today as it was when Hopkins wrote and taught it personally.

Several features of the retreat require special mention. Eliza Sutherland designed a prayer panel where workshop participants volunteered to take a specific time during the day to pray. Each hour on the half hour, participants were requested to pray "The Light," beginning, "I AM in the Light of the Christ. This light is a revealing, inspiring, illuminating Light; it is a strengthening, healing, life giving, revitalizing and reenergizing Light," and ending, "God the Good Omnipotent is meeting that need and more, right here, right now, easily, effortlessly, and lovingly . . . and so, it is!" In addition to this prayer, Flotron prepared an affirmation envelope for each person in attendance with an individualized spiritual passage for meditation taken from Hopkins's book *Drops of Gold*.[11]

The Ministry of Truth International in Chicago has a price-list pamphlet for "The Works of Emma Curtis Hopkins." Flotron carries books that have been reprinted and manuscripts that she has had typed and photocopied into bound editions. Costs range from $1.50 for individual booklets of a specific chapter to $15.00 for *Class Lessons, 1888*. The latest pamphlet from this ministry indicates it is continuing to grow and expand its outreach program.

For thirty years, the Lighthouse of Truth in Tampa, Florida, under the direction of the Reverend William L. Lamb, carried some texts of Hopkins. This ministry was not restricted to the exclusive use of Hopkins's work. The book room carried a wide variety of metaphysical, self-help, and psychology books. Lamb, now retired, has an abiding interest in the academic study of new religious movements. As an antique collector, he has gathered many old texts from spiritualism, New Thought, and New Age sources. He has conducted workshops and seminars in various teachings, including Hopkins's. During the latter part of 1990, he used *High Mysticism* as a foundation for twelve lectures during Sunday services. Lamb, though eclectic in his spiritual focus, has provided Flotron in Chicago with financial assistance to keep Hopkins's books in print. Flotron says in the afterword of *Class Lessons, 1888*, "We are grateful to Reverend William

Lamb . . . whose loving support made possible the publication of this second printing of this volume. Reverend Lamb is dedicated to keeping the priceless works of Emma Curtis Hopkins available to all men everywhere."

There are other New Thought ministries—namely, Divine Science, Religious Science, Unity, and independent metaphysical churches—that carry some of Hopkins's works in their book rooms and sponsor Flotron to teach weekend workshops in Hopkins's materials. Today, people continue to read and study metaphysical messages written by Hopkins, yet they know little about the mystical messenger.

Personal Contacts

I attempted to contact persons who might have known Hopkins or had personal information about her or her life. Most leads were not fruitful. There were, however, several people who had studied with Hopkins's students and hence were of the second generation.

Lamb saw an article in a Unity magazine about ninety-eight-year-old Louise P. Ramey, and sent the article to me on the outside chance she had known Hopkins. Ramey was an ordained Unity minister from a prominent pioneer family in Tampa. I contacted her via the telephone, and she agreed to meet with me at her home, overlooking Tampa Bay. Several months later, in 1990, she and I met and talked of New Thought and the healing movements. She had first come to Unity Village to study in 1928. Hopkins had died in 1925. Ramey did not personally know Hopkins, but studied with Myrtle Fillmore and Charles Fillmore and was a close friend of Harley B. Jeffery. She had no special information on Hopkins, but recalled having used Hopkins's materials many times. Ramey attended a Methodist church in Tampa because they sponsor a school for children in which she was interested. In the late 1980s, she visited Unity Village, Missouri, with her grandson, Stephen. Conversation with Ramey centered on spiritual issues, and she frequently used phrases and ideas that might have come from Hopkins or Myrtle Fillmore.[12] She did use a biblical phrase several times that Hopkins frequently used: "Be still and know that I am God."

J. Gordon Melton gave me the name of someone whose teacher was one of the last persons to study with Hopkins. I contacted him at his home in the

San Francisco Bay area in 1990. He relayed that his teacher, Kenneth "Thane" Walker, had studied with Hopkins. Unfortunately, Walker had died the previous year. He did, however, recall the following story. He said he thought Thane had told him that he was traveling in Europe, heard Hopkins was there, went up to her residence (he thought it was in the south of France), introduced himself, and asked to be taught by her. Hopkins allowed him in and taught him her twelve lessons in about two weeks. Thane departed to go in search of Gurdjieff, who was also active in Europe at that time. (This encounter was probably in the early twenties.) According to Robert Ellwood, retired professor of religious studies at the University of Southern California and noted author of various texts in comparative religion and new religious movements, Thane Walker was a "modern magus in his own right." He had a "magnetic personality" that was "awe inspiring." He claimed to have modeled his "Prosperos" after "New Thought literature, Freud, Jung," and "Gurdjieff's music and exercises," combined with "modern psychology, occult and astrological traditions." Ellwood said that Walker's groups assume a "monistic idealism" and that "Prosperos has an inner circle called the High Watch." Hopkins used the term *High Watch,* and it is the name of the group that perpetuated her teachings after her death.[13] According to an anonymous student of Walker, the use of this specific term is Walker's salute to Hopkins for her contributions to his spiritual and mystical development. I spoke briefly with Ellwood in November 1990 about Hopkins and Walker, and he was aware that Hopkins had also used the term *High Watch.* He reported that "Prosperos" continues today under the directorship of a disciple of Thane Walker.

Conclusion

It has been reported in the *New Thought Bulletin* that Hopkins, who was "Teacher of Teachers" of the New Thought movement, had taught more than fifty thousand persons in her lifetime.[14] No statistics are given to back this claim. Hopkins, by her own admission, was busy. It is realistic to assume that she might have seen many thousands of people, particularly if large classes are counted. From the appointment times mentioned in her letters, it is obvious she saw people from early morning until early evening.

This fact may well compute to fifty thousand people over a thirty-year career, but a number of the people would have been ones who came many times. It was who Hopkins taught that determined her subsequent influence in U.S. religion. During the Chicago years, she actively focused on New Thought development. In New York, with the movement safely launched, she could be selective in her teaching and channel her missionary zeal into the individual spiritual development of her clients.

As records have shown, her indirect influence during the New York years touched civil-rights issues for both Native Americans and African Americans, as she lived her life in service to humanity. As teacher and healer, her progressive ideas on mysticism and religion took a pragmatic focus as she ministered to some of the "movers and shakers" who were creating new expressions in theater, journalism, art, and music. Only a few names are known among her clientele during the New York years. The recovery of her appointment books would be invaluable in creating a flowchart to determine the universality of her influence. Without proper documentation, one can only extrapolate from existing sources how extensive her influence was. New Thought as a decidedly U.S. religious phenomena entered mainline Christian traditions through Robert Russell, Glenn Clark, Norman Vincent Peale, Robert Schuller, and other lesser-known ministers. Secular contemporaries of Hopkins such as Ralph Waldo Trine and Henry Wood wrote best-selling classics in that field that indicate a strident receptivity of New Thought principles around the nation. However, it was Hopkins and her students that developed the organizations and trained leaders who would propel New Thought forward and ensure its tenets into the next generation. As scholarship continues in New Thought, one hopes that more material on Hopkins and others of her time will come to light and find its way to the historians of U.S. religion. That her teaching has permeated mainline churches is undeniable.[15] Although rarely cited as the source for modern writers and speakers, her positive ideas about spiritual healing and prosperity have enriched both religious and secular areas of contemporary life. Perhaps future research will further strengthen appreciation of her achievements as a pioneer feminist, mystic, writer, prophet, egalitarian, and organizational founder of New Thought.

Within the parameters of patriarchal societies, many exceptional women have etched a sphere of autonomy by virtue of their independent natures, their charisma, and the perception that they constituted a direct pipeline to the divine. However, the majority of these notable women do not challenge the existing social order or restructure the traditional theologies. Hopkins is one of the few nineteenth-century women who created religious movements that continue to empower women. She is an important yet overlooked figure whose centrality to U.S. religious history has almost been forgotten. Using her innovative qualities, she created and established a unique theological seminary that trained more women than men and dispatched them into the world as healers and heralds of the Second Coming of Christ. Her charismatic influence continued into the twentieth century as she extended her ministry to reach and teach the individuals of the avant-garde the "newer ways." Hopkins's trenchant interpretations of theology as both a pragmatic and a mystical path remain as a stable infrastructure of the positive-thinking movement.

That Hopkins perceived divine healing to be a renaissance of spiritual enlightenment is clear. She challenged her students to continue the heritage she founded and attain greater summits in consciousness for the history of the human race. Setting the stage, she closes *Résumé* with this blueprint for the next magnum opus:

Fill . . . blank pages
with quotations from
philosophers, poets,
mystics, on the foregoing
twelve points.

Put them in your own
original inspirations as
they come to you.

So will you write your
name with the stars, and
make the foundation of an
original book.

It has been prophesied
that a little book is to
come to the world,
altering its life and
ushering in a new dispensation.

No station in life, no
age, no sex, no color, no
previous acquirements,
shall indicate the writer
of the book.

Only the Keeper of the
Name and the High Watch
can write it.

Should your hand pen the
revolutionizing doctrine,
no heart so praiseful as
mine.

E. C. H.[16]

NOTES

GLOSSARY

BIBLIOGRAPHY

INDEX

NOTES

Introduction

1. It should be noted that Hopkins never claimed to be the first or only person in history to make this assertion.

2. William James, *The Varieties of Religious Experience,* 94.

3. These schools were called academies in New England. Students usually attended the academy in their home community.

4. W. James, *Varieties of Religious Experience,* 94, 100.

5. Catherine Albanese, *The Spirituality of the American Transcendentalists,* 13, 21. Their record on devoting themselves to "contemporary efforts for social reform" is mixed, she says. (Underlined or italicized words are in original text and will be duplicated accordingly throughout this text.)

6. Ibid., 21, 22. For a more thorough discussion of the concept of correspondence, see Catherine Albanese, *Corresponding Motion: Transcendental Religion and the New America.*

7. One notable exception is the library for the Institute for the Study of American Religion in Santa Barbara, California, under the direction of J. Gordon Melton.

8. Gerda Lerner, "Placing Women in History," in *The Majority Finds Its Past: Placing Women in History,* 161–67.

9. Lerner, "Placing Women in History: Definitions and Challenges," in ibid., 148.

10. Eddy, on the other hand, taught primary and normal classes in Christian Science at her Massachusetts Metaphysical College in Boston. Normal-class instruction authorized students to teach Christian Science themselves. Eddy revised the structure of church services in 1895. Two readers read "Lesson-Sermons" consisting of citations from the Bible and *Science and Health with Key to the Scriptures.* The lessons were centered around twenty-six subjects supplied by Eddy in 1898; the citations were prepared by the Bible Lesson Committee at church headquarters in Boston. The introduction of new lesson subjects was not allowed. Eddy remains the only person to receive ordained status.

1. The New England Years

1. *Commemorative Biographical Record of Tolland and Windham Counties, Connecticut*, 815.

2. Margaret Cushing, "Emma Curtis Hopkins: The Teacher of Teachers," 4. "Oral tradition" and other sources, such as Charles S. Braden in *Notable American Women, 1607–1950: A Biographical Dictionary*, edited by E. James, J. W. James, and Paul S. Bayer, have erroneously reported that Emma was the oldest of three daughters. "Oral tradition" reports they all had first names beginning with *E*. In fact, only her sister Estelle had a first name beginning with *E*.

3. Ferne Anderson recovered the Census reports too late for them to be included in her master's thesis, "Emma Curtis Hopkins: Springboard to New Thought." She sent them to me.

4. *Commemorative Biographical Record*, 814.

5. Ibid., 815.

6. Ibid., 814.

7. Ibid., 814–15. The information about Lewis Lincoln Grant was confirmed by an archivist at Phillips-Exeter Academy. According to their records, he was a good student with a grade average of 89–90.

8. Smith reported that at times of peak enrollment, bright or accomplished students functioned as teaching assistants.

9. There was no record he was ever employed there.

10. For more information on Mary Baker Eddy and her development of Christian Science, see Robert Peel's three-volume work, *Mary Baker Eddy*. Peel is a Harvard-educated historian and Christian Scientist whose biography of Eddy attempted to bridge the gap between critics and apologists of Eddy and Christian Science.

11. The finer points of this controversy will be discussed later.

12. Mary F. Berry was one of eight women who had studied with Eddy at the Massachusetts Metaphysical College in Boston in the Oct. 23, 1882, primary class. E. S. Bates and J. V. Dittemore list the members for each of Eddy's classes *(Mary Baker Eddy: The Truth and Tradition*, 463). Bates and Dittemore had access to Christian Science archives when Dittemore was a member of the Christian Science Board of Directors. After their research, they wrote a biography hostile to Eddy that is continually repudiated by the church. They had access to lists in the archives and compiled material that is not available elsewhere.

13. Ibid., 464.

14. Quinsy sore throat is a localized bacterial infection on the tonsils that is rare today due to the advent of antibiotics.

15. Ibid., 252.

16. Robert Peel, *Mary Baker Eddy: The Years of Trial*, 139.

17. Emma Curtis Hopkins, "Teachers of Metaphysics," 112. Hopkins was referring to Mary Baker Eddy, *Science and Health with Key to the Scriptures.*

18. Eddy is reported to have nicknamed Swarts "Spectator, Graduate of five lessons" (Bates and Dittemore, *Mary Baker Eddy,* 264).

19. I find no record that Frye was a doctor of any type. Apparently, this title was used as a sign of honor for some of the men in the movement. I can find no references to women in Christian Science being called "Doctor." Charles S. Braden, *Spirits in Rebellion: The Rise and Development of New Thought,* 141.

20. Ibid.

21. For more information on the development of Christian Science, see Stephen Gottschalk, *The Emergence of Christian Science in American Religious Life.*

22. Peel, *Years of Trial,* 145, 170.

23. Ibid., 177; original letter in Mary Baker Eddy Papers, copy with author. Emma Curtis Hopkins, editorial, *Christian Science Journal* 2 (Oct. 1884).

24. Plunkett is not mentioned by name in Hopkins's letters to Eddy or Bartlett. Peel insinuates that this gap is deliberate. Gottschalk says Mary Plunkett was "asked to leave one of Mrs. Eddy's classes in 1883" (*Emergence of Christian Science,* 101). Plunkett did not enroll in Eddy's class until Sept. 14, 1885. Hopkins had matriculated in a primary class of Eddy on Dec. 27, 1883. See Bates and Dittemore, *Mary Baker Eddy,* 464, 466.

25. Peel, *Years of Trial,* 179. Sarah Crosse, who assumed editorship of the journal after Hopkins, had more seniority than Hopkins. She had matriculated in the Aug. 16, 1882, class. This class was only the second taught by Eddy after the establishment of the Massachusetts Metaphysical College. It is possible that Hopkins's presence and appointment as editor made the "senior" students competitive and envious. Also, Hopkins was the first person beside Eddy to hold the rank of editor, which, of course, made her a powerful figure. There was rapid turnover in the editorship of the *Christian Science Journal.* In the five years after Hopkins, there were four editors. See Bates and Dittemore, *Mary Baker Eddy,* 308.

26. Peel, *Years of Trial,* 179.

27. Peel had more access to Hopkins's letters than I did.

28. Mary Baker Eddy, "Questions and Answers," *Christian Science Journal* (Sept. 1885): 113.

29. Mary Baker Eddy, "Pro Bono Publico," *Christian Science Journal* (July 1886): 105.

30. Peel gives accounts of the lawsuits in *Years of Trial* (31–58). Stillson Judah gives a brief account of the dispute with Dresser in *The History and Philosophy of the Metaphysical Movements in America* (270–72).

31. Quoted in Peel, *Years of Trial,* 179–80.

32. J. Gordon Melton, *The Encyclopedia of American Religions,* 616.

33. Ann Braude, "The Perils of Passivity: Women's Leadership in Spiritualism and

Christian Science," 60; Gail Thain Parker, *Mind Cure in New England,* 11; Braude, "Perils of Passivity," 61.

34. Peel says, "Two months later, on Christmas Day" *(Years of Trial,* 180).

35. Emma Curtis Hopkins to Mary Baker Eddy, Dec. 25, 1886, Eddy Papers.

36. F. Anderson, "Emma Curtis Hopkins," 12, 13.

37. Peel, *Years of Trial,* 160. See also Bates and Dittemore, *Mary Baker Eddy,* 471.

38. Peel, *Years of Trial,* 161.

39. Gottschalk, *Emergence of Christian Science,* 102; Braden, *Spirits in Rebellion,* 58; Judah, *Metaphysical Movements,* 271. Actually, the term was first used in 1850 by the Reverend Joseph Adams, who wrote a book with these two words in the title, *The Elements of Christian Science.*

40. Judah, *Metaphysical Movements,* 272.

41. Ibid.

42. Hopkins, "Teachers of Metaphysics," 112.

43. Gottschalk, *Emergence of Christian Science,* 164–65.

44. Ibid., 165, 166.

45. Ibid., 116.

46. Ibid., 146.

47. Charles Braden, *Christian Science Today,* 399; James D. Freeman, *The Household of Faith,* 59.

48. Melton, "New Thought's Hidden History: Emma Curtis Hopkins, Forgotten Founder," 11.

49. Peel, *Years of Trial,* 177.

50. See Margaret Fuller, *Woman in the Nineteenth Century;* and Paula Blanchard, *Margaret Fuller: From Transcendentalism to Revolution.*

51. See Blanchard, *Margaret Fuller,* 56, 86, 146, 147, chaps. 15–17; and Barbara Welter, "The Feminization of American Religion."

52. Donald Meyer, *Sex and Power: The Rise of Women in America, Russia, Sweden, and Italy,* 324.

53. Catherine Albanese, *Nature Religion in America: From the Algonkian Indians to the New Age,* 115.

54. Penny Hansen, "Women's Hour: Feminist Implications of Mary Baker Eddy's Christian Science Movement, 1885–1910," 405.

55. R. L. Numbers and R. B. Schoepflin, "Ministries of Healing," 381. Hansen named Frances Lord, Augusta Stetson, Clara Choate, and Josephine Woodbury as Eddy's "celebrated apostates." Records indicate that Frances Lord never took a class with Eddy. Lord studied with Hopkins and mentioned this fact in the preface to her book *Christian Science Healing: Its Principles and Practice* (xiv). Hansen, "Women's Hour," 392.

56. The term *paranoid temperament* is used not in a pejorative, but in a descriptive sense. Hansen, "Women's Hour," 402. Hansen says Mark Twain and Joseph Pulitzer at-

tacked her for this reason. She was acting with "an unfeminine audacity." Hansen says, "Founding a religion . . . represents a truly audacious act" (393).

57. Quoted in Peel, *Years of Trial*, 180.

58. Quoted in Braden, *Spirits in Rebellion*, 143, 144.

59. *Christian Science* (Chicago) (July 1889): 332. (Not to be mistaken for *Christian Science Journal* of Eddy published in Boston.)

2. The Chicago Years

1. Melton, "New Thought's Hidden History," 17.

2. Bates and Dittemore, *Mary Baker Eddy*, 464.

3. Emma Curtis Hopkins, "What Is Plagiarism?" 81.

4. In a footnote, R. R. Ruether and R. S. Keller state that Hopkins broke with Eddy in 1886 *(Women and Religion in America*, 3:386). She was excommunicated by Eddy and resigned from the Christian Science Association on Nov. 4, 1885, and arrived in Chicago in 1886. Judah says in *Metaphysical Movements* that Hopkins left Christian Science a defector. She was not a defector; she was fired. She relocated to Chicago after that event.

5. Emma Curtis Hopkins to Mary Baker Eddy, Dec. 25, 1886, Eddy Papers.

6. Ruether and Keller state that Emma Curtis Hopkins founded the Illinois Metaphysical College *(Women and Religion*, 3:8, 386). Rather, she founded (with Mary Plunkett) the Emma Curtis Hopkins College of Christian Science in 1886. In 1888, after Plunkett's defection, she redesigned her ministry and founded the Christian Science Theological Seminary. The Illinois Metaphysical College was founded by Lizzie Charles and George Charles. The *Christian Metaphysician* that was mentioned as one of Hopkins's methods of disseminating information was owned by the Charleses and was only one of the numerous journals and magazines for which Hopkins wrote. Hopkins did write the lead article for the first edition.

7. Melton, "New Thought's Hidden History," 13.

8. Ibid., 12.

9. Sarah Crosse, "Beware of False Teachers," 157. See Robert Ellwood and Catherine Wessinger, "The Feminism of Universal Brotherhood: Women in the Theosophical Movement," in *Women's Leadership in Marginal Religions: Explorations Outside the Mainstream*, edited by Wessinger, 68–87. It is beyond the scope of this book to go into Theosophy; however, Ellwood and Wessinger cover a number of salient features that are informative about that group. Bates and Dittemore, *Mary Baker Eddy*, 272.

10. Eddy, "Questions Answered by Mary Baker Eddy," 25, 54.

11. Braden, *Spirits in Rebellion*, 143; Wessinger, *Women's Leadership*, 9; Mary Farrell Bednarowski, "Widening the Banks of the Mainstream: Women Constructing Theologies," in ibid., 211. Also see J. Gordon Melton, "Emma Curtis Hopkins: A Feminist of the 1880s and Mother of New Thought," in ibid., 88–101.

12. [Charles Fillmore?], "Newsbriefs."

13. Alan Anderson, "Horatio Dresser and the Philosophy of New Thought," 156; Peel, *Years of Trial*, 145.

14. Emma Curtis Hopkins, "God's Omnipresence."

15. For an insightful reference to "religious technology," see Dell deChant, "New Thought and New Age," in *New Age Encyclopedia: A Guide to the Beliefs, Concepts, Terms, People, and Organizations That Make Up the New Global Movement Toward Spiritual Development, Health and Healing, Higher Consciousness, and Related Subjects,* edited by J. Gordon Melton, Jerome Clark, and Aidan A. Kelly, 326–31. In brief, because metaphysical concepts were established and stabilized so they could be repeated and would produce the same results in each treatment, they were similar to replication in scientific endeavors. This new movement's members, because of the advent of industrialization, believed their advances were sterling examples of how religion and technology could be wedded for the illumination of the human race. Today, quantum mechanics and physics attempt to bridge the gap between science and religion.

16. Peel, *Years of Trial*, 228. Marston quoted in Hulda B. Loud, "A Skeptic and the Mental Healers," *Truth* 1 (Nov. 1887): 23; and *Mental Health Monthly* 2 (Nov. 1887). Melton, "New Thought's Hidden History," 14.

17. Quoted in Peel, *Years of Trial*, 228.

18. Gottschalk, *Emergence of Christian Science*, 101; Peel, *Years of Trial*, 260–61.

19. Melton, "New Thought's Hidden History," 17.

20. Bates and Dittemore, *Mary Baker Eddy*, 178; Peel, *Years of Trial*, 131. I was informed that a great deal of material about A. Bently Worthington was available. The material claims Worthington was an alias for Samuel Oakley Crawford, who was a con-artist type with eight living wives. When Worthington "melted away," he went to Christchurch, New Zealand, with Mary Plunkett, where they published a pamphlet called "Comforter." They were both associated with the Students of Truth Home. The last bit of material seems to be from 1892–1893. In an interesting twist to this saga, Gary Ward quoted from A. Bently Worthington, "Talk to Men," *Unity* 3 (June 1893): 5. Worthington wrote "a fascinating article on a woman's perspective on sexuality." Worthington says that "chastity is necessary for true godliness, a major reason being that sex has been the occasion for men dealing poorly with women. Practically every household, Worthington said, contains women who have suffered outrageously in sexual relations. Somewhere, sometime, at the bar of Truth, the manhood of the world changes place with the womanhood of the world and reaps what it has sown in the selfish indulgence of untrammelled lust." One wonders how autobiographical this article was. On Jan. 26, 1991, an article was forwarded to me that had been secured from a source in New Zealand. There was a write-up of Worthington in the *Encyclopedia of New Zealand*, 3:689. It states that Worthington arrived in New Zealand in Jan. 1890. He was successful in establishing a congregation of Students of Truth, said to have numbered two thousand. Apparently, someone checked and found he was a bigamist. His eighth wife,

Plunkett, "confirmed the charges." In 1895, he married again, fled to Tasmania, came back to Christchurch in Sept. 1897, and sought to reestablish his Students of Truth; however, riotous crowds, "numbering in the thousands . . . stifled his sermons." Worthington returned to New York and was subsequently "gaoled for fraud." He died there in 1917. Plunkett remained in New Zealand and remarried. She became mentally unstable every evening for several hours and committed suicide during one of these episodes in 1900.

21. Peel, *Years of Trial*, 261; Gottschalk, *Emergence of Christian Science*, 102–3; Melton, "New Thought's Hidden History," 17.

22. Melton, "New Thought's Hidden History," 18. Melton cites *Christian Science* 1 (Sept. 1888): 16 as his source.

23. Melton, "New Thought's Hidden History," 18. Melton quotes from ads for the Christian Science Theological Seminary in the 1888 issues of the *Christian Metaphysician*.

24. Emma Curtis Hopkins, *Christian Science* 1–2 (Oct. 1888): 43–48.

25. Hopkins promised to write only for *Christian Science* "to help set this young candidate for favor quite on its feet" *(Christian Science* 1 [Sept. 1888]: 20). Melton, "New Thought's Hidden History," 19. In fact, one can see the growth of Christian Science-New Thought through the press runs of the various organs. During the editorship of Eddy's *Christian Science Journal,* Hopkins believed specific press runs of two to three thousand copies augured well for that 1884 journal.

26. Emma Curtis Hopkins, *Christian Science* 1–3 (Nov. 1888): 68.

27. Ibid.; Meyer, *Sex and Power,* 325.

28. Braden, *Spirits in Rebellion,* 89; Albanese, *Nature Religion,* 113, 108; Judah, *Metaphysical Movements,* 25; Melton, *The Encyclopedia Handbook of Cults in America,* 27.

29. Melton, *Handbook of Cults,* 27; Melton, "New Thought's Hidden History," 9.

30. Alan Anderson, "Contrasting Strains of Metaphysical Idealism Contributing to New Thought," 38.

31. Ruether and Keller, *Women and Religion,* 1:301, 307.

32. This obscurity is seen in Kali Herman, *Women in Particular: An Index to American Women,* 540. Hopkins is mistakenly called a "Spiritualist teacher" of the New Thought movement. Hopkins was never a Spiritualist. The fact that so much confusion exists in today's literature demonstrates the cloud eclipsing her life and accomplishments.

33. Gary Ward, "The Feminist Theme of Early New Thought," 2. He and Melton, in "New Thought's Hidden History," differ in their figures for the association in 1887. Melton says there were seventeen associations. (This disparity could be due to recovery of more material.)

34. Ward, "Feminist Theme," 17. Braden, Judah, Melton, Freeman, and others all support this statement with similar lists.

35. Loud, "Skeptic and Healers," 23, quoted in Melton, "New Thought's Hidden History," 14.

36. Ruether and Keller, *Women and Religion,* 1:47.

37. Melton, "New Thought's Hidden History," 21.

38. Ibid., 9; Peel, *Years of Trial,* 96.

39. Melton, "New Thought's Hidden History," 6.

40. Ibid., 6, 7.

41. Emma Curtis Hopkins, *Class Lessons, 1888,* 49.

42. Ibid., 162, 164.

43. Ibid., 186.

44. Ibid., 210–12.

45. Ibid., 219.

46. Ibid., 220.

47. Ibid., 234.

48. Ibid., 43.

49. Ibid., 246–47.

50. Melton, "New Thought's Hidden History," 15.

51. Lord, *Christian Science Healing,* xiv; Braden, *Spirits in Rebellion,* 410–11. Braden said that the Coleses were members of Eddy's famous class of Mar. 1888. This spelling of the names of Mr. and Mrs. Graves Colles, who were from England, is incorrect. Hannah Laramine, an American from the same class, returned with them to the British Isles at Eddy's request to start missionary activity there. See Bates and Dittemore, *Mary Baker Eddy,* 468.

52. The late Elizabeth C. Bogart compiled the lessons in book form after Hopkins's death. Bogart was a secretary to Myrtle Fillmore and owned her own book business. She was instrumental in locating and publishing Hopkins's work after her death in 1925. Without Bogart's foresight and dedication, much of Hopkins's work might have been lost.

53. Hopkins, *Class Lessons, 1888,* 149, 282. Hopkins said, "People call Christian Science a new doctrine, but it is only the old doctrine explained" *(Christian Science* [Jan. 1889]: 4).

54. Lord used these examples to explain the process used by practitioners: "John is not ill" is a denial; "John is well" is an affirmation; "John will be well" is a prophecy *(Christian Science Healing,* 48). The process of affirmation and denial came to be a source of contention in Divine Science and remains controversial today among different factions.

55. Arthur Christy, *The Orient in American Transcendentalism,* xi; A. Anderson, "Contrasting Strains," 35.

56. Braden, *Spirits in Rebellion,* 153; Van Anderson, *The Right Knock,* vi.

57. The article is unsigned, but is no doubt the work of Hopkins ("The Trinity, Part Two," 111).

58. Emma Curtis Hopkins, "Christian Science Ordination Address," *Christian Science* 1 (June 1889): 271; Ida Nichols, "Personal Mention," *Christian Science* 1 (Mar. 1889): 200.

59. Hopkins, "Christian Science Ordination Address," 271–74.

60. Melton, "New Thought's Hidden History," 21.

61. Emma Curtis Hopkins, "Healing Drops," *Christian Science* (Nov. 1888): 63.

62. She discussed this idea in "The Trinity, Part One," 79–80.

63. Hopkins, "The Trinity, Part Two," 111; Emma Curtis Hopkins to Mary Baker Eddy, Dec. 12, 1883, Eddy Papers.

64. Ida Nichols reported, "A large party of scientists and their friends . . . on April 9 . . . proceeded to the Seminary at 2019 Indiana Avenue to meet Prof. G. I. Hopkins, who was spending his vacation in Chicago. . . . A most delightful evening was passed" ("Special Healing," *Christian Science* 1 [May 1889]: 250).

65. Emma Curtis Hopkins to Mary Baker Eddy, Apr. 3, 1884, Eddy Papers.

66. Copies of this catalog were sent to me by J. Gordon Melton of the Institute for the Study of American Religion and Patricia Delks of the Archives of the International New Thought Alliance.

67. Judah says that Charles was ordained by Hopkins in 1890 *(Metaphysical Movements,* 234). In fact, both Myrtle and Charles were ordained in 1891. Judah is quoting from James Teener, "Unity School of Christianity" (Ph.D. diss., Univ. of Chicago, 1939), 109. He also quotes Freeman as saying that Hopkins established the Illinois Metaphysical College *(The Household of Faith,* 19–40). Judah says Teener refers to it as the Christian Science Theological Seminary. Teener's is the accurate designation. Hopkins did not establish the Illinois Metaphysical College.

68. Ruether and Keller list James D. Fillmore as the author of *The Household of Faith* when it should be James D. Freeman *(Women and Religion* 3:386). Freeman, *The Household of Faith,* 43.

69. Freeman, *The Household of Faith,* 75–76.

70. Ibid., 100.

71. Ibid., 101. Unity School Library responded to my request for documents supporting the Hopkins-Fillmore association. Included with material from their archives was a letter stating, "The wording and content [of the letters] imply a trusting friendship between Emma Curtis Hopkins and the Fillmores."

72. Freeman, *The Household of Faith,* 102.

73. Ibid., 106; Dell deChant, "Myrtle Fillmore and Her Daughters: An Observation and Analysis of the Role of Women in Unity," in *Women's Leadership,* edited by Wessinger. For an abbreviated treatment of the significance of Unity, see Gail M. Harley, "New Thought and the Harmonial Family," 325–30.

74. Emma Curtis Hopkins to Myrtle Fillmore, Nov. 8, 1890, Charles Fillmore and Myrtle Fillmore Papers. Copy in Archives of the Institute for the Study of American Religion, Santa Barbara, Calif. Unless otherwise noted, all the letters quoted in this section are in the Charles Fillmore and Myrtle Fillmore Papers.

75. The covenant reads: "We, Charles Fillmore and Myrtle Fillmore, husband and wife, hereby dedicate our selves, our time, our money, all we have and all we expect to have, to the Spirit of Truth, and through it, to the Society of Silent Unity. It being understood and agreed that the said Spirit of Truth shall render unto us an equivalent for this dedication, in peace of mind, health of body, wisdom, understanding, love, life and an abundant supply of all things necessary to meet every want without our making any of these things the object of our existence. In the presence of the Conscious Mind of Christ Jesus, this 7th day of December, 1892 A.D." (Braden, *Spirits in Rebellion,* 241). It is signed by both.

76. Emma Curtis Hopkins, "Hopkins Metaphysical Association," *Christian Science* 1 (Oct. 1888): 40.

77. Dean Halverson, "Mind Power: A History and Analysis of the New Thought Movement," 6–7.

78. Emma Curtis Hopkins, "The New Religion," *International Magazine of Christian Science* (July 1888): 5.

79. Emma Curtis Hopkins, *Scientific Christian Mental Practice,* 50. An example might be the con artist who comes to believe his own story and in decreeing it so faithfully causes the good to come about. Hopkins believed that these types of people get their hardship in life in another manner, such as a physical disability.

80. Ibid., 57, 63, 48, 240.

81. Braden, *Spirits in Rebellion,* 152–53.

82. Marjorie Procter-Smith, *Women in Shaker Communities and Worship,* ix, quoted in Rosemary Ruether and Eleanor McLaughlin, "The Feminist Thrust of Sectarian Christianity," in *Women of Spirit: Female Leadership in the Jewish and Christian Traditions* (New York: Simon and Schuster, 1979).

83. See Robert Ellwood, "Shakers and Spiritualists," in *Alternative Altars: Unconventional and Eastern Spirituality in America,* 65. See also Ruether and Keller, *Women and Religion,* vol. 1. Ruether, *Women and Religion,* 1:48.

84. Welter makes the point that the "male principle was rarely challenged by Trinitarians or Unitarians" (*Insights and Parallels,* 310).

85. Rosemary R. Ruether demonstrates the sexist foundations of Protestant and Catholic dogma that deprive women of humanity and divinity *(Women-Church: Theology and Practice,* 89). She recommends a "ministry of function," which would allow "the ministerial needs of the community to be defined and met" in order to initiate a balance of power (90–91). Hopkins was aware of the victimization and oppression of women within patriarchal religion and a religious movement that equalized power. She promoted a paradigm shift more than one hundred years ago that was a major watershed for contemporary feminist theology. Ruether and Keller, *Women and Religion,* 1:51.

86. Louise Southworth, "Baccalaureate Address," *Christian Science* 1 (Feb. 1889): 141–45; Elizabeth Boynton Harbert, "Right Hand of Fellowship," *Christian Science* 1 (Feb. 1889): 141.

87. Emma Curtis Hopkins, "Christian Science Ordination Address," *Christian Science* 1 (Mar. 1889): 174.

88. Ward, "Feminist Theme," 11–12.

89. Hopkins, "The Trinity, Part One," 110–11.

90. Ida Nichols, "Minutes of Hopkins Association," *Christian Science* (Aug. 1889): 353.

91. Ida Nichols, "Minutes of Hopkins Association," *Christian Science* (Dec. 1888): 66; Ida Nichols, "Minutes of Hopkins Association," *Christian Science* (Jan. 1889): 95.

92. Ida Nichols, "Minutes of Hopkins Association," *Christian Science* (Feb. 1889): 155, 159.

93. Melton points out that this idea had been spoken of by Joachim of Fiore ("New Thought's Hidden History," 9). Hopkins was well read, but there is no evidence she had come into literary contact with this idea.

94. Ida Nichols, "Hopkins Metaphysical Association," *Christian Science* (Feb. 1889): 193.

95. Burnell, "Edemic Cherubim," *Christian Science* 1 (Sept. 1888): 1. A news brief from the Department of Religious Studies at Stanford University states that the "Book Fund, established by the anonymous donor who endowed the George Edward Burnell Professorship in Religious Studies has attained an aggressive level of acquisitions . . . in New Thought," including "a very large number of sermons addressed by Burnell" *(New Thought* 4 [winter 1982]). Burnell met and married Mary Lamereaux while they were affiliated with Hopkins. He became a prominent voice in New Thought.

96. Lerner, *Majority Finds Its Past,* 145.

97. Ibid., 161; Hansen, "Women's Hour," 397. Gilman used New Thought material, but did not formally affiliate with a New Thought ministry. For a more thorough discussion, see Gail Thain Parker, *Mind Cure,* 870–94.

98. Lerner, *Majority Finds Its Past,* 161.

99. Ibid., 162, 166.

100. Frank Podmore quotes Eddy as saying, "In 1895 . . . I ordained the Bible and *Science and Health with Key to the Scriptures,* as the Pastor, on this planet" *(From Mesmer to Christian Science,* 276). This statement appeared in her book *Miscellaneous Writings* (382–83).

101. See the salient discussion of this and related concepts in Wessinger, introduction to *Women's Leadership,* 1–19.

102. Ward, "Feminist Theme," 11; Hansen, "Women's Hour," 380.

103. Southworth, "Baccalaureate Address," 144; Helen Wilmans, "The New Cult," *Christian Science Thought* (June 1890): 10, quoted in Ward, "Feminist Theme," 11.

104. Emma Curtis Hopkins, "The Ideal of Woman," *Christian Science Journal 3* (Apr. 1885): 16; Hopkins, "Justice," *Christian Science Journal 3* (June 1885): 64–65; Hopkins, "New Publications," *Christian Science Journal 3* (July 1885): 82; Hopkins, "NWCTU," *Christian Science Journal 3* (Aug. 1885): 100–101.

105. The Queen Isabella Association was a group for women who were social activists.
106. Melton, "New Thought's Hidden History," 17.

3. The New York Years

1. This fact leads one to conjecture that Estelle may have been the person who filled out the *1880 Census Report* and made everyone but the five-year-old child younger.

2. Mabel Dodge Luhan, *Movers and Shakers,* 193. There were twenty-four chapters in the book. Chap. 17 was titled "Emma Curtis Hopkins," although she is mentioned in other places. There were chapters devoted to Elizabeth Duncan and her progressive school for children, John Reed, Maurice Sterne (a Russian-born artist), and other notable people of the times.

3. There is some doubt that these letters were ever mailed; however, I believe that they were.

4. For a chatty, unfootnoted biography on Luhan, see Emily Hahn, *Mabel: A Biography of Mabel Dodge Luhan.* For a more thorough critical study, see Lois Rudnick, *Mabel Dodge Luhan: New Woman, New Worlds.* Rudnick's book is a carefully researched work on Mabel. However, she does not have basic information about the New Thought movement, and her assumptions about it are inaccurate. For instance, she stated Horatio Dresser was the "founder of the New Thought movement" (130). Her grasp of New Thought and its reverberations throughout society was the weakest part of an otherwise strong book. The most recent book on Mabel is good, too: Winifred Frazer, *Mabel Dodge Luhan.*

5. Neith Boyce was the author of various works, including *The Folly of Others* (1904; reprint, Freeport, N.Y.: Books for Libraries Press, 1970). She was originally a newspaper writer under the tutelage of Lincoln Steffens at the *Commercial Advertiser.* Boyce was a writer of short stories, a playwright, and a facilitator of the Provincetown Players. She was married to Hutchins Hapgood.

6. A portion of Jack Reed's life was portrayed in the 1982 film *Reds,* directed by Warren Beatty, who also starred as Reed. Mabel made several trips to Europe with Reed, but had terminated her liaison with him prior to the time the film depicts. In fact, Reed was prompted to marry Louise Bryant because she had been seeing Eugene O'Neill, who was his classmate's (Bobby Jones's) business partner. Mabel considered Louise an opportunist and was hurt when Jack snubbed her after their breakup. She never bore him any ill will and dedicated part 1 of *Movers and Shakers* to "Jack Reed the Poet."

7. See Judith Schwarz, *Radical Feminists of Heterodoxy, 1912–1940.*

8. Luhan, *Movers and Shakers,* 143.

9. Rudnick, *New Woman, New Worlds,* 132.

10. Emma Curtis Hopkins to Mabel Dodge Luhan, June 12, 1917, Mabel Dodge Luhan Papers. Unless otherwise noted, all the letters quoted in this section are in the Mabel Dodge Luhan Papers.

11. Elizabeth was the older sister and teacher of Isadora, who dressed "in comfortable soft draperies and glove like shoes." Elizabeth, like all the Duncans, "had a vision" and "was a great teacher." She said of herself, "My teaching is a way of living" (Luhan, *Movers and Shakers*, 332–35).

12. Ibid., 520.

13. Rudnick, *New Woman, New Worlds*, 141.

14. Ibid.

15. Luhan, *Movers and Shakers*, 529.

16. Ibid., 534.

17. Ibid., 534–35.

18. *New Thought Bulletin* 28, no. 3, taken from a copy in the Archives of the Institute for the Study of American Religion in Santa Barbara, Calif.

19. This material was supplied by Betty Jean House, officer of the alliance.

20. Rudnick, *New Woman, New Worlds*, 144.

21. Bobby Jones is Robert Edmond Jones. "He was associated with Eugene O'Neill in managing the Greenwich Village Theatre." Jones was also a gifted stage designer. "He was a devotee of Emma Curtis Hopkins," and after Hopkins's death Mabel raised "funds" for him to go into analysis with Carl Jung in Europe in 1926 (Rudnick, *New Woman, New Worlds*, 184).

22. Luhan, *Movers and Shakers*, 48.

23. Maurice, at Mabel's insistence, had put aside his paints and begun to do sculpturing. He had done a bust of two beautiful Indians. The heat melted them while they were being shipped to New York. For Maurice's version of these two years, see Charlotte Leon Mayerson, ed., *Shadow and Light: The Life, Friends, and Opinions of Maurice Sterne.*

24. Rudnick, *New Woman, New Worlds*, 154.

25. The Duncan School was created by Elizabeth Duncan to give children an exceptional education. Movement and dance were a large part of the curriculum. The money to fund the project came from wealthy socialites such as Mabel (see Luhan, *Movers and Shakers*, 341–48). Mayerson, *Shadow and Light*, xxvi.

26. Luhan, *Movers and Shakers*, 46, 55, 59. Hutchins Hapgood at the time had written *The Autobiography of a Thief* (1903; reprint, New York: Johnson Reprint, 1970); and *The Spirit of the Ghetto* (1902; reprint, Cambridge: Harvard Univ. Press, 1967). He is probably remembered best for *A Victorian in the Modern World* (New York: Harcourt, Brace, 1939).

27. Rudnick, *New Woman, New Worlds*, 105.

28. Luhan, *Movers and Shakers*, 60, 66.

29. Hopkins wrote in lesson form, usually pamphlet or booklet style—probably because it was less expensive to publish. Many of her texts were not bound together in book form until after her death. Today, *Résumé* contains scriptural references in parentheses that were not in the original work by Hopkins, but have been added recently by a New Thought

minister. This text is the only one that I have been able to find that has been altered. See afterword of book for specifics.

30. Emilie Hapgood was heavily involved in securing civil rights for African Americans. She was instrumental in bringing to New York the first all-black dramatic production. See Luhan, *Movers and Shakers*, 535.

31. Tony was a full-blooded Native American of the Tiwa Nation from the Pueblo, near Taos. Mabel was not the first American woman to choose a Native American mate, nor was theirs a frivolous affair. They had remained together for more than forty years when death separated them. See Annette Kolodny, *The Land Before Her: Fantasy and Experience of the American Frontiers, 1630–1860*. This book is a collection of case studies of American women who preferred relationships with Native American men. Mary was the first wife of artist John Young-Hunter. He was originally from Scotland and painted western scenes.

32. Luhan, *Movers and Shakers*, 468. Mabel obviously felt special because Hopkins called her "child from Atlantis." Hopkins explained that Mabel's behavior could be understood only by another Atlantean. I think the connotation was that an Atlantean was an old soul, one who had experienced many lives and could help others along the way, because of their experience. Hopkins seems to be suggesting that Mabel's behavior might at times be exceptional.

33. Frazer, *Mabel Dodge Luhan*. The biographical chronology for Mabel shows that Arthur Brisbane had paid Mabel thirty dollars for each article of hers he had used in the *New York Journal* from Aug. 1917 to Feb. 1918.

34. Mayerson, *Shadow and Light*, xxvi.

35. Lotus Dudley was probably a spiritualist medium who was delivering messages from a trance state. The term that Hopkins used for her, however, was *occultist*. There were hints that this person might have been practicing some form of black magic, although this term was never used by Hopkins.

36. Selena Chamberlain would become the teacher of Emmet Fox, "one of the most renowned New Thought leaders in this century" (Judah, *Metaphysical Movements*, 184).

37. This person was probably Eve Schoer. If it was, she is the one Mabel credited with introducing her to Hopkins. Eve was a bright and promising student of Hopkins and also a good friend of Mabel.

38. Hopkins used this term to mean maintaining an elevated consciousness that looks up to heaven to find God.

39. I think she means E. B. Weeks, a Truth teacher whom she had known and was associated with in her Chicago days.

40. This letter indicates that Elizabeth Duncan might have gotten to Taos, after all.

41. On Alice Sprague, see Luhan, *Movers and Shakers*, 349. Mabel maintains that Sprague "embedded naturally without need of teaching the doctrines of Emma Curtis

Hopkins whom Bobby, Eve, Nina and even Maurice, later spent hours and dollars trying to learn and live by." Sprague was from Buffalo and a few years older than Mabel. She was from a wealthy family also. She was reputed to be a dark-haired, serene beauty who saw beauty wherever she looked.

42. See J. Gordon Melton, Jerome Clark, and Aidan A. Kelly, *New Age Almanac* (Detroit: Visible Ink Press, 1991). This tome is helpful for understanding the history of the New Age.

43. Rudnick, *New Woman, New Worlds,* 166. Santa Fe and Taos had artist colonies that were competitive. Mabel "began to advertise the merits of Taos in her last column for the Hearst newspapers published on February 1918" (ibid.). As a true entrepreneur, Mabel did not want to associate with an established artist community, such as Santa Fe. She chose Taos because she could stake out this virgin territory for another artist enclave.

44. It can be assumed that this charge occurred during the breakup of Maurice and Mabel when Hopkins was supportive of Maurice in his time of grief over Mabel's affair with Tony.

45. Hutch was a special person in Hopkins's life, if in fact the initials "N. B." do refer to Neith Boyce. Nina was a childhood friend of Mabel who grew up in the same Buffalo neighborhood. She married Harry Bull. Nina was a Divine Science practitioner who knew Hopkins also (and may have introduced Mabel to Hopkins).

46. The reference to Eve and John together meant that John Young-Hunter and Mary Young-Hunter were seeking a divorce. Eve was apparently involved with John prior to the divorce and later married him. Eve and John were continually thrown together because John's property in Taos abutted Mabel's. Again, this relationship was not a short-lived fling. They were married until death separated them. John dedicated his book, *Reviewing the Years,* "To Eve, not my original ancestress, but my wife, who guides my hesitating insufficiencies with a ministering devotion, so that I appear more adequate than I am" (iii). By "John shall have some unseen helpings," I think Hopkins meant that spiritual forces, such as angels, might help John.

47. Bobby was, by this time, Hopkins's favorite "child."

48. John Evans was Mabel's son by her first marriage. His father was killed in a hunting accident when he was a baby. The only father he could remember was Edwin Dodge, Mabel's second husband. Mabel included some short letters he wrote as a child in *Movers and Shakers,* 466.

49. Ibid., 314–18.

50. Hahn, *Biography of Luhan,* 172.

51. This reference could be to Emilie Hapgood, wife of Norman, or Neith Boyce, wife of Hutchins. Emilie's mission was civil-rights issues for black people, and Neith was a playwright. It was most likely Emilie, who may have been taking a troupe of black actors abroad. Hopkins probably would not have called Neith "Mrs. Hapgood."

52. Dudley was the occultist whom Mabel had consulted originally in 1919 when she was dismayed about her relationship with Tony. Dudley told Mabel she had a mission in Taos because "the great souls will be drawn there." For a thorough discussion, see Rudnick, *New Woman, New Worlds*, 165. Apparently, Mabel went right to work on this prophecy. Hopkins did not quibble about the importance of Mabel to the world. Her concern was that occultism was a wrong path that could damage people spiritually. She believed occultism took people further from the path to God and not closer. This difference with Dudley could have been interpreted as a case of rivalry between two gurus for the commitment of some wealthy clients; however, it is my conclusion that Hopkins had a genuine spiritual concern. It is not unusual for spiritual seekers and searchers to go into rebel mode against the original authority figure. New gurus are enthralling if they are flamboyant and tell the students what they want to hear. Dudley apparently captured their imaginations for a while, and possibly they were afraid of what they perceived to be her power.

53. Clarence Thompson did go to Taos. This "aesthete from New York" arrived in time to drink with D. H. Lawrence (who rarely drank). At a party, Alice Sprague and Clarence were guests. Clarence danced with Frieda, Lawrence's wife. Mabel grabbed Lawrence, "who danced as seldom as he drank." The dancing group ended by splitting up and Clarence going off with Frieda Lawrence. Apparently, Frieda told Clarence "that Lawrence had vowed to destroy Mabel." This statement caused quite a disturbance. Another version of this encounter was also told. According to historian Christopher Lasch, Mabel lied in her rendition, and the dancing partners were Dorothy Brett with Lawrence and Mabel with Clarence. The point Lasch makes is that "Luhan could have imagined . . . seeing herself as Lawrence's 'battering ram' " *(New Radicalism in America,* 137–39). Lasch's comments about Mabel seem scathingly Freudian, and he picks her personality to shreds, insinuating that she had penis envy.

54. This use of the term *New Age* was Hopkins's first in her letters to Mabel. *New Age* to Hopkins was not the same as *New Age* in today's parlance. Hopkins would certainly take issue with the occult propensity of today's New Age. She herself moved closer than usual to acknowledging the occult when she spoke of using formulas for healing. New Age for her was the metaphysical healing movement that drew on all the religious traditions of the world for sacred texts and signified an advancement in human social and spiritual progress. For instance, experiencing the oneness of the immanent transcends the duality of gender and racial bias because all are one in the Divine Mind.

55. Mrs. Darrow is Hopkins's younger sister Estelle, who managed to muddy the waters about Hopkins's marriage, death, and true age.

56. Andrew Dasburg, who had painted Mabel's portrait and was a "leader of the avant-garde," was the first of Mabel's New York social set to respond to the call. Later in the decade, Willa Cather, Georgia O'Keeffe, D. H. Lawrence, Dorothy Brett, Marsden Hartley, Leo Stein, and John Young-Hunter would all check out the Taos scene. Some, such as Young-Hunter (from Scotland), stayed for the rest of their lives. Young-Hunter bought the

property adjoining Mabel and Tony in a business arrangement negotiated by Tony. By 1925 (the year of Hopkins's death), this young artist colony was "on the map." The ensuing years would see even more famous artists and writers come to the pristine desert for nourishment. There is no question that Mabel believed she was fulfilling a prophecy.

57. Mary H. Austin, in *The Land of Journey's Ending,* prophesied that Native American culture might promote a rebirth of the United States. She also wrote *Earth Horizon: An Autobiography.* For a fuller discussion, see Frazer, *Mabel Dodge Luhan.* In brief, Frazer says, "Mary was a close friend of Mabel and Tony." She realized that there was a growing opposition to Mabel and Tony's relationship. She encouraged Mabel to divorce Maurice Sterne "and to make an allowance to Tony's wife, Candelaria" (97). This demonstration helped the Pueblo community calm down with regard to Tony's having married a white woman. However, he did lose, for a number of years, his seat on the Pueblo council.

58. Luhan, *Movers and Shakers,* 467.

59. Ibid., 467, 469.

60. Ibid., 469.

61. Ibid., 465–73.

62. Donald Gallup, "Mabel Dodge Luhan Collection," 100, quoted in Frazer, *Mabel Dodge Luhan,* 107–8.

63. Lasch, *New Radicalism in America,* 114, ix. Lasch argued in his book that "radicalism or liberalism can best be understood as a phase of social history of the intellectuals" (114).

64. All quotes in this section are taken from "Ernest Studies with Emma Curtis Hopkins." Copy in the Archives of the Institute for the Study of American Religion, Santa Barbara, Calif.

65. Hopkins, "Teachers of Metaphysics," 112.

66. Evelyn Underhill, *Mysticism* (New York: New American Library, 1974); W. T. Stace, *Mysticism and Philosophy,* 87 (emphasis in original), 88, 94, citing Jan van Ruysbroeck, *The Adornment Spiritual Marriage, The Book of the Supreme Truth,* and *The Sparkling Stone,* translated by C. A. Wynschenk (London: J. M. Dent and Sons, 1916), 185–86. For a thorough discussion of introvertive and extravertive mystical status and a diagram, see Stace, *Mysticism and Philosophy,* 41–133. It is beyond the scope of this biography to delve into the topic of mysticism in great depth.

67. Stace, *Mysticism and Philosophy,* 61.

68. James, *Varieties of Religious Experience,* 410 (quoted in Stace, *Mysticism and Philosophy,* 42–43), 406. In James's parlance, a "mystical classic" was a master at mysticism, and this ability transcended culture, race, and religion. Hopkins is an example of a "mystical classic."

69. Stace, *Mysticism and Philosophy,* 61; Mabel Dodge Luhan, *Edge of the Taos Desert,* 245–46.

70. On Sept. 12, 1998, Louise Boehme and I traveled to Killingly, Connecticut, and lo-

cated the cemetery for the Curtis family. We photographed the family plot that had a three-tier granite monument identifying the persons who were buried there. Essential data were recorded on the large monument. For Hopkins, only her name and date of death, Apr. 8, 1925, were reported. Individual markers on each grave designated the person's first name only. The individual grave marker for Hopkins simply states "Emma." The Congregational church the Curtis family attended was dedicated in 1845. Currently, the church is in a state of disrepair and is for sale. The church and cemetery are approximately five hundred yards apart.

71. Braden, *Notable American Women,* edited by James, James, and Bayer, 219.

72. "Obituary Column," *Windham County (Conn.) Paper,* Apr. 9, 1925.

73. A certified copy of George Hopkins's death certificate is in my possession.

4. The Continuation of Hopkins's Teaching

1. I called the personnel office at the Unity School of Christianity at Unity Village, Mo. The records do not go back far enough to indicate the years that Bogart was there. A relative did verify in a phone conversation that she was employed by Unity. He was not clear about the years of her employment.

2. Braden, *Spirits in Rebellion,* 148. Hopkins would not have minded his use of her material. As early as 1887–1888, she had given Frances Lord permission to use her work. The mission was more important to her than self-promotion.

3. Judah, *Metaphysical Movements,* 300.

4. John Gayner Banks, *Truth That Heals,* 1–5.

5. Ibid., 7.

6. Carmelita Trowbridge, "Emma Curtis Hopkins: Christian Mystic for Today" (Alhambra, Calif.: Sanctuary of Truth, n.d.).

7. Ibid.

8. Flotron, "Newsletter" (June 1987).

9. Flotron, "Sharing III Seminar" (Chicago: Ministry of Truth International, n.d.).

10. Ibid.

11. This affirmation was on a small card given to each person. The affirmation assigned to me was that for "June 19th." It read: "Your nature can be trained to be satisfied and at peace. Therefore, while doing the best you can be not restless; be at peace. Keep this word close: *There shall no evil happen to the just.*"

12. In search of someone who knew Hopkins, I interviewed Louise P. Ramey, who had recently celebrated her ninety-eighth birthday. Ramey had been ordained by Charles Fillmore. When asked what Myrtle was like, Ramey replied, "She was a lovely person." It is interesting she used the same word, *lovely,* for Myrtle that Myrtle used for Hopkins. Ramey frequently used terms that Hopkins used in her books. She said she had come into Unity in 1928 after being healed of a physical illness. She stated they used Hopkins's work as a foun-

dation in New Thought. In 1932, after Myrtle Fillmore's death, Ramey was ordained by Charles Fillmore as a minister of the Unity School of Christianity. This meeting is the closest I have been able to come to someone who knew Hopkins. Ramey knew Myrtle Fillmore and Charles Fillmore well, but Hopkins had died in 1925. In keeping with the original intent of Unity to supplement the work of existing denominations and not replace them, Ramey had retained her membership in the Methodist church in Tampa, Florida, and was active there. Louise Ramey died in 1994. Her grandson, Stephen, donated many valuable books from her personal library to the Institute for the Study of American Religion in Santa Barbara, Calif.; the Unity-Progressive Seminary Library in Clearwater, Fla.; and the Emma Curtis Hopkins Theological Seminary in Chicago.

13. Robert Ellwood, *Religious and Spiritual Groups in Modern America,* 164–68. Ellwood discusses Kenneth Thane Walker and "The Prosperos," which is a variation of the orthodox Gurdjieff schools. Walker is the founder of this variation on "Fourth Way Schools." On High Watch, see ibid., 141.

14. Cushing, "Teacher of Teachers," 4.

15. Judah's report on the Order of St. Luke is an example of this influence. See also Braden, *Spirits in Rebellion,* 379–405.

16. Hopkins, *Résumé,* 65.

GLOSSARY

Animal magnetism: A belief that thoughts could be transferable.

Christian Science: A monistic religion with a healing component founded by Mary Baker Eddy in Boston in 1879, reported after her miraculous recovery from a fall in 1866.

Christian Science healing: A type of silent healing denying sickness and affirming perfect health. Because humans are divine, illness is based on erroneous thinking.

College of Christian Science Healing: See **Massachusetts Metaphysical College.**

Cosmic substance: See **Truth-Principle.**

Deity: See **God.**

Divine Science Church: See **International Divine Science Association.**

God: A metaphysically perfect being beyond gender qualities who is in everything. God is all, all is God.

Healing: See **Metaphysical healing.**

Heterodoxy Club: An association of women prominent in Greenwich Village during the twentieth century who were devoted to suffrage and egalitarian principles and agitated for social-justice legislation while living heterodox lifestyles.

High Watch Farm: The farm near Kent, Connecticut, where the work of Emma Curtis Hopkins was taught and published in her later years and after her death in 1925.

Hopkins Metaphysical Association: A coast-to-coast network of former and current students of Hopkins made up of teachers, ministers, publishers, and writers embracing New Thought tenets as healing modalities for a variety of issues confronting humankind. This organization gave Hopkins the pacesetting position in the founding of New Thought.

International Christian Science Association: An organization formed in 1888 by Mary Plunkett in New York to rival the Hopkins Association.

International Divine Science Association: An organization formed by students of Melinda Cramer, Kate Bingham, and the Brooks sisters.

International Order of St. Luke the Physician: The healing industry founded by John Gaynor Banks, a student of Hopkins and an Episcopal priest.

Lessons in Truth: A classic New Thought text authored by H. Emilie Cady, a homeopathic physician and student of Hopkins.

Lighthouse of Truth: An eclectic contemporary educational ministry based in Tampa, Florida, that supported the work of Hopkins and other New Thought and metaphysical proponents for more than thirty-five years.

Malicious magnetism: An attempt to harm based on thinking evil thoughts about someone. Mary Baker Eddy coined the term. It was never an idea of Hopkins.

Massachusetts Metaphysical College: The teaching institute founded by Mary Baker Eddy to train students in Christian Science principles.

Metaphysical healing: A method of spiritual communication that affirms metaphysical perfection as the means to good health. Because God is all and God is pure, sickness is ignorance of the divine state.

Ministry of the High Watch: A later group of disciples formed by Hopkins during her New York years that kept her work in print for some time after her death.

Ministry of Truth International: A contemporary ministry, based in Chicago, devoted to Hopkins's work and the republishing of her books.

Mother principle: The postulation that God or Divine Mind supports comforting principles based on the nurturing skills of women.

New Thought: The term coined for generic Christian Science or metaphysical idealism in the 1890s.

Prosperos: An eclectic school founded by Thane Walker based on Gurdjieff's teachings, astrology, and various metaphysical tenets. Its inner circle is called "High Watch."

Race law: Hopkins's theory that was similar to Carl Jung's ideas of the collective and individual unconsciouses.

Religious Science: A church and association founded by Ernest Holmes who was one of Hopkins's last students in 1924.

Right Knock: A book about Hopkins written by Helen (Nellie) Van Anderson who disguises Hopkins as Mrs. Pearl.

Sanctuary of Truth: A ministry in Alhambra, California, founded by Carmelita Trowbridge, a student of Ernest Holmes, who taught the work of Hopkins prior to her death.

Science of Mind: The primary text written by Ernest Holmes that proved the catalyst for founding a ministry.

Shakers: A group of men and women who lived communally and observed celibacy, organized by the charismatic Mother Ann Lee. Shakers spoke of deity as "Father-Mother God."

Silent Truth Principle: A form of healing prayer affirming harmony, symmetry, and perfection in one's life.

Spiritualism: A phenomenon, based upon the reports of the Fox sisters in Hydesville, New York, in 1848, that a spirit was communicating with them. This communication was in a series of knocks or raps upon a wall that was interpreted by the Fox sisters. Talking to the dead became a popular form of religious expression generally not accepted by mainstream religious groups.

Suffragists: Women who, collectively and actively, campaigned for a woman's right to vote.

Swedenborgians: Followers of Emanuel Swedenborg, a prominent scientist in Sweden, who reported he had access to beings dwelling in the invisible realms and communicated with them about a variety of topics. They have a seminary in Bryn Athyn, Pa.

Theosophy: An occult organization cofounded by Helena Blavatsky and Henry Steele Olcott who proclaimed they had established communication with the mahatmas of higher spiritual realms that would lead humanity into a spiritually enlightened age.

Transcendentalists: A New England group headed by Ralph Waldo Emerson that supported monistic ideas and nature mysticism among other radical theses of the 1840s.

Trinity: Recast by Hopkins to include the Holy Spirit or Comforter as the feminine principle.

Truth-Principle: The construct that God is good, God is all.

Truth Students Association: Formerly the Hopkins Metaphysical Association.

Unity School of Christianity: A New Thought ministry cofounded by Myrtle Fillmore and Charles Fillmore who were ordained by Hopkins in 1891. The institution is currently headquartered at Unity Village, Missouri, and is the largest and most influential of New Thought ministries.

Women's Bible: A reinterpretation and rewriting of Scripture by a collective of noted women from various fields of endeavor. Elizabeth Cady Stanton was the editor.

Women's movement: A collective promoting egalitarian and social-justice ideals that would eliminate sexist discrimination against women. The movement continues to grow, adding various components to its agenda of social action.

BIBLIOGRAPHY

Works by Emma Curtis Hopkins

"Christian Science." *Christian Science Theological Review* 30 (Nov. 1893): 3.

Class Lessons, 1888. 2nd ed. N.d. Reprint, Chicago: Ministry of Truth International, 1987.

Drops of Gold. 4th ed. N.d. Reprint, Chicago: Ministry of Truth International, n.d.

"Faith." *Christian Metaphysician* 1 (Jan. 1887): 2.

The Genesis Series, 1894. N.d. Reprint, Chicago: Ministry of Truth International, n.d.

"God's Omnipresence." *Christian Science Journal* 2 (Apr. 1884): 5.

High Mysticism. N.d. Reprint, Marina del Rey, Calif.: De Vorss, 1983.

"International Bible Lessons." *Christian Science* (Jan. 1888-Aug. 1889): 156–397.

The Judgement Series. 1889–1894. Reprint, Chicago: Ministry of Truth International, n.d.

"Ministry of the Holy Mother." Undated pamphlet. Copy obtained from the Institute for the Study of American Religion, Santa Barbara, Calif.

"The Power That Heals." *Truth* (Mar. 1888): 103.

The Radiant I Am. Putnam, Conn.: Emma Curtis Hopkins Publications, n.d.

Résumé. N.d. Reprint, Chicago: Ministry of Truth International, n.d.

Scientific Christian Mental Practice. N.d. Reprint, Marina del Rey, Calif.: De Vorss, n.d.

"The Songs of Zion." *Truth* (May 1888).

"Teachers of Metaphysics." *Christian Science Journal* (Sept. 1885): 112.

"The Trinity, Part One." *Christian Science* 1 (Dec. 1888).

"The Trinity, Part Two." *Christian Science* 1 (Jan. 1889).

"We Need Not Die." *Truth* (Apr. 1888): 152.

"What Is Plagiarism?" *Christian Science Journal* 3 (July 1885): 81.

Other Sources

Albanese, Catherine. *Corresponding Motion: Transcendental Religion and the New America*. Philadelphia: Temple Univ. Press, 1977.

———. *Nature Religion in America: From the Algonkian Indians to the New Age*. Chicago: Univ. of Chicago Press, 1990.

———. *The Spirituality of the American Transcendentalists*. Macon, Ga.: Mercer Univ. Press, 1988.

Anderson, Alan C. "A Comparison of Some New Thought Statements of Belief." Forthcoming.

———. "Contrasting Strains of Metaphysical Idealism Contributing to New Thought." Unpublished paper.

———. "Horatio Dresser and the Philosophy of New Thought." Ph.D. diss., Boston Univ., 1963.

———. "New Thought and Postmodernism." Unpublished paper.

———. "New Thought and Process Thought as Complementary Aspects of the Revolution of Spiritual Power." Unpublished paper.

Anderson, Ferne. "Emma Curtis Hopkins: Springboard to New Thought." Master's thesis, Univ. of Denver, 1981.

Atkins, Gaius G. *Modern Religious Cults and Movements*. Westwood, N.J.: Fleming H. Revell, 1923.

Austin, Mary. *Earth Horizon: An Autobiography*. Boston: Houghton Mifflin, 1932.

———. *The Land of Journey's Ending*. 1924. Reprint, New York: AMS Press, 1969.

Banks, John Gayner. *Truth That Heals*. N.p.: St. Luke's Press, 1947.

Barker, Raymond. *Miscellaneous Writings of Raymond Charles Barker*. New York: First Church of Religious Service, 1958.

———. *Power for More Successful Living*. New York: Dodd, Mead, 1953.

Bates, E. S., and J. V. Dittemore. *Mary Baker Eddy: The Truth and Tradition*. New York: Alfred A. Knopf, 1932.

Bedell, Geo. C., L. Sandon Jr., and Charles T. Wellborn. *Religion in America*. 2nd ed. New York: Macmillan, 1982.

Bednarowski, Mary Farrell. "Outside the Mainstream: Women's Religion and Women Religious Leaders in Nineteenth-Century America." *Journal of the American Academy of Religion* 48 (June 1980): 207–31.

Bentov, Ishtak. *Stalking the Wild Pendulum.* New York: E. P. Dutton, 1977.

Blanchard, Paula. *Margaret Fuller: From Transcendentalism to Revolution.* New York: Delacorte Press, 1978.

Bordin, Ruth. *Frances Willard: A Biography.* Chapel Hill: Univ. of North Carolina Press, 1986.

Bowden, Henry Wainer. *Dictionary of American Religious Biography.* Westport, Conn.: Greenwood Press, 1977.

Braden, Charles S. *Christian Science Today.* Dallas: Southern Methodist Univ. Press, 1958.

———. *Spirits in Rebellion: The Rise and Development of New Thought.* Dallas: Southern Methodist Univ. Press, 1963.

———. *These Also Believe.* New York: Macmillan, 1951.

Braude, Ann. "The Perils of Passivity: Women's Leadership in Spiritualism and Christian Science." In *Women's Leadership Roles in Marginal Religions: Explorations Outside of the Mainstream,* edited by Catherine Wessinger, 55–67. Chicago: Univ. of Illinois Press.

Bucke, R. M. *Cosmic Consciousness: A Study in the Evolution of the Human Mind.* New York: E. P. Dutton, 1946.

Cady, Emilie. *Lessons in Truth.* Unity Village, Mo.: Unity School of Christianity, n.d.

Christy, Arthur. *The Orient in American Transcendentalism.* New York: Columbia Univ. Press, 1932.

Collingwood, R. G. *The Idea of History.* Oxford: Oxford Univ. Press, 1956.

Commemorative Biographical Record of Tolland and Windham Counties, Connecticut. Chicago: J. H. Beers, 1903.

Crosse, Sarah. "Beware of False Teachers." *Christian Science Journal* 5 (July 1887): 157.

Cushing, Margaret. "Emma Curtis Hopkins: The Teacher of Teachers." *New Thought Bulletin* 28 (spring 1945); reprint, summer 1978.

Dresser, Horatio, ed. *The History of the New Thought Movement.* New York: Thomas Crowell, 1919.

———. *The Quimby Manuscripts.* Seacaucus, N.J.: Citadel Press, 1961.

Eddy, Mary Baker. *The First Church of Christ Scientist and Miscellany.* Boston: Allison V. Stewart, 1918.

———. "Important Offer." *Christian Science Journal* 5 (July 1887).

———. *Miscellaneous Writings*. Boston: Christian Science Publishing, 1896.

———. *No and Yes*. Boston: Christian Science Publishing, 1891.

———. Papers. Church History Department, First Church of Christ, Scientist, Boston.

———. "Questions Answered by Mary Baker Eddy." *Christian Science Journal* 5 (Apr. 1887): 25.

———. *Retrospection and Introspection*. Boston: Christian Science Publishing, 1920.

———. *Science and Health with Key to the Scriptures*. Boston: Christian Science Publishing, 1934.

Ellwood, Robert, Jr. *Alternative Altars: Unconventional and Eastern Spirituality in America*. Chicago: Univ. of Chicago Press, 1979.

———. *Religious and Spiritual Groups in Modern America*. Englewood Cliffs, N.J.: Prentice-Hall, 1973.

Evans, Richard J. *The Feminists*. London: Croom Helm, 1977.

Fillmore, Charles. "Newsbriefs." *Modern Thought* 2 (Nov.-Dec. 1890): 229.

———. "Teacher Visits." *Modern Thought* 2 (1889): 227.

Fillmore, Charles, and Myrtle Fillmore. Papers. Archives of Unity School of Christianity, Unity Village, Missouri.

Fillmore, Myrtle. *Letters*. Lee's Summit, Mo.: Unity School of Christianity, 1956.

Frazer, Winifred. *Mabel Dodge Luhan*. Boston: Twayne, 1984.

Freeman, James D. *The Household of Faith*. Lee Summit, Mo.: Unity School of Christianity, 1951.

Frothington, Octavius. *Transcendentalism in New England*. Philadelphia: Univ. of Pennsylvania Press, 1972.

Fuller, Margaret. *Woman in the Nineteenth Century*. New York: Sheldon, Lampart, 1855.

Gallup, Donald. "Mabel Dodge Luhan Collection." *Yale University Library Gazette* 37 (Jan. 1963): 100.

Gestefeld, Ursula N. *Jesuitism in Christian Science*. Chicago: Ursula N. Gestefeld, Central Music Hall, 1888.

Gilman, Charlotte Perkins. *Women and Economics: A Study of the Economic Relation Between Men and Women as a Factor in Social Evolution*. 1898. Reprint, New York: N.p., 1966.

Gottschalk, Stephen. *The Emergence of Christian Science in American Religious Life*. Berkeley and Los Angeles: Univ. of California Press, 1973.

Hahn, Emily. *Mabel: A Biography of Mabel Dodge Luhan.* Boston: Houghton Mifflin, 1977.

Halverson, Dean. "Mind Power: A History and Analysis of the New Thought Movement." *SCP Newsletter* 2 (spring 1985): 1, 5–10.

Hansen, Penny. "Women's Hour: Feminist Implications of Mary Baker Eddy's Christian Science Movement, 1885–1910." Ph.D. diss., Univ. of California at Irvine, 1981.

Harbert, Elizabeth Boynton. "The Right Hand of Fellowship." *Christian Science* 1 (Feb. 1889).

Harley, Gail M. "New Thought and the Harmonial Family." In *America's Alternative Religions,* edited by Timothy Miller, 325–30. New York: State Univ. of New York Press, 1995.

Herman, Kali. *Women in Particular: An Index to American Women.* Phoenix: Oryx Press, 1984.

Holmes, Ernest. *Science of Mind: A Complete Course of Lessons in the Science of Mind and Spirit.* New York: Robert M. McBride, 1926.

James, E., J. W. James, and Paul S. Bayer, eds. *Notable American Women, 1607–1950: A Biographical Dictionary.* Vol. 2. Cambridge: Harvard Univ. Press, Belknap Press, 1970.

James, William. *The Varieties of Religious Experience.* Cambridge: Harvard Univ. Press, 1982.

Johnsen, Thomas C. "Christian Science and the Puritan Tradition." Ph.D. diss., Johns Hopkins Univ., 1983.

Judah, Stillson. *The History and Philosophy of the Metaphysical Movements in America.* Philadelphia: Westminster Press, 1967.

Katz, Steven, ed. *Mysticism and Philosophical Analysis.* New York: Oxford Univ. Press, 1978.

Kolodny, Annette. *The Land Before Her: Fantasy and Experience of the American Frontiers, 1630–1860.* Chapel Hill: Univ. of North Carolina Press, 1984.

Larson, Martin. *New Thought or a Modern Religious Approach.* New York: Philosophical Library, 1984.

Lasch, Christopher. *New Radicalism in America.* New York: Alfred A. Knopf, 1965.

Leavitt, Judith E., ed. *Women and Health in America.* Madison: Univ. of Wisconsin Press, 1984.

Lerner, Gerda. *The Female Experience: An American Documentary.* Indianapolis: Bobbs-Merrill Educational Publishing, 1977.

————. *The Majority Finds Its Past: Placing Women in History*. Oxford: Oxford Univ. Press, 1979.

Lord, Frances. *Christian Science Healing: Its Principles and Practice*. Chicago: Lily Publishing, 1888.

Luhan, Mabel Dodge. *Background*. Intimate Memories Series. New York: Harcourt, Brace, 1933.

————. *Edge of the Taos Desert*. Intimate Memories Series. New York: Harcourt, Brace, 1937.

————. *Movers and Shakers*. Intimate Memories Series. New York: Harcourt, Brace, 1933.

————. Papers. Beinecke Rare Book and Manuscript Library, Yale Univ., New Haven.

Martin, Alfred W. *Psychic Tendencies of Today*. New York: D. Appleton, 1918.

Mayerson, Charlotte Leon, ed. *Shadow and Light: The Life, Friends, and Opinions of Maurice Sterne*. New York: Harcourt, Brace, and World, 1952.

Melton, J. Gordon. *Biographical Dictionary of American Cult and Sect Leaders*. New York: Garland, 1986.

————. *A Directory of Religious Bodies in the United States: Compiled from the Files of the Institute for the Study of American Religion*. New York: Garland, 1977.

————. *The Encyclopedia Handbook of Cults in America*. New York: Garland, 1986.

————. *The Encyclopedia of American Religions*. 3rd ed. Detroit: Gale Research, 1989.

————. *The Encyclopedia of American Religions and Religious Creeds: A Compilation of More Than 450 Creeds, Confessions, Statements of Faith, and Summaries of Doctrine of Religious and Spiritual Groups in the United States and Canada*. Detroit: Gale Research, 1988.

————. "New Thought's Hidden History: Emma Curtis Hopkins, Forgotten Founder." *JSSMR, the Journal of the Society for the Study of Metaphysical Religion* (Clearwater, Fla.) (spring 1995).

Melton, J. Gordon, Jerome Clark, and Aidan A. Kelly, eds. *New Age Encyclopedia: A Guide to the Beliefs, Concepts, Terms, People, and Organizations That Make Up the New Global Movement Toward Spiritual Development, Health and Healing, Higher Consciousness, and Related Subjects*. Detroit: Gale Research, 1990.

Meyer, Donald. *Sex and Power: The Rise of Women in America, Russia, Sweden, and Italy*. Middletown, Conn.: Wesleyan Univ. Press, 1987.

Miller, Perry. *Errand into the Wilderness*. Cambridge: Harvard Univ. Press, Belknap Press, 1956.

Miller, Timothy. *America's Alternative Religions*. New York: State Univ. of New York Press, 1995.

Mott, Frank Luther. *A History of American Magazines, 1885–1905*. Cambridge: Harvard Univ. Press, 1957.

Numbers, R. L., and R. B. Schoepflin. "Ministries of Healing." In *Women and Health in America,* edited by Judith W. Leavitt. Madison: Univ. of Wisconsin Press, 1984.

Parker, Gail Thain. *Mind Cure in New England*. Hanover, N.H.: Univ. Press of New England, 1973.

Peel, Robert. *Mary Baker Eddy*. 3 vols. New York: Holt, Rinehart, and Winston, 1966–1977.

———. *Mary Baker Eddy: The Years of Trial*. New York: Holt, Rinehart, and Winston, 1971.

Podmore, Frank. *From Mesmer to Christian Science*. New Hyde Park, N.Y.: University Books, 1963.

Proctor-Smith, Marjorie. *Women in Shaker Communities and Worship*. Lewiston, N.Y.: Edward Mellen Press, 1985.

Rudnick, Lois. *Mabel Dodge Luhan: New Woman, New Worlds*. Albuquerque: Univ. of New Mexico Press, 1984.

Ruether, Rosemary R. *Woman Guides: Readings Toward a Feminist Theology*. Boston: Beacon Press, 1985.

———. *Women-Church: Theology and Practice*. San Francisco: Harper and Row, 1988.

———. *Women of Spirit: The Female Leadership in the Jewish and Christian Traditions*. New York: Simon and Schuster, 1979.

Ruether, R. R., and R. S. Keller. *Women and Religion in America*. 3 vols. New York: Harper and Row, 1981–1990.

Satter, Beryl. *Each Mind a Kingdom*. Berkeley: Univ. of California Press, 1999.

Schwartz, Judith. *Radical Feminists of Heterodoxy, 1912–1940*. Norwich, Vt.: New Victoria, 1986.

Scott, Anne F., Andrew Scott, and Harold Hyman, eds. *One Half the People: The Fight for Woman's Suffrage*. Philadelphia: J. B. Lippincott, 1975.

Stace, W. T. *Mysticism and Philosophy*. Philadelphia: J. B. Lippincott, 1960.

Stocker, Clara. *Realization Through Concentrated Attention*. New York: Church of the Truth, n.d.

Stone, Merlin. *When God Was a Woman*. San Diego: Harcourt Brace Jovanovich, 1976.

Van Anderson, Nellie. *The Right Knock*. Chicago: by the author, 1889.

Van Dusen, Wilson. *The Presence of Other Worlds: The Psychological/Spiritual Findings of Emanuel Swedenborg*. New York: Harper and Row, 1974.

Ward, Gary. "The Feminist Theme of Early New Thought." Unpublished paper, 1987.

Welter, Barbara. "The Feminization of American Women." In *Insights and Parallels: Problems and Issues of American Social History*, ed. William L. O'Neill. Minneapolis: Borgess, 1973.

Wessinger, Catherine, ed. *Women's Leadership in Marginal Religions: Explorations Outside the Mainstream*. Urbana and Chicago: Univ. of Illinois Press, 1993.

Young-Hunter, John. *Reviewing the Years*. New York: Crown, 1963.

Zweig, Stefan. *Mental Healers: Anton Mesmer, Mary Baker Eddy, Sigmund Freud*. Garden City, N.Y.: Doubleday, 1932.

INDEX